FOREVER TWENTY

By
Nicholas Timmer, Ph.D

MARSHALL - MICHIGAN
800PUBLISHING.COM

Forever Twenty

Copyright © 2011 by Nicholas Timmer Ph.D

Cover design by   Donald Semora   www.donsemora.com

Author photo by   Courtesy of Author

The opinions expressed in this manuscript are solely the opinions of the author and do not represent the opinions or thoughts of the publisher. The author represents and warrants that s/he either owns or has the legal right to publish all material in this book.

ISBN-13: 978-1-937580-08-7

First published in 2011

10 9 8 7 6 5 4 3 2 1

Published by   2 MOON PRESS
123 West Michigan Ave, Marshall, Michigan 49068
www.800publishing.com

All Rights Reserved. This book may not be reproduced, transmitted, or stored in whole or in part by any means, including graphic, electronic, or mechanical without the express written consent of the publisher except in the case of brief quotations embodied in critical articles and reviews.

PRINTED IN THE UNITED STATES OF AMERICA

This book and Robert Timmer's legacy
are dedicated to his nieces and nephews.
If not us, who?

"The fighters are our salvation,
but the bombers alone provide the means of victory."

--Winston Churchill
September, 1940

CONTENTS

Preface		1
Forever Twenty		4
Chapter 1	Prelude – Africa	7
Chapter 2	Heritage	19
Chapter 3	Robert	39
Chapter 4	Canada	73
Chapter 5	Wings	93
Chapter 6	RAF	121
Chapter 7	The Circus	149
Chapter 8	The Liberator	169
Chapter 9	The Approach	197
Chapter 10	Ploesti	217
Chapter 11	Utah Man	237
Chapter 12	Bremen	257
Chapter 13	Home	271
Epilogue		283
Author's Notes		293
Acknowledgements		303
Bibliography		309
Notes		320

Preface

A young boy, maybe nine or ten years old, lay on his bed, staring at the framed photograph carefully positioned on his dresser. He looks at the World War II officer, an Air Force pilot his hero and wonders. He remembers the tall, good-looking uncle who could raise his 3-year-old body up to the ceiling without any effort. He remembers, too, the crying women in the kitchen. His mother, his Granny... his Aunt Eileen. He wonders some more.

Six decades later, triggered by information that "just happened" to come his way, he made the decision to quit wondering and find out. Who was this man, this hero, whose memory he still cherished?

So began my husband's passion to capture the legacy of his uncle Robert Timmer. His pursuit has taken him to distant places, and led him to people long forgotten or never before known to him; people who knew Bob Timmer and helped to complete the picture of who he really was. Nick's original goal in writing this story was simple: to preserve the memory of his fallen hero and to present it to his family as part of its heritage. What evolved was the recounting of the life of a gifted young man who was crazy about flying, deeply in love with his high school sweetheart, and determined to join the fight against aggression in the world, even before the bombing of Pearl Harbor.

Nick's research covers an airman's journey from training, to combat, and ultimately to the grave, and is a tribute to the men who were willing to put their lives on the line during WWII. In the telling of one story, he provides a glimpse into the bravery and sacrifices of many.

He has accomplished his original goal and more in these pages. It has been a privilege and an adventure helping him to complete this project. Our hope is that it will be shared with generations to come.

Michele Timmer
August, 2011

FOREVER TWENTY

Weary eyes look through misty glasses
at the smiling face in the yellowing photo.
It never grows old. And as weary eyes grow older,
the face seems younger still. Forever twenty.

Somehow this, the fate you knew might come,
with your flying and your war.
You were a boy and fast became a man.
Too fast. They made you a warrior.

Instead of soaring with eagles and
flying to the stars, over mountains, oceans,
rivers and cities, seeing the beauty in
what God has made,

You flew where few would ever go.
Places where there was no beauty,
only fire, blood, destruction and death.
Your friends went with you.

Your machine was uncomfortable,
cold and noisy and scary.
You were afraid, but you went
to your place, over and over again.

Until it seemed there couldn't be
a tomorrow for you, because so many
fell around you; but it mattered not,
you and your friends went still.

And then, it was you.
Trapped in your place,
twisting and spinning and falling from the sky.
In an instant, your future became your past.

What are those medals, anyway?
Pieces of metal, now dusty and stained.
Did they heal the heart of a crying girl?
Did they dry a mother's tears?

Do they tell of children who never were?
Or of projects never started,
a future full of promise and
love, no longer given or received?

Those you left behind believed that
your sacrifice was for a reason.
But in their sadness wondered,
was this the will of God?

There were no bands to play for you,
nor did you march to people's waves.
Only a lonely flag is there,
a silent symbol of shattered dreams.

The weary eyes return their gaze
to the worn image of so long ago
and ask, "What do you want from us?"
And lips forever silent seem to whisper,
"Remember me, remember me."

—Nicholas Timmer, 2011

CHAPTER I PRELUDE-AFRICA

Sand. Hot, blowing, shifting, stinging, unrelenting sand. It was in their tents, clothes, cots, food and water. They breathed it. They tasted it. There was no escaping its violent barrage. The sand blew so frequently that the landscape changed daily, and the newly arrived men of the Ninety-third Heavy Bombardment Group quickly learned that things left out in the open were soon buried. It was also hot. One hundred and twenty-five stifling degrees, and that was in the shade. Any shade, of course, was man-made, yet tents were ovens during the day and offered no relief. It was June, 1943, and summer in the Libyan desert.

They were called "Ted's Travelling Circus" after their first commander, Col. Ted Timberlake. They had been in existence a little over a year and were already the most famous bomb group in the war. The "travelling" (with the two 'l's of the British spelling) part of the name was because of their frequent travels to the nastiest places of World War II. "Circus" fit well because they were colorful fun-loving perfectionists who performed their deadly tricks against fascism in three rings, each one on a different continent. Simply called "The Circus" by the world media, they were back in Africa for a second tour of duty and had no idea why.

The aircraft they flew were B-24s, nicknamed "Liberators," the largest planes in the American Army Air Force. These huge ships carried a crew of ten and more bombs than any aircraft yet designed. Forty-four of these monsters had left their home base in cool Hardwick, England on June 25, 1943, bound for Africa. In one of the planes, called *The Duchess,* was a twenty-year-old copilot named Robert Timmer. Bob, a recent transfer from the Royal Canadian Air Force where he had learned to fly bombers, had never flown in combat. That was about to change.

It was at Hardwick that, late in May 1943, the Ninety-third Heavy Bomb Group had its bombing missions to Europe suspended. They began practicing low-level flying over the English countryside, obviously training for a different kind of mission. Even though they did not know where they were going, the men knew that something was brewing, and rumors began to fly around the base. Maybe they were going to Russia, or China. Or perhaps they were going after Hitler in one of his concrete lairs? "What kind of target would they bomb at fifty feet altitude?" they wondered. Concern grew among the crews. All they really knew was that they were ordered to make their huge machines fly at treetop level. These behemoths were never designed to fly that low. They were built to climb to 20,000 feet, find the target, drop their payload, and head for home. B-24s were difficult to fly even in the best of circumstances. It took talented pilots to fly that low, especially in tight formation.

In the Libyan desert, sand wasn't the only problem facing the airmen. They were welcomed by sparrow-sized grasshoppers, scorpions the size of lizards, and huge kangaroo rats who actually were quite friendly in contrast to the scorpions who could inflict a very painful sting. Sergeant Lewis Smith, a gunner on *The Duchess,* remembers that in addition to those critters, large ants and flies were ever present. The food was terrible. Chow lines were long, hot, and tedious, only to get food that was of one kind—bad! Breakfast was often pressed ham and dried cabbage or powdered eggs and coffee. Lunch was a peanut butter sandwich, and dinner was usually dehydrated cabbage, powdered potatoes, and dried beef or Spam. All of this was typically eaten with a sprinkling of sand. The old military reference for chipped beef on toast (SOS) was changed to "Sand on a Shingle."[1] Diarrhea was rampant and, according to Major Ramsay Potts, pilot of *The Duchess,* everyone lost weight.

The Libyan Desert 1943

Their forlorn tents, hand-me-downs from departing forces, were threadbare and often patched with pieces of scrap war materials left by the Germans and Italians. Around the tents were "desert lilies," cone shaped latrines made from piled up gas cans and palm leaves, with their uncomfortable privies fashioned from oil drums. Water, of course, was in short supply. The men got one full canteen a day. They often "cleaned" their clothes by dunking them in high octane airplane fuel and drying them in the desert sun. They had a unique way of cooling their beer. It was easy to find a plane that needed to fly a "test run." That plane was then loaded with beer and flown at high altitude in below zero temperatures until the beer got cold. It landed to the cheers of the waiting, thirsty men.[2]

Despite the limitations morale was high. Men wearing nothing but shorts and boots were lean, strong and brown. Their faces had scruffy beards (water for shaving was limited) and most sported sun bleached hair. They felt tough as they battled and conquered their hostile desert environment. They were tough. Ramsay Potts said that they felt like warriors[3] and believed they could take on anything.

The schedule was monotonous. When they were not on a mission or practicing low-level flying, the men organized baseball games, played cards or craps, and tinkered with equipment. Some restored beat-up, discarded German cars, motorcycles, and even planes, and got them running. Many went to the races, betting on captured kangaroo rats that raced each other on a specially built track. Speedy rats were bought, sold and traded, just like thoroughbred horses. All activities, baseball and missions alike, were often disrupted by the inevitable sand storm. High winds and blowing sand during the day often forced maintenance crews to work at night when the winds were milder. That schedule took its toll on the men, because the heat during the day made sleeping difficult.

The surroundings wreaked havoc on the machines. Each plane had four huge fourteen-cylinder Pratt and Whitney engines that had to be cleaned constantly because of sand. Conditions and equipment permitting, however, the men of the 93rd continued to practice their low-level flying over the Libyan desert. Even though few knew why they were flying low-level, they knew that the target had to be special. They also knew that low altitude flying avoided radar detection and conserved fuel, so speculation on their ultimate mission was often fairly accurate. However, no one knew for sure, and the brass were not going to let them in on it until the appropriate time. So the planes continued to roar fifty feet over the desert, dropping dummy bombs on dummy targets, over and over again.

Flying in formation, which was essential for the "Big One," (as the men began to call it) was extremely difficult. Controlling a huge Liberator at low altitude with another just off each wingtip was not for the faint of heart. But they had to get it right, and they practiced in a variety of small formations that were eventually joined to form larger ones. Soon, dozens of planes were in tight formations as they thundered over the desert. However, lest the men began to think that the Army Air Force had sent them on a desert vacation, orders came down to send them on regular missions while waiting for the Big One.

Allied forces, led by General George Patton and British General Bernard Montgomery, were preparing for the imminent invasion of Sicily. The Italian and German forces there, along with bridges, roads and other infrastructure, needed softening up. The "Heavies" of the 93rd and the 44th Bomb Groups were called on to do the job.

On July 2, 1943, just one week after they had arrived in Africa, pilot Jack Jones and copilot Robert Timmer lifted *The*

Duchess off the desert sand and headed out over the Mediterranean toward Italy. The target was the San Pancrazio Aerodrome on Italy's heel. Captain Jones was sitting in for Ramsay Potts, the regular pilot of *The Duchess* and the leader of the 330th Squadron, who took the day off for administrative tasks. Jones was one of the originals of the 93rd and had flown training flights with Lt. Timmer back at Hardwick when the young pilot was learning to fly the B-24. For his first combat mission, Bob could not have had a better man sitting next to him in the cockpit.

Robert Timmer was excited. Like many of his mates, he had chosen to be a warrior. That is why he had given up a full college scholarship to learn to fly. This is what all those months of training, first with the Canadians and then with the Americans, had come down to, and he was pleased about it. Like most after learning to fly, he longed to get into combat. Since receiving his wings in October of 1942, it had been nine months of training and waiting, and he was ready. He had some anxiety and apprehension. He was, after all, an inexperienced twenty-year-old and second in command of a huge "battleship" carrying nine other men, most of whom had combat experience. Fear of combat came with the territory and he must have felt some of it. Even the most experienced crew member of these huge machines had some "butterflies" before leaving on a mission.

It was a beautiful day for flying, sunny and clear. *The Duchess* was accompanied by twenty two other B-24s. Their objective at San Pancrazio was to damage or destroy the airfield's hangers and parked planes. Shortly before 11:30 a.m., as they approached the target, Lt. Timmer, for the first time, watched as anti-aircraft fire exploded harmlessly around them. When their bomb run began, Capt. Jones turned over control of the plane to his bombardier, Captain Claude Culpepper, who salvoed their 500 pounders at 11:28. The run on the target took place at 22,500 feet and lasted ninety seconds. The results were disappointing. Some of the hangers were damaged but no enemy planes were hit. Historian Cal Stewart notes, "Although the dispersal areas were fairly well hit, most bombardiers weren't satisfied.[4] All the planes returned safely to their base, but a few days later *The Duchess* was again called into action.

Rail installations at Messina, Sicily, were attacked on July 5 by the 93rd and four other groups. This time the regular pilot of *The Duchess* was back in the pilot's seat. In contrast to Bob's inexperience, Ramsay Potts was one of the most experienced pilots in the bomb group. Potts was more than six years older than his copilot and, at twenty-six, an old man among Liberator pilots. He was from Memphis, Tennessee, the son of a cotton merchant, and a commerce graduate of the University of North Carolina where he was a highly ranked collegiate tennis player. He taught economics at a junior college before joining the Air Corps and received his wings four days after Pearl Harbor. He was one of the original pilots of the Circus. Potts was promoted rapidly, going from lieutenant to major in nine months, one of the fastest rises through rank in the Army Air Force. He had flown many missions prior to having Bob join his crew and had already won several medals for bravery, including the Distinguished Flying Cross.

The raid on Messina involved twenty-two planes. Some rail facilities were hit, but about two thirds of the bombs fell into the sea. Lt. Timmer had another first, however; as he watched, six fighter planes rose to greet them as they left the target. The attack was not pressed in earnest, but 200 rounds were fired by the Libs at the enemy planes. The flak was intense, but all planes returned to base—another mission with disappointing results.

Lt. Timmer flew his third combat mission, with the regular crew of *The Duchess*, to Italy on July 12, where the Circus and their friends bombed a ferry slip at San Giovanni. Again, the flak was intense and, again, the results were disappointing. The mission was compromised by flak smashing into the nose of the lead plane and mortally wounding the mission's navigator. Several Circus ships were riddled by flak but *The Duchess* was not one of them. A few days later the *Duchess* was again war bound, this time with Captain Hugh Roper in the pilot's seat. Another of the Circus's legendary pilots, Roper had spent time helping to train Timmer when he first encountered B-24s. They had a special bond. They finally had a productive mission, destroying six planes on the ground and four hanger facilities at the Foggia Aerodrome on Italy's heel.

The Circus participated in two other missions in July, but Bob did not fly in either. Not all planes flew every mission and crew members did not always fly in the same plane. On July 17, the 93rd successfully bombed Naples and didn't lose a plane, despite attacks by a host of German and Italian fighters. In one of the most interesting raids of the war, they bombed facilities around Rome on July 19. Catholic crew members were given the option of not flying on the mission, but most of them went. Bombing had to be precise because if they hit any holy sites there would be worldwide outrage. Hundreds of British and American planes participated with very positive results and no damage to church facilities.

Chaplain James A. Burris was a Methodist minister from the Ozarks in Missouri. Photographs show him skinny and not very old, maybe in his thirties. He loved to fly. He often hitched a ride on one of the Liberators and went into combat with the crew. He held regular Sunday protestant services in the desert, with the men sitting on gas cans or cross-legged on the sand. Walt Stewart, a Mormon from Utah, often played a portable organ while sitting on one of the cans. Bob Timmer attended these services. "Chappy" Burris had other responsibilities as well. Young men halfway around the world from home and undergoing enormous stress, both from homesickness and combat, had special needs and, whether they were believers or not, often sought out the chaplain for counseling and advice. The rough part for Chappy, however, was when the planes came back from missions carrying mangled young men hit by shrapnel or gunfire. Often in agony, and sometimes minutes from death, it took all the spiritual strength he could get from God for Chappy to meet their needs. By all reports, he was good at what he did and was an essential part of the Ninety-third's efforts.

In late July, 1943, the missions supporting the invasion of Sicily ceased and all efforts were devoted to "Hipper Dipper." Five Heavy Bombardment groups from the Eighth and Ninth Air Forces, which included the 93rd, were gathered in the desert of Libya. It was the greatest massing of the most experienced heavy bomber men the world had ever known.[5] While they waited to get the word to go, the men hunkered down in the sand as the Liberators continued to skim the desert, their prop wash creating mini-storms of their own. There were stories of shearing the humps off camels and scratching paint off the underbellies of the huge planes as they scraped the desert floor. Extra fuel tanks were being installed on the planes, and one didn't have to be a genius to figure out that it was going to be not only a low-level mission but a long low-level mission.

Finally, in meetings held by senior officers, first the flying officers and then the sergeants were informed, officially, of what some had already figured out. They were going to fly an unprecedented, low-altitude attack on the heavily-fortified, German-occupied oil fields at Ploesti, Romania. The operation was code-named "Tidal Wave." The mission had been months in the planning and was conceived at the highest levels of the Allied command. Many senior officers had serious objections to the low-level plan, thinking it absolute suicide, especially with the cumbersome Liberators, but the Joint Chiefs of Staff had approved it, and it was going to happen, objections or not.

So, now they knew. The months of speculation, preparation, and sacrifice were all for what probably was going to be the adventure of their lives. Many reacted with a sense of "let's get it over with." Apprehension was normal and expected. Lt. Walt Stewart's prayer groups increased in size, but all went about their business with the determination to do the job, no matter how dangerous—characteristic of men of courage.

Because Major Ramsay Potts was the leader of the 330th Bomb Squadron, *The Duchess* and its crew would have a special role to play in the attack. John Sherman, the tail gunner, had a lot of respect for Potts and appreciated flying with him. He was an excellent flyer and that was good for everyone on board. But Potts, as squadron leader, had much to do, and he was not one of the boys. On the other hand, according to Sherman, his copilot, Second Lieutenant Timmer, was very approachable. Even though they had not been together very long as a crew, Sherman recalls Timmer visiting the tents of his men just to engage in small talk and get to know them. "Everyone liked him," Sherman recalls.[6]

Timmer might not have known it, but he almost missed flying

with Sherman and the others. The Circus was going to be split into two forces, one led by Colonel Baker and the other by Colonel Ted Timberlake, the former commander of the 93rd. Timberlake had just been promoted to brigadier general, and he planned on flying the mission in the copilot's seat of *The Duchess*, next to his friend Ramsay. According to Potts, however, just prior to the mission, Gen. Lewis Brereton (commander of the Ninth Air Force to which the 93rd was temporarily attached) ordered Timberlake not to go because there were already too many generals going.[7] Timberlake was bitterly disappointed that he was grounded, but Robert Timmer had his spot.

On July 30, two days before the mission, General Brereton, in one of the most incredible statements of the war, told the men on one of his rounds that if half the bombers failed to return, a successful bombing mission will be worth it.[8] Maps of the refineries were drawn in the sand, using urine instead of scarce water for the planes to 'bomb" as they passed over. Mock models of the Ploesti complex were trucked around the camp so crews could get some kind of perspective of their target. Three hundred new engines (undamaged by sand) arrived two days before the mission and mechanics worked around the clock for the next forty-eight hours to get them installed.[9]

The next day, the eve of "Tidal Wave," the weather was clear and sunny, and the fliers were briefed on the final practice mission. All five bombardment groups would participate. They would fly with live ammunition simulating the real thing. They took off, gathered over the Mediterranean, then came in low out of the west, forming a five-mile-wide front. Observers on the ground couldn't believe their eyes (and ears) as wave after wave of the huge planes, skimming the dunes, roared overhead. Their powerful prop wash was so intense that tent stakes were pulled out of the ground and a major dust storm was created. It was a sight to behold, almost beyond belief.[10] Most importantly, it was a successful simulation and gave hope that this mission could be a success.

After practice, there was an unusual quiet around the tents. The generals and a few VIPs (World War I Ace Eddie Rickenbacker was one of them) made their rounds of the camps, giving pep talks and emphasizing the importance of the mission. In the meantime, ground crews were loading the planes with fuel and munitions. That evening, men wrote their "last letters" and left them with the chaplains. Chaplains received lots of worldly goods before tough missions: family photos, high school rings, medals, camel whips and money, "just in case." After dinner many gathered in small groups to read Scripture and pray. They discussed life, death, resurrection and the life to come. The pastors served communion and heard confessions. Second Lieutenant Robert Timmer, on the eve of a battle of historic proportions, retired to his tent, read a verse from his New Testament and said a silent prayer. He looked longingly at his photograph of Eileen, and tried to get some sleep.

Chapter II Heritage

He was Dutch, or in today's hyphenated society, a "Netherlander-American." In the days of his youth, there were not many people in his hometown of Wyoming Park, Michigan, who were not Dutch. However, those who weren't often referred to those who were as "Hollanders": not necessarily a term of endearment, but not offensive. The term was frequently applied to those who were "yust the boat off" — recent immigrants who, with their broken English, old-world habits, and ignorance of things American, stood out from those who were one or more generations removed from immigrant status. As a matter-of-fact, the Americanized Dutch often used the "Hollander" term in describing their recently arrived country men and women. Another description applied to recent arrivals from the Old Country was "Dutchie." It was not uncommon to hear something like, "Their furniture is so Dutchie." Regardless, whether new or old, rich or poor, pretty or plain, "Dutchie" or not, the Dutch are proud to be Dutch and Robert Timmer's family was no exception.

The Dutch had, after all, a rich history of incredible achievements as a people, both in Europe and America. From their tiny little enclave (much of which was recovered from the North Sea), they sailed the world, ruling portions of it that were hundreds of times the size of their own land. They established a culture and lifestyle in Europe that produced great geniuses of the art world, and they became adept at trading and negotiations, which enhanced their reputation of being shrewd in the art of the deal. (They really did buy Manhattan Island for the equivalent of twenty-four dollars!)

They were some of the earliest arrivals on the shores of America, founding Albany and New Amsterdam (New York) in 1624-25, only four years after the Pilgrims landed at Plymouth. After helping finance the American Revolution, they embarked on a relationship with the United States that has, for over 225 years, remained one of the closest between nations in the history of the modern world.

While the Netherlanders who were the early settlers on the East Coast came to the New World primarily for economic opportunities, (pursuit of profit being the motivating factor in Dutch settlement and achievement), those who emigrated in the mid-nineteenth century came for somewhat different reasons. By the 1830s and '40s, the Dutch government, whose policies were aimed at state control of all religious denominations, had become increasingly meddlesome in its citizens' religious affairs. Persecution of church leaders, who openly opposed the actions of their government, included fines, jail, and the billeting of the rougher elements of the Dutch army in their homes.[11] This was happening during a period when hard economic times had fallen on most of central Europe. The Dutch character holds two things most dear: the right to worship God without interference, and a full stomach - in that order! A Dutch government that messes with number one, and doesn't help with number two, is risking widespread dissatisfaction among its people. Many, especially the common, poorer citizens living under the monarchy of the Netherlands, were disgruntled and hungry.

As hardships continued for the people of Europe, "America fever" began gripping them, leading to emigration to the United States by the thousands in the 1840s. In the Netherlands, local ministers who, for the most part, were well educated, articulate and uncompromising, had significant influence over their flocks. It was only a matter of time before many of them began making plans to bring their people to the New World. After much deliberation and prayer, different congregations began emigrating to different parts of North America. Primarily unskilled laborers or farmers looking for land, the new immigrants to the United States bypassed the earlier Dutch settlements in the East and headed for Iowa, Wisconsin, Illinois, and Michigan. Indeed, leaders of this so-called "Great Trek" were men of the cloth.

The Michigan contingent was led by Pastor Albertus Van Raalte who established the colony of Holland, Michigan, on the shores of Lake Michigan in 1847. The colonists first built their houses (huts they were called) and then their churches. After some very severe conditions, sickness, and death, the settlement began to thrive. So much so that letters back to the "Old Country" told of the land of plenty and encouraged those who were still experiencing difficulties to come to the New World.

Despite the hardships, the early settlers, a hearty bunch, began to make progress and grow. They soon spread north and east of Holland and founded the villages of Zeeland, Overisel, Drenthe, Groningen and Vriesland. Life was difficult, and early visitors to their communities often commented on how hard they worked. Using only axes and hatchets, for example, they cleared thousands of acres of virgin forests. Other land in the area was swampy bottom land, called "muck," that, once drained and prepared, was excellent for growing vegetables, especially celery and onions. They crawled through it on hands and knees, planting and harvesting, coming home in the evening covered with smelly, black, swamp dirt. Children learned early on to "crawl" and, generations later, kids who worked the muck were still being called "crawlers" by their friends. Good muck, however, meant good money, and even though the crawlers may have come to church on Sunday with dirt under their fingernails, the church coffers prospered because of them. Dairy and crop farms also sprouted in the area so that a variety of products were shipped to the population centers of Grand Rapids, Kalamazoo and even across Lake Michigan to Chicago and Milwaukee.

The new settlers were very parochial, tending to cling to their old-country ways against the creeping "Americanism" that soon began to affect their children. They were not given to frivolity and outsiders were not likely to say that the early Dutch were fun to be around. Observers noted that they prayed often: not just in their homes and churches, but throughout the day, just as if God were standing right beside them. (They, of course, believed He was.) They could be not only stern, strict, stubborn, frugal and narrow-minded, but also honest, faithful, and fair. Their attempts at humor were often directed at themselves. They valued cleanliness not only in their personal habits but also in their homes and yards, and, whether they ultimately lived in a mansion or a shack, chances were that it was immaculate. More than anything else, however, religion was the backbone of their culture in West Michigan.

Their belief system was wrapped around Calvinism—Dutch Calvinism. Nowhere, except perhaps in John Calvin's Geneva, was Calvinism more imbued into a culture than it was into the Netherlanders who practiced it. When the Calvinist interpretation of the Scriptures and catechisms came into their lives it spoke to who they were: Biblical literalists prone to believe in their own unworthiness, economically depressed but hard working, freedom seeking but oppressed, and very spiritual. John Calvin's writings, with its emphasis on redemption through faith in Christ and the freedom that results from that belief, seemed to sort their issues out for them and gave them what they so desperately sought: hope of heavenly salvation and a better earthly life. It fit them like a well-carved pair of wooden shoes.

They loved their churches, where they would spend the better part of every Sunday, not only listening to a two-to-three-hour sermon from a pastor they referred to as "Dominie," but also socializing with their fellow congregants. Sunday, the Sabbath, was strictly observed, but it was the highlight of their week, their only day off.

Often found in tight-knit immigrant communities was a certain amount of intolerance toward people not of the majority's background or religion, and many Dutch were adept at practicing it. Some were quick to look down their sanctimonious noses at those who they felt were not as proficient in the art of holiness as they. The tenants of their catechisms —sin, redemption, and thanksgiving— were to them such a simple, easy to understand road to eternal bliss, that they could not understand why others didn't get it. This often led to a pious attitude toward non-Calvinist neighbors who might labor on Sundays, engage in "worldly" pleasures such as dancing, theater attendance, and card playing, or frequent taverns instead of church.

Seemingly in contrast, but absolutely in line with their belief of reaching out to others less fortunate, they began to put their faith into practice by establishing and supporting institutions of mercy wherever they settled. Early on in West Michigan, they established and supported Pine Rest Hospital and Bethany Christian Services, each becoming a world-class organization in their respective specialties. Through the years, The Hope Network, Wedgewood Acres, Van Andel Institute, and DeVos Children's Hospital in Grand Rapids; Hope Haven and Village Northwest in Iowa; and institutions in Illinois and South Dakota, all sprang from the faith of their Dutch founders.

After churches, their emphasis was schools, and although the early arrivals were for the most part uneducated, it did not take long for them to make education a priority. Most pressing was the need to train their ministers. Following the example of their eastern brethren, who founded Queens College (now Rutgers University) in New Jersey, the West Michigan faction quickly founded Hope College in 1866 and Calvin College ten years later. Out west, Dordt and Northwestern were established in Iowa. Christian elementary and high schools sprang up wherever there were Dutch Calvinists. Christian in their perspective, these schools not only educated but also helped to perpetuate the culture.

They called their church "Reformed." It was the denomination of many of the Dutch settlers of 200 years previous who had located primarily in New York and New Jersey. The Easterners were prospering and reaching out to the newcomers with supplies and money. But they were different from these recent immigrants. They were Americans and, by this time, they lived in American-style homes, ate American food, married non-Dutch Americans (as long as they weren't Catholic), and, of course, spoke English. They did, however, desire close fellowship with those of the same faith and culture. To that end, the Reformed Church of North America extended full membership to the churches in West Michigan, which, after much debate, was accepted and approved by the General Synod on June 5, 1850. Even though there was now one

Dutch Reformed Church in America, the seeds of discontent had been sown.

It was not only the Union that bothered some people; friction among the various early congregations often had its roots in the Netherlands where, for example, the Frisians didn't always see eye-to-eye with the Gelderlanders. The people, lack of education aside, knew their Bible and could debate the finer points of Scripture and Calvinist doctrine, ad infinitum. That, combined with an innate Dutch stubbornness, often led to hard feelings among and within the congregations.

There was also increasing frustration, and even hostility, from outlying churches toward Van Raalte and his flock in *de Kolonie* (Holland), for their perceived "broadminded" ways. Among other things, they were accused of allowing other Christians to partake of the Lord's Supper and of singing hymns instead of Psalms during services.[12] One particular meeting became so unruly that Dominie Van Raalte was threatened with violence.[13]

Hostile, accusatory communications setting forth their respective views on doctrinal and non-doctrinal issues flew between factions, and the first of several "splits" among Dutch Calvinists in America was fostered. Mulder writing in 1947 noted, "Although they have won the reputation of being phlegmatic, the Hollanders have proved many times during their century of life in America that there is plenty of dynamite in Dutch nature. They have often fought at Armageddon with an abandon that had something splendid about it. To many non-Hollanders, however, those battles of ecclesiastical titans usually seemed incomprehensible, even somewhat comic."[14] Talk of secession from the Reformed Church became more prevalent and a serious issue for Classis Holland.

The break formally occurred in 1857, when several West Michigan congregations informed the Classis of Holland that they were leaving the Reformed Church. Many believe that those who left were more concerned with retaining their Dutch culture and language than with conflicting doctrinal interpretations between the two groups, although there was some of that as well. "The Secession of 1857, in America, which was first and foremost a church matter, was not exclusively religious in nature. As mentioned before, we may see in it also a "clash between two cultures — Dutch and American."[15]

The congregations that left soon formed the Christian Reformed Church and the two denominations went their separate ways. (Existing side-by-side in Dutch settlements across Canada and the United States, they stopped competing for Dutch souls years ago and now exist in harmony with each other. Most of the members of both groups neither understand nor care about the issues that divided them so long ago.) Rev. Albertus Van Raalte, who faithfully withstood years of abuse finally had had enough and, with his health failing, quit the ministry in July of 1867. He continued to lead the community however, and "remained the soul of the whole colony until his death."[16]

~~~~~~~

During the 1850s and '60s, conditions in the Netherlands improved somewhat, and, with the advent of the American Civil War, immigration from the Old Country slowed. However, in 1872, seven years after the war ended, a twenty-three-year-old farm laborer from the Dutch province of Groningen named Matthew Timmer married his sweetheart Grace Giebles, said a last good-bye to family and friends, and headed for America.

They ended their journey in West Michigan and settled in the area around Jamestown, in Ottawa County, where Matthew found work on area farms.

Matthew Timmer

In 1877, approximately five years after they emigrated, Matthew and Grace were living on Thomas Street, near Union, in the third ward of Grand Rapids in what was referred to as "the south side." The couple likely rented and moved a couple of times, but always to different houses on Thomas. They were both twenty-eight years old.

[Note: Attempting to track the early wanderings of Matthew is made difficult by the different spellings of his first name. Early documents have six different spellings: Matheus, Mathias, Matthias, Mathew, Matthew and Mattheus. The variances most likely had to do with difficulty understanding the Dutch sounds when attempting to spell his name in English. While that may excuse people like the census taker, his own family called him "Mattheus" in his obituary and had "Matthew" chiseled on his tombstone! The spelling on his tombstone will be used in this narrative, as it is the final say on the matter.]

In Grand Rapids, Matthew worked as a laborer and later as a mason; while working as a laborer, he gained the skills needed to become a bricklayer and a stonecutter. Grand Rapids was booming in the 1870s, and brick and stone buildings, like the Water Treatment Plant, the Post Office and City Hall, were rising from the riverbanks. It is likely he worked on one or more of those projects. There was much work in the building trades, and Matthew and Grace, with no children to feed and clothe, saved their money.

While living on Thomas Street, their first child, daughter Edie, was born in 1882, fully ten years after they had arrived in America. It is a startling statistic, given that most immigrants quickly began having lots of children, for even though it meant more mouths to feed, it also meant more help for the family farm or business. There could be a number of reasons for Grace's long infertility, but it is possible that, contrary to what was happening in their Dutch community, they wanted to accumulate some resources before having children. Be that as it may, it was an amazing birth control performance, considering there were none of our modern methods to rely on. Once Grace got started having babies, however, they came at regular intervals. Their second child, Nicholas, arrived in 1884, and in 1885, John was born, both in Grand Rapids.

Sometime during the late 1880s, Matthew and Grace, along with their three small children, left Grand Rapids, took out a mortgage, combined it with their savings, bought a farm in Jamestown Township, Ottawa County, and began having more children. Gerritt came along in 1886; Matthew Jr. in 1890; and, finally, Bertha in 1891. Grace had her first child when she was thirty-three and the last at age forty-two. The family harbored a sense of pride that all the children were born in America, and all grew up speaking English. None of them, however, went into farming. With the exception of Gerritt, who had a rough time financially, they all eventually prospered. In 1905, tragedy struck the family when fifteen-year-old Matthew Jr. died, possibly from being kicked by a horse. Nick kept a memorial to his brother on the wall in his home for many years.

Fifteen-year-old Nick quit school after the end of the school year in 1900, just before his sixteenth birthday in July. He left the farm and moved to Grand Rapids where he went to work clerking for Lambert Vander Honing. Mr. Vander Honing owned a meat market on College Avenue, near the downtown area (where currently the I-196 expressway passes under College). Nick also boarded at the Vander Honings, whose house and market were in the same building. It was here that he began to learn the meat cutting business. He also delivered meat, often to the nearby Heritage Hill mansions. An undated photograph shows him, at approximately eighteen years of age, driving a nicely painted, horse drawn delivery wagon with "L. Vander Honing" neatly lettered on the side. He is wearing a dark jacket and pants, white shirt and skinny dark tie. Of average height, but with his feet dangling over the buggy's foot rest, he is thin, sort of wiry, and wearing a cap over his dark wavy hair. Hanging from a long strap over his left shoulder is a leather change purse. It looks exactly like those he bought for his paperboy grandsons decades later, insisting that it was a necessity when collecting money. In the photo, judging from the pleasant look on his face, he seems to be enjoying what he is doing, as does the horse.

In contrast to Matthew and Grace, who emigrated from the Netherlands when times were relatively good, the Klaas Zwijghuizen family found themselves caught in an agricultural crisis that plagued all of Europe in the late 1870s. Due in part to competition with America, the economies of many nations were affected, which led to depressed prices. The Netherlands fell into a major economic depression. Finding work became extremely difficult, and food was scarce. Klaas, his wife Kornelia Meinardi, and their five children lived in the town of Zandeweer, in the province of Groningen. Klaas was an unskilled day laborer, and it was a struggle just to put food on the table for a family of seven. That, and his dissatisfaction with the state-dominated church, led Klaas to make the decision to move his family to the New World. In March, 1892, they left family and friends and traveled to Rotterdam, where they boarded the ss *Veendam,* and headed for America. Their destination was Grand Rapids, Michigan. It is very likely they had sponsors who paid for their trip. This patronage sometimes came as a loan which had to be repaid with either money or work, or as an outright gift. Churches often sponsored immigrants.

Upon arriving in Grand Rapids, the family began changing their names to more Americanized versions–Zwijghuizen became Zwyghuizen. Klaas remained Klaas, but Kornelia began spelling her name with a "C." Sixteen-year-old Pieter (named after his grandfather) was now Peter, fourteen-year-old Antje was Anna, while twelve-year-old Eisse became Isaac, called "Ike." Nine-year-old Aafke's name was changed to Effie. Surprisingly, the kid with the strangest name, seven-year-old Hemmo, stayed a Hemmo, although his family called him "Mo."

They moved into a home at 210 Underhill Street in the Grandville Avenue area, where there was a substantial Dutch immigrant settlement. Here they were living when a survey was taken in the fall of 1894. It revealed some things of interest about this recently-arrived family. Klaas was still a laborer (who was unemployed for four months of that year) and Cornelia still a housewife. Nineteen-year-old Peter was living at home and working at a furniture shop. Isaac was fifteen and he, like his father, was working as a laborer and living at home. The youngest two, Effie and Hemmo, were in school, while seventeen-year-old Anna remained at home, making and selling dresses. It is very likely that some of the salaries of the three working kids were going into the family coffers. The oldest three children were also listed as boarders, thus paying their parents for room and board. Surprisingly, all the children could read and write English, even though they had only been in the United States for two years. According to the survey, however, their parents could only write and read "Holland."

America was good to the Zwyghuizens. By the turn of the century, they had moved to a farm in Wyoming Township. The house was a large, two-story, wood-framed farm house, with a nice front porch supported by fancy posts and topped by a dormer with carved wooden sunbursts in its peak. In an undated photograph, probably taken in the late 1890s, the family is gathered in front of the house, dressed in their Sunday best. Klaas and Cornelia are seated, while the children are standing. Anna and Effie, almost six years apart in age, look so much alike they could be twins. The two older boys are tall and thin, like their father. Hemmo looks to be about thirteen, and he is holding his bicycle, which must have been a very precious machine to be able to appear in a rare family photo. It is obvious however, that one piece of equipment they apparently did not own was a lawn mower. The house still stands on the corner of Prairie and Byron Center Avenue and looks now just as it did more than a hundred years ago.

Effie enrolled in the Grandville Public Schools after the move to the Wyoming farm. She graduated in June of 1901, just after her nineteenth birthday - the first of her family to graduate from high school. The ceremony for the six seniors was held at the First Reformed Church in Grandville. Her graduation photo shows a tall, attractive woman, with a proud look on her full, round face, and flowers in her dark hair. She is wearing a white blouse and a floor length white skirt. Around her neck is a long ribbon with some kind of a fob at the bottom, perhaps a lanyard denoting an academic honor for the new graduate. Soon she was teaching school in a one-room school house on 36th Street, a few blocks from the farm. It was called Newhall No. 2; she had twenty-five students of all sizes and shapes, apparently ranging in grades from kindergarten to the eighth.

Turn-of-the-century America was growing under the dynamic leadership of President Theodore Roosevelt, he of Dutch ancestry, who suddenly ascended to the presidency with the assassination of William McKinley. He inherited an essentially rural, agrarian society and began to bring it, or, more appropriately, drag it, into the industrial and imperial giant it became. He broke up huge monopolies called "trusts" and used the power of the federal government to regulate them. He made a deal with newly independent Panama for a canal across their skinny country and began to build the "Big Ditch." He got involved in settling a horrible war between Russia and Japan and won the Noble Peace Prize for his efforts. (He also won the Congressional Medal of Honor for bravery in the Spanish-American War, making him the only world personality ever to win highest honors for both war and peace.) He embarked on a campaign of conservation for protecting the natural resources of this country unequaled by any president before or since.

TR's foreign policy was epitomized by the theme of "speak softly and carry a big stick," so he painted his "bully" battleships white and sent them around the world, demonstrating to friend and foe the emerging power of the United States. And when Congress balked at the cost, the commander in chief sent them anyway, telling Congress that if they wanted to get their "Great White Fleet" back, they'd have to cough up the money. He permanently changed the nature of the American presidency and did it all with unbridled energy and joy. In 1904, he won his only election to the presidency by an unprecedented majority.

During that election year, Nick left the employ of Mr. Vander Honing and returned to his parents' farm in Jamestown. He began apprenticing as a meat cutter with Lee Edson, who owned a large slaughter house (now called a meat processing plant) near Hudsonville, not too far from the farm. Nick learned the business, and when Lee saw an opportunity for a retail meat outlet in the growing community of Beverly, he encouraged his young protégé to explore it

In order to set up the new business, Nick had to travel from the Jamestown farm to Beverly. When he couldn't borrow one of the horses from his father, he had to walk. It was approximately ten miles from the farm to the market—and ten miles back. The most direct route was along Byron Center Avenue where one of the few, but more prominent, farms along the way belonged to the Zwyghuizen family. From time to time Cornelia would invite the weary young traveler to help himself to a cup of water from the pump and even offer him a goody or two. The stops became more frequent as Effie began showing more interest in taking over some of the hospitality duties from her mother. Noticeable sparks of affection were kindled between the butcher's apprentice and the school teacher and soon there was an engagement announcement.

The Zwyghuizens were long time members of the Holland Church of Grandville, Michigan, aka First Reformed Church. To attend services there, they hitched up their finest buggy and drove about a mile and a half down Prairie Street. Living that close it was easy to be involved in church activities and they were. It was there, on April 25, 1906, that Nicholas Timmer and Effie Zwyghuizen were married by Dominie John Ossewaarde. They moved in with Effie's parents and later that year Nick's new meat market opened on Porter Street in Beverly.

The first settlers in the area that came to be called Beverly were Dutch immigrants who realized that Whalen swamp, along muddy, mostly impassable, Burlingame Avenue south of Porter Street and north of the wagon track called 28th Street, had real potential. They purchased five, ten, and twenty acre parcels and used their old-country expertise to turn the swampland into soggy farmland, suited to their style of farming. Soon onions, carrots, watermelons, and celery were sprouting from the muck, and people began to prosper from land no one else wanted. (Apparently vegetables were not all they produced. Years later, Ty Timmer recalled that the local boys referred to the pretty, blond, Dutch girls who lived there as "Swamp Angels.)"[17]

The southwest suburbs of the city of Grand Rapids began to grow as developers purchased plats and built houses along the Grand Rapids-Holland interurban railway, which had a stop in Beverly. The settlement grew quickly.

Nick and Effie on their wedding day

With marriage and a new business, 1906 was a pivotal year for Nick and Effie, and an interesting one for our country. On April 18, a week before their marriage, a huge earthquake rocked San Francisco. The incredible damage it caused, along with the fires it created, destroyed two-thirds of our most prosperous Pacific Coast city. On Wall Street, the Dow-Jones industrial average closed above one hundred for the first time, while on Broadway, George Cohan was singing "You're a Grand Old Flag" in the musical "George Washington, Jr." The first train tunnel under the Hudson River, between New Jersey and New York, was opened. In February, the social event of the young century occurred when Alice Lee Roosevelt, the oldest of the president's six children, was wed in the East Room of the White House to Congressman Nicholas Longworth. While in sports, the Chicago Cubs' vaunted airtight infield of "Tinkers to Evers to Chance" ran away with the National League season with 116 wins, only to lose the World Series to the cross-town White Sox, four games to two.

The Timmer market did well and grew along with Beverly and its new neighbor to the west, Wyoming Park, which was platted in 1910. (Avon Street, which ran next to the meat market, was the eastern boundary of the new settlement, but soon the two communities blended and few knew, or cared, about boundary lines.) A hundred years later, many homes built during that era, including the building that once housed the Timmer Meat Market, still stand along Porter Street in the city of Wyoming.

Unlike Matthew and Grace, Nick and Effie wasted no time having children, and the little ones started coming at regular intervals. Matthew (Ty) arrived in 1907, and his sister Cornelia (Connie), two years later. Nicholas Jr. (Nick) came along in 1911, and Grace in 1913, followed by Anna (Anne) in 1914. In

1916, the Timmers tragically lost twin boys in their infancy, causing a gap between Anne and Gerald, who was born in 1919. Anne, born in September, was the only one not born in the first three months of the year. The children were all named after someone in the family: Ty, Connie and Grace were named after grandparents, Nick after his father, and Anne and Gerald after an aunt and uncle.

Chapter III Robert

Times were good in 1922. America was four years removed from the slaughter of World War I and, although the trauma of the tragedy still lingered, the country was moving on. In 1920, Republican Warren G. Harding was elected president on a campaign that promised "Normalcy," but, among the nations of the world, the United States was far from normal. Our factories, transitioning to peacetime production, were booming, led by the country's insatiable appetite for automobiles. Electricity was reaching into rural America and transforming lives, especially on the farms. Food production and distribution were being modernized, and most Americans had "a full dinner bucket," although there were pockets of extreme poverty, especially in the South. In 1922, the Roaring Twenties, with flappers dancing the Charleston, were in full swing. Prohibition was the law of the land, but the partying continued unabated as illegal booze was readily available.

If the Dutch of West Michigan, with their religious conservatism, took any notice at all of the worldly pleasures going on around them, it was only to condemn those lifestyles in their homes and from their pulpits. With few exceptions, they didn't drink, they didn't dance and they certainly did not participate in the roaring of the twenties. What they did do, however, was jump on the economic bandwagon and take advantage of the financial goodies that America had to offer. People just a generation or two removed from their starving immigrant forefathers were prospering. The Nicholas Timmer Sr. family was no exception. Nick and Effie had recently moved from a large house on Meyer Avenue, in Beverly, to a house owned by the family at 1933 Porter Street. They had lived in this home previously and kept it as rental property after they left. Now they were back, temporarily, because they were building a new home on Avon Street a block away. With the exception of a short stay at a farm in Byron Township, most of this buying, selling, building, and moving, over about a ten-year period, took place within a couple of city blocks.

Nestled in the middle of all this Timmer residential property sat the Timmer Meat Market. In a 1915 photograph, Nick and his hired man, John Westdorp, (who later became a Catholic priest) are seen standing in front of the market next to a delivery wagon attached to a team of two horses. In neat lettering on the side of the wagon is "Traveling Meat Market" with "N. Timmer" painted near the door. (This photo forms the cover of the 1984 edition of the book, *The City of Wyoming – A History.*) He uniquely peddled meat to customers in Beverly, Wyoming Park and Grandville while John, and later Nick's sons, minded the market. The business must have done well. Not only did the Timmers build several new houses, which were among the largest in the area, but also Nick's daughter Connie recalled that they had one of the first automobiles in the Wyoming Park community. She also remembered that all of the children always had nice clothes and that her dad often kept regular customers supplied with meat, even when they were behind on their accounts. But in 1920, after fourteen years of business, Nick temporarily closed the meat market and went to work at the nearby gypsum mines as a laborer. He began remodeling the market, expanding it and adding a brick smokehouse and sausage-making apparatus. He proudly reopened his establishment in 1922, calling it the "New Suburban Market."

The six kids had very fond memories of the Meyer Avenue home and were sad when they left it. Their father had it built for his family of nine, which included their maternal grandfather, Klaas, whom they called "Opa" (Grandpa in Dutch). The children liked that house because it had more room than they'd had in their previous homes. The family was able to walk across the street to Beverly Reformed Church where they were regular attendees and where Nick Sr. was a deacon. However, in 1920, Nick Sr. decided to sell the house to the church, which wanted it for a parsonage. He must have received a good offer to entice him to sell, but his daughter Grace recalls that getting the money from the church was difficult. It seems that Beverly Reformed was without a pastor at the time and apparently didn't feel any urgency about payments to her dad, since they didn't have anyone to move into it anyway. The hassles involved in the sale must have led to some hard feelings because, in 1921, Nick transferred the membership of everyone in the family out of Beverly Reformed to First Reformed Church of Grandville where Nick and Effie remained members for the rest of their lives.

The house on Porter Street, next door to the meat market, had three bedrooms: one for the folks, one for the boys and Opa, and one for the girls. The rooms were not large enough to hold a multitude of beds, so they had to sleep together -three each in a regular-sized bed! One can only speculate where Opa slept. Someone would have had to have slept on the floor, probably Gerald who, at four, was the youngest. The home had only one toilet and that, of course, was outside. Fortunately, living there was only temporary.

Managing this active household in 1922 (the oldest, Ty, was fifteen) with its comings and goings, baking and cooking, washing and mending, building and moving, was forty-year-old "Mother," Effie Zwyghuizen Timmer, who, unbeknownst to her children, was also pregnant. Because of her age, it was decided that she would have the baby at Butterworth Hospital in downtown Grand Rapids, even though all of her other children had been born at home. All went well, and on New Year's Day, 1923, her seventh and last child, a boy, came into the world.

In a break with family tradition, the baby was not named after a relative. His parents delegated the baby-naming process to their other children. Sibling negotiations produced two finalists which were popular names of the time: Donald and Robert. After some difficult discussions, "Robert," with the middle initial "J," was chosen. He was a chubby and smiling baby who was, of course, doted on by his older siblings

Nine-year-old Grace was surprised that she had a baby brother and disappointed that, at her age, she was not allowed to go into the hospital to see him. Grace eventually saw more than enough of him, however, as she was his primary babysitter and remembers having to push him, seemingly endlessly, in his brown buggy, up and down the street, even before she left for school. Sidewalks were rare in Beverly, but there was one by their former house on Meyer Avenue, so she often took him there where pushing was easier.

In April, when Bob was four months old, he was baptized in the First Reformed Church of Grandville. That same month, the new house on Avon was finished, and the family moved from their temporary home around the corner to their new home half a block away. Nick and Effie never moved again and, decades later, each passed away in the house on Avon that they had built for their family in 1923.

The new house had four bedrooms and the only one downstairs went to the folks, with Bob in the crib next to his parents. Not much changed for the other kids, however, because the additional bedroom, with the only upstairs heat register, went to Opa, while the three (soon to be four) boys and three girls shared the other two. At least they now had inside facilities.

Klaas (Opa) Zwyghuizen

Klaas "Opa" Zwyghuizen must have been someone special. His grandchildren always spoke of him with love, respect and admiration. When Cornelia, his wife of thirty-two years, died of pneumonia in April, 1907, he sold the farm and moved in with the Timmer family. Even though in those days it was common to have a live-in parent, Klaas lived with his daughter, her husband, and their children for eighteen years! Their house was his house. He was raised doing farm work and so, for something to do and to earn some money, he would walk to Groelsema's muck farm on 28th Street to lend a hand with their crops. Often on Saturdays he would dress up, fill a basket with fresh vegetables, and visit friends from the Old Country, dropping off the veggies as he went. When he returned, he brought home cinnamon rolls that his grandchildren ate before church on Sunday mornings. A tall man, he had a very distinct walk. Stooped over, arms swinging, looking more at the ground than straight ahead, he quickly made his way to his destinations around the neighborhood and beyond. He never learned to speak English, so communication with his grandchildren, who didn't speak Dutch, was unique. They had a special language all their own. It was based, in part, on his knowing only a few English words and phrases and they the same in Dutch. Most likely, non-verbal communication, based on the love they had for each other, dating from the time he held them as newborns, was all the language they needed.

He spent a good share of his days walking around Beverly (where everyone knew him and liked him) talking to his Dutch-speaking friends. He was called Opa by everyone-sort of a grandpa to the community. With rare exception, every Sunday morning, through all kinds of weather, he walked the two miles from his home in Beverly to Grandville Avenue Christian Reformed Church for their Dutch language services. He adored his newest grandson, of course, and Grace remembers the toddler holding grandpa's finger as the baby took his earliest steps. Opa passed away in September of 1925, but not before his influence and his love were embedded into his little two year old grandson. He died on a Friday at his son Isaac's home. On Saturday he was taken to the Timmer house, where he lay in repose until Monday. Before the funeral at Beverly Reformed Church, a short service was held at the house, which was interrupted by little Bobbie, who wandered through the gathering until his sister Grace corralled him and took him outside.

Also part of the household when Bob was a schoolboy was a very large Newfoundland named Major. He was so big and gentle that he could easily carry small children on his back. Major, however, was not so gentle when it came to cats. He hated them, and that was bad news for the cat that he occasionally caught. Nick Jr. loved telling the story of how, during winter, Bob's brothers would put him on a sled and tie the sled to Major. Then one of them would release a cat a few blocks away. Major's predictable response was to tear through the neighborhood, chasing the cat, giving Bob, who screamed with delight, the ride of his life for as long as he could stay on the sled.

The fact that Bob grew up in a Dutch Calvinist household defined who he was and what he became. Typical of Dutch homes, the children were encouraged to achieve and education was valued. Their mother, perhaps remembering her school-teaching days, instilled in her kids a love of learning, whether it was learning a trade or studying in school. They were expected to speak and read English. Dutch, while not discouraged, was not promoted. In a household that large, there were rules, roles, and responsibilities, and enforcement was generally left up to Effie. It seemed that if Nick observed an infraction, he told Mother and she had a "little talk" with the offender. Grace does not remember anyone ever getting a spanking.

As little ones they were taught to pray. Their mother gave them Bibles at an early age and expected them to read it regularly. They ate meals together whenever possible, and devotions were part of every meal and family gathering. Interestingly, their father led mealtime devotions, as was the practice in "Reformed" households, but he prayed and read Scripture in Dutch, even though the kids could not understand it. If he was making some kind of point with this practice, it escaped the children. Church attendance was mandatory and so was Sunday school, which followed the worship service. The biblical day of rest was practiced on Sunday afternoons with limits on what the kids could do before heading off to church again for evening services. As teens, they participated in a program called Christian Endeavor (CE) on Sunday afternoons, and if need be, took the bus to Grandville to attend. The Bible made the Sabbath special and different from other days, and so did the Timmer family.

The girls in the family were expected to help with the many household chores that were necessary in those days: baking bread, cooking, cleaning, shopping for groceries, and helping their mother with the younger children. According to Grace, the boys, other than having to mow the lawn, were pretty much free to do as they pleased. In accordance with societal values of the 1920s, girls were trained to be housewives and mothers. Work was a family value. It was valued because hard work was what God expected, and it brought additional revenue into the family.. Nick also had a *Grand Rapids Press* route, which he took to pay back his folks for the violin they had purchased for him. He soon lost interest in both the violin and his route. Grace frequently peddled his papers while younger sister Anne took over the violin and became very good at it. When they were old enough, Ty and Nick, began working for their father at the meat market and were meat cutters all their working lives

Although family trips were rare, Grace recalls an outing (probably sometime in the mid-twenties) to Fennville to visit friends who had moved there. It seems that her father had replaced his horse-drawn wagon with a Model T Ford pickup truck. The truck was equipped with an insulated box which kept the meat fresh during delivery. For the Fennville trip, the box was removed and replaced with seven kids. With the folks in the cramped seats, the three girls sat on a plank laid across the truck box near the cab, and the two oldest boys, Ty and Nick, were at the rear of the bed, draping their feet over the back edge. Sitting on the truck bed, protected by siblings fore and aft, were the little boys, Gerald and Bob. It is amazing that they all stayed within the confines of the truck with the roads of the day being little more than two-track, bumpy ruts. (Given the name of the community where they lived, it is hard to resist conjuring up the image of them going down the road as sort of a Dutch version of the television show *The Beverly Hillbillies*.)

The Dutch of West Michigan loved their new land. After all, it had treated most of them very well. The Timmer family was no exception. Nick and Effie purposely modeled a love of country in their home, instilling a strong sense of patriotism in their children. There was always an American flag flying in front of the house on Avon.

The older kids in the family went to Porter School on the corner of Porter Street and Byron Center Avenue. Nick Jr. was proud of the fact that he had been in the school's first eighth grade graduating class. (Eighth grade graduation was a big deal in those days.) Although Ty took the interurban trolley to

South High School in Grand Rapids, the other kids went to Grandville High School, because there was not a secondary school in the Wyoming Park/Beverly area. In 1926, Boulevard Elementary School was built, and Bob started kindergarten there a year later, at the age of four and a half. It was only a few blocks from home and an easy walk for a four year old, especially when accompanied by his brother Gerald, who was eight. Years later, several of his Boulevard teachers remembered him as a good student and a well-behaved little boy. Dorothy Beverwyk DeWitt, who was in his class from kindergarten through graduation, recalled that he was a very good student and well-liked.

Bob's six older brothers and sisters were involved in many activities. Their mother required that they participate in music of some kind. She herself played the piano. Practice on a variety of musical instruments —piano, flute, and violin—became part of the sounds of the house. A regular feature of their family life was singing hymns around the piano while Mother played. And although Dad did not lend his voice to the concert, they knew he enjoyed the playing and singing by the way he rocked back and forth to the music. They also participated in sports. The girls played basketball (the six-person girls' variety) and the boys were involved in baseball, basketball and football. Bob soaked up all of it. It was while he was in elementary school, however, that his real passion in life emerged: a love for airplanes and the dream of learning to fly.

In 1919, Kent County began turning a field at Madison and 36th Street into an airport. However, it wasn't until 1925 that the County Board of Supervisors, pressured by the Grand Rapids community, granted a group of businessmen a five-year lease to develop the property into a serviceable airport.

Their efforts, combined with a desire by the Army Air Service to install a military air control system, led to the completion of an all-weather airport. Forty thousand people were on hand in July of 1926, when the airport officially opened.[18] Soon, regular passenger and freight service were inaugurated, and planes were taking off and landing on a daily basis. Interestingly, one of the early leases granted by the county prohibited Sunday flying.

Given the new airport's close proximity to Wyoming Park, Bob often observed planes flying overhead. This also was the era of barnstorming, where daredevil pilots traveled the country showing off their flying skills and taking people for rides. It is possible that Bob saw these shows as a young boy, but it is not very likely that he took his first plane ride with a barnstormer. His parents would not have allowed it, even if he could have come up with the fifteen dollar charge. His brother Nick also liked planes and, given the fact that he was twelve years older and could drive a car, meant that his young brother frequently got rides to the airport to watch the planes.

When no ride was available, as was often the case, Bob (even as young as twelve or thirteen) would hitchhike to the airport just to hang around the planes and pilots. The flyers must have enjoyed having him around because they began to give him rides and even took him to Chicago on one occasion. What a thrill plane rides must have been for a young boy. Many of the small planes of the early 1930s were double-winged biplanes with an open cockpit for the pilot and one for his passenger. So with goggles on and wind in his face, Bob got the thrill of flying into his bones at an early age. However, the fact that he sometimes "forgot" to tell his parents where he was going, and occasionally neglected to tell them about the rides until after they had occurred, was of great concern around the house and led to some "understandings" about his airport activities.

Nick Sr. sold his meat cutting business in the late 1920s and began working at a meat market in Hudsonville owned by his former boss Lee Edson. Besides his slaughterhouse, Lee owned a retail market and wanted Nick to manage it. Effie could not understand why he would get rid of a business half a block from their house and commute ten miles or so to work for someone else. Apparently one of the perks of his job was to be able to hire his sons to work for him, just as he did when he had his own business. Unlike his two oldest brothers, Bob had no desire to follow in his dad's footsteps and become a butcher, but he too, worked at the Hudsonville store when he was in junior high and early high school. Teammate Jay Van Sweden remembers that when Wyoming played Hudsonville in football, it was like old home week for Bob because he knew many of the opposing players. (In 1940, Wyoming beat Hudsonville 25-0!)

~~~~~~~~

Boulevard Elementary School was located at the intersection of Boulevard and Wrenwood Streets in Wyoming Park. Wyoming school authorities scrambled to keep classrooms, teachers and a curriculum in front of the growing number of students moving through Boulevard. A new high school soon was being planned for the same site, which would eventually become a K-12 complex. In the school year 1934-35, a ninth grade was added to the K-8 school and each year thereafter, another grade was formed. Unfortunately, the construction of the new high school complex could not keep up with the advancing classes. The building wasn't finished when the first freshmen class was ready to begin their sophomore year, so the students were farmed out to Grandville, Lee, and Grand Rapids Central. Even though they were officially Wyoming High School students, they did not return to their own high school until the fall of their junior year.[19] They were the first Wyoming Park senior class and graduated in 1938.

The new building, finally completed, was dedicated in November, 1936. (It was first called Wyoming, then later Wyoming Park, and today it is known as "The Park.") Bob Timmer, unlike his brothers and sisters, did not have to leave his neighborhood to go to high school. He entered Wyoming as a ninth-grader in the fall of 1936. By this time his older siblings had begun leaving the house through marriage or employment, and the younger kids began to enjoy bedrooms of their own. Major, however, was never relegated to a doghouse, so room still had to be made for his bulk as well.

Nick Timmer Sr. Family: Seated: Connie, Grace, Anne. Middle Row: Gerald, Bob, Standing: Effie, Ty, Nick, Jr., Nick, Sr.

The Wyoming High School that Robert Timmer entered did not have a twelfth grade. The students must have been excited, that fall of '36, to move into a brand new high school with its modern facilities: science labs, music rooms, a home economics room, a gymnasium, and a library. It was also conveniently located within walking distance for most of them. The far-flung juniors, after a year apart, rejoiced at coming together again, even though for them there was very little tradition: no athletic teams, no music program, no mascot, no yearbook, and no student newspaper. In addition to getting to know each other again, they also had to enter classrooms with unfamiliar teachers. It is obvious from class sizes that many who could have returned to Wyoming chose not to do so, preferring to stay at the various schools they had attended as sophomores. The class of '38 had forty members, while Bob's freshman class had about seventy.

In photographs, the new freshman looks rather shy and reserved, a skinny thirteen-year-old, one of the younger ninth-graders with his fourteenth birthday some four months away. Nothing, however, kept him from plunging into high school life. He went out for football that first fall and played on the JV team. The junior varsity boys did not have a regular schedule, but they played a few games and practiced with the varsity players, who were all juniors. Bob was also on the JV basketball team.

It is difficult to determine where he developed his love of sports. There were no Little League or city recreation teams around in those days, so he and his neighborhood buddies played their games in fields and playgrounds around Beverly. While Bob was growing up, his brother Nick did play basketball and baseball on sponsored teams, and most likely taught his little brother some of the basics and encouraged him to be an active participant. Bob sang in the school choir that first year, which, hopefully, satisfied his mother's desire to have her kids involved in music, because he did not play an instrument. Outside of school he was a Boy Scout and continued to spend time at the airport. He was an excellent student.

On an application he filled out in 1941 for the Royal Canadian Air Force, Bob stated that he worked as an "apprentice airplane mechanic" at the Kent County Airport during the summers of 1936 and `37. It is highly unlikely that, in the depths of the Great Depression, a fourteen or fifteen-year-old boy would hold down a paying job as an apprentice, which required significant mechanical ability. There is no doubt, however, that he continued to be a presence at the airport, and because he had known many of the pilots and mechanics for several years, they allowed him to play a role similar to a "surgical assistant" and hand them tools and even tighten a few nuts while they worked on their planes. Whatever his role, it was a great learning experience and, of course, looked good on his application.

Late the summer of 1937, while Bob was roller-skating toward home along Porter Street from Wyoming Park to Beverly, he was hit by a car driven by a nineteen-year-old young man. He was skating in the street because there were no sidewalks. The driver stated that he did not see him until it was too late. Even though the driver swerved, the bumper and headlamp of the vehicle struck Bob, breaking his leg. Luckily, it happened right in front of Beverly Park Dairy, operated by the Bergman family, who were good friends of Bob's father. Mr. Bergman ran around the corner and got Bob's brother-in-law, Bill Van Hoeven, who was living on Avon. Bill carried the boy home and from there he was taken to St. Mary's Hospital to be treated. He thus began his sophomore year in a cast and on crutches.

Bob seemed to really enjoy athletics, especially football, and participation in sports occupied a great deal of his time in high school. With his leg in a cast, his sophomore football season was unfortunately over, but he stayed involved in the sport by becoming the student manager of the varsity team. Wyoming finally had a senior class and a good football team, finishing with a 4-1-3 record; the three ties were 0-0 scores against Zeeland, Godwin and Coopersville. Not bad, considering they had not yet held a graduation ceremony. It seems playing football was the only thing the broken leg limited Bob from doing that year. He was again on the JV basketball team, and they played a full schedule of seventeen games, losing only three. Strangely, they played to a 9-9 tie with Hudsonville.

The class of 1938 was the first to graduate from Wyoming High School. That year they published the first Wyoming yearbook, the *Orbit*, with photographs showing Bob in a variety of activities. In addition to football and basketball, he again was in the choir which staged *Miss Cherryblossom*, a musical comedy about a "white girl brought up in Tokyo, Japan." Bob must have had some talent because he played the role of Kokemo, one of only eight speaking roles. He joined the Forensic Club, which was formed to "foster interest in speech activities." Membership was limited to those who had taken a course in public speaking. The Hi-Y Club, one of the more active school clubs, was open only to boys and existed "to create, maintain, and extend throughout the school and community, high standards of Christian character." It was affiliated with the national, state, and local YMCA organizations. There were Hi-Y clubs in most of the high schools of that day. The Wyoming club sponsored speakers and school events and sold school emblems and sweaters. Apparently, the first club (1935-36) was given some responsibility in selecting the school mascot, and came up with "Vikings," which they are to this day. Bob was a member of Hi-Y each of his high school years and served as vice-president his senior year.

Wyoming Park H.S. 1940

There were no accidents, that summer of 1938, to prevent Bob from starting football practice in the fall of his junior year at Wyoming. Coaches Swanson and Davis picked him as the starting center. It is obvious from his pictures that he had begun to fill out and add inches. His friend, Jay Van Sweden, stated that the reason Bob played center was because he was so slow. "They always picked the slowest kids to play center," he remembered.[20] In the single wing formation that most schools used in that era, the center had to snap the ball to a back by looking between his legs (the quarterback rarely took the snap), exposing himself to getting crunched by opposing linemen who often hit him while he had his head down, probably the reason photos show very little blue and white paint left on his leather helmet. The team, the first with seniors, led by all-around athlete Jay Stalsonberg, went 3-3-2. Bob seemed to have been better at football than basketball because, as a junior, he was again assigned to the junior varsity team that went 10-6. Jay Van Sweden said that he had "two left feet," which may have been the reason for another JV season.[21]

The first debate team was organized in 1938 and Bob was a member, along with his continuing involvement in forensics. He also added writing for the school newspaper, *The Beacon*, to his list of activities. As a junior he successfully campaigned for election as treasurer of his class of 1940. While in high school, he never participated in spring sports (baseball and track in those days), but in the spring of his junior year he went into rehearsals for the operetta, *The Sunbonnet Girl*, performed on May 18, where he played Ezra McSpavin, a police constable. He continued to excel in the classroom, taking college preparatory courses in math, science, social studies, and English.

When he joined the military, Bob estimated that he had about two-hundred flying hours as a passenger. Obviously, with that many hours in the air, he was still spending a lot of time at the airport, despite his full high school schedule. In the summer of 1939, as he approached his senior year, all of his siblings had left the house for jobs and marriage, so it was just Bob, Major and his parents in what was now a house with plenty of room. He was also a proud uncle to three nieces and a nephew, and spent time visiting with his married brothers and sisters, all of whom were still in the area.

Late that same summer, two events occurred that would have a profound effect on Bob's life. World War II began on September 3rd when German armies swept into Poland, and that same month, a fifteen-year-old girl, transferred from Grand Rapids South High School, and began attending Wyoming. Her name was Eileen Donna Koopman, and it did not take long for the good-looking sixteen-year-old senior to notice the pretty new junior.

It would be difficult to imagine that anyone could have had more fun in his or her senior year of high school than did Robert Timmer. Now grown to about 6'0 and 180 pounds, he again was the starting center on a football team that went 5 and 3. Unfortunately, more was expected of that team as they had eleven returning letterman, one at each position. They started the season in great fashion, winning their first three games without being scored on, but then lost three of their next five. The *Orbit* speculates that they lost games due to "sensational" reporting by area papers that led to overconfidence on the part of the "Dream Team."[22] Based on comments from some of his classmates, Bob must have held some aspirations of playing college football although, at this point in his senior year, his attention turned to other things.

He finally made the varsity basketball team, but due to the two-left-feet syndrome, was not one of the starting five on the 8 and 6 squad. Given his size, however, he was an early substitute, usually at the center position. In a game against powerhouse Holland Christian on Tuesday, February 13,

1940, which Wyoming lost 27 to 24, the *Grand Rapids Herald,* with the headline, "Holland Quint Whips Wyoming High Cage Five," reports, "Timmer was lost to Wyoming Park late in the third quarter when he collected four fouls."[23] It was too early in the game to be getting into foul trouble, so he must have been out there hacking at his opponents. Before going to the bench, however, he had scored four points, not bad when your team totaled only 24. He was also a substitute at guard, an interesting position for someone slow afoot.

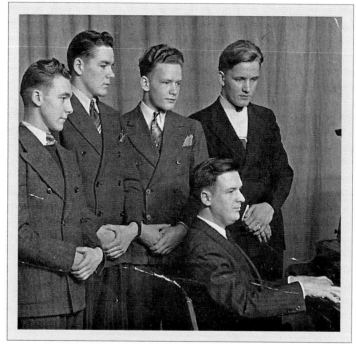

Singing Bass in the Quartette

In addition to his fourth year in the large, all-school mixed chorus, Bob participated in the school's first Boys Glee Club. From it a male quartet was formed with Robert Timmer singing bass. The yearbook states, "The members of this quartette found themselves very popular with their listeners, and the versatility of this quartette is proved by its repeated demand to appear before varied audiences."[24] He left the staff of *The Beacon* and joined the yearbook staff, doing the writing for boys' sports. He probably wrote the piece on "sensational reporting" mentioned above. He joined the Dramatics Club and again had a part in the school play, *Icebound*. All of this while serving as an officer in Hi-Y and treasurer of his class. As if his own interests weren't enough to occupy his time, he was involved in his friend Jay Van Sweden's campaign for Student Council President, Class of 1941. It seems that Jay began by running unopposed, which was unacceptable to class sponsor Mr. Ken Davis, who recruited two girls to run against him. That split the girls' vote and Jay was elected president for his senior year.[25]

On New Year's Day, 1940, Bob celebrated his seventeenth birthday. His mother gave him a small Bible containing the New Testament and Psalms which she inscribed, "To Bobbie from Mother on his 17th birthday."

> *[Note: The Bible, which is still in the family, is in fairly good shape, despite the fact that it was later stuffed into pockets, duffle bags, boxes, and lockers, and hauled across three continents while being exposed to the elements of rain, blowing sand and forty below temperatures.]*

Public Confession of Faith is a common practice in churches with a Reformed perspective. It is a religious rite of passage somewhat comparable to the first communion ritual in the Roman Catholic Church or Bar Mitzvah in the Jewish tradition. A person moved by God to make profession will meet with the church consistory and answer questions relating to his or her understanding of God's word and church doctrine.

The consistory, if confident of the person's commitment, will grant approval to him or her to become a communicant member of that denomination. The person must then publicly proclaim his or her faith by standing in church on a Sunday morning and answering "yes" or "I do" to questions contained in a ritual read by the minister. The person is then welcomed into full communion with the church, the body of Christ, and is able to partake of the Lord's Supper. The overwhelming majority of people who do this are in their teenage years. Robert Timmer made his Confession of Faith on March 18, 1940, before the congregation at First Reformed Church of Grandville. It was a significant event in his life.

In the summer of 1939, Eileen Koopman's parents had moved from Jefferson Street in Grand Rapids to Porter Street in Beverly, which was only a few blocks from the Timmer home on Avon. It is difficult to know exactly when Eileen became his girlfriend, but they may have become acquainted while walking to school because they would have taken the same route. They sang together in the choir, which was their only class together. Once they got to know each other, however, it didn't take long for her to become a big part of his life. Eileen was described by those who knew her as pretty, quiet, and a good student. "A sweet personality that goes far," is the quote by her senior picture. It would be easy to speculate that this big, handsome, all-everything senior swept the shy fifteen-year-old junior off her feet just as she was trying to get comfortable in a new high school where she had few, if any, friends. Eileen, however, seemed to have her head about her and did not seem to be the type who would quickly fall hopelessly and helplessly in love, or be swept off her feet by anybody.

Dating for high school couples in those days centered around school events, and that was the case for Bob and Eileen. Boys did not have the money to take their girlfriends out, even to inexpensive events. There were, of course, games and concerts, banquets and parties that were mostly free, and dating couples would often be in attendance. Absent from the things-to-do-with-a-date list were sock-hops and proms because dancing was not allowed at Wyoming High School. Occasionally, a class would rent a skating rink for a class outing, and there is a photo in the yearbook of Bob and Eileen, with arms locked, roller-skating at such an event.[26] He is wearing his white letter sweater with the big blue "W" on the front, common attire for high school boys of the time. She is wearing a white blouse and plaid skirt, and her long hair reflects the "dos" of the early forties. They are an attractive couple who looked older than they were.

Often, Bob would walk the few blocks to Eileen's house and would just hang out there, sitting around talking to the folks and teasing Eileen's younger sister Jean. He was easy to be with—friendly, but somewhat shy unless around people he knew. He laughed often. Occasionally, the couple would go for a date walk and just stroll around the neighborhood. Henry Vander Velde, who lived near the Koopman home, used to watch them coming and going, holding hands.

During their walks, they would often stop at brother Nick and wife Tressa's house a few blocks from Eileen's and bounce around his first baby nephew. They would also show up at his folks, especially if his sisters were there with his nieces. In those days, kids could get their drivers licenses at the age of fourteen, so if a car was available (few had their own) the couple could leave Wyoming Park for a date, maybe even go to Grand Rapids. Bob's dad, however, was rather stingy about letting his kids use his car, but from time to time, his brothers and sisters would let him use theirs for special occasions. Eileen's parents thought the world of Bob, just as his parents did about Eileen.

Not surprisingly for teenagers in love, things did not always go smoothly between Bob and Eileen. The note Eileen wrote in Bob's senior yearbook says, "Dear Bob, It's been fun (?) knowing you. Lots of luck in the future and I hope you make the team at State. Sincerely, Eileen" —a rather chilly note to share with a boyfriend she had been dating for some time. One can only speculate on the meaning of the (?) but it seems that on the eve of his graduation, things might have been a little shaky between them. Somewhat more telling about their relationship, perhaps, is the note next to Eileen's, written by Norma M. It says, "Dear Timmer, I probably should have chosen a different page— this won't be seen next to this (with an arrow drawn to Eileen's note)—but— I certainly wish you loads of good luck— it sure was swell you're getting to M. State— I'm sure you will make good— You will be missed in Wyoming by many— including E.K." Chilly notes aside, there is little doubt that by the time Bob left high school, these talented teenagers had fallen hard for each other.

In the spring of his senior year, Bob applied for the Michigan State College Alumni Undergraduate Scholarship. Three hundred "outstanding" high school seniors were considered, with 170 selected to take the comprehensive exam. The letter of notification, dated May 23, 1940, states, "On the basis of your high school record, the recommendations of the local committee, and the comprehensive examination—you have been awarded a scholarship. . . We congratulate you on being one of the sixty-four so honored. Your competition in this contest was very keen." His college fees would be waived for the first year, and annual renewal was contingent upon keeping his grades "sufficiently high."

So, in June of 1940, after giving as much to his school as he could give, and getting a lot back in return, Robert Timmer, head over heels in love, and with a full ride to Michigan State in his pocket, graduated from Wyoming Park High School.

~~~~~~~

Wyoming Park was nice place to be living that warm summer of 1940. Most families were doing well as the economy began to pull out of the Great Depression, and summer jobs were available for kids who wanted to work. Houses were being built throughout the area, so vacant lots were not as plentiful for pickup baseball games among neighborhood kids.

People were getting rid of their old ice boxes and the need for the weekly ice delivery man and were replacing them with new refrigerators, which cost around $150. (The Timmer family had their icebox well into the 1940s, however.)

Most small businesses had a telephone and they soon became a necessity in private residences. Milk was delivered from Beverly Park Dairy with horse-drawn wagons and cost ten cents a quart, while a loaf of bread was six cents.

Horses were very much in use in those days. Their workload ranged from Pete Stalsenburg's team digging fresh basements for new homes, by pulling a huge scoop through recently platted house sites, to pulling huckster Frank Noel's wagon through the streets of Beverly, supplying fresh vegetables to housewives every Tuesday and Friday. There were numerous corner grocery stores in the area, but the Timmers purchased their groceries a few doors from their house at Vanderwal's on

Porter Street. The store was owned by Levi Depuit and George Vanderwal, who had ice cream available every Saturday.

There were no supermarkets. Large families, with limited space in the kitchen and the icebox, went shopping for food almost every day, and there were numerous small mom-and-pop grocery stores dotting the neighborhoods to serve that purpose. In some stores, customers were able to fill their own orders, but in most, shoppers gave their grocery lists and baskets to the clerk who would then walk among the shelves filling the order by placing the desired items in the customer's basket. While waiting at the counter, customers often entertained themselves by watching flies struggle unsuccessfully to free their feet from the numerous strands of sticky fly paper hanging from the tin ceilings. The paper was made locally by the Thum brothers at their Thum Tanglefoot Flypaper Company on Byron Center Avenue.[27] Over-the-counter drugs, prescriptions and things medical were purchased at Ganzel's Drug Store in Wyoming Park.

The Timmer family never had to shop for meat, but gradually grocery stores began adding a meat department. With improving refrigerated trucks, large hunks of meat were delivered to their doors from area slaughterhouses and stored in rather large walk-in coolers. Inside, hanging from hooks, were a side or two of beef and pork and other slabs of varying sizes. On shelves were boxes of chickens and processed meat like lunch meat and hot dogs. Large metal pans held pounds and pounds of freshly ground hamburger and strings of homemade sausage, frequently manufactured according to a secret, family recipe. The floors were covered with sawdust to soak up blood dripping from the hanging carcasses.

Outside of the cooler in the work area, there was always meat on the chopping block in various stages of dismemberment, and bolted to a counter was a metal grinder waiting for chunks of meat to be shoved into its top and turned into hamburger. Next to the block were a couple of metal garbage cans containing scrap - hunks of fat and bones that had been removed from the slabs. Tools of the trade, hanging from hooks and sticking out of racks and crevices, consisted of knives of all sizes and shapes, various kinds of hack saws, and gruesome short-handled axes called cleavers. A sausage machine, which looked like a hamburger grinder but with a nozzle for a nose, stood ready to receive the gut casings into which the sausage meat would be squirted. On a counter near the glass case was a dispenser holding a large roll of butcher paper, above a spool of string hanging from the ceiling. The end of the string dangled over the paper. Once a customer selected the meat she wanted, an experienced butcher could wrap and tie it in a split second. The package would then be weighed and priced using the large round-faced scale sitting on top of the display case.

Many meat departments had a back door for deliveries where, at the same time every day, neighborhood dogs would gather for their daily bone. If the bones were passed out at ten o'clock each morning, the dogs would start gathering at about 9:58. There were enough to go around so there was no fighting, and neighbors smiled at the look of pride on the dog's faces as they trotted home with their treats. The dogs were not the only ones getting treats. Neighborhood kids would often stop by for a raw hot dog that some thought was better than candy.
People also went shopping in downtown Grand Rapids and usually took a Grandville-Wyoming Transit Co. bus to get there. (The interurban was gone by the late 1930s.) A man could buy a nice suit at Jurgens and Holtvluwer on Grandville Avenue for about fifteen dollars. Coal was delivered by the

Wyoming Park Lumber and Fuel Co., where every chilly day in every home, it had to be shoveled from the coal bin into the furnace - a dirty job. Staying cool in the summer heat was difficult, especially in second floor bedrooms, so a good fan was a necessity. Neighborhood kids, though, got relief from summer heat by swimming in one of the numerous gravel pits in the area.

Wyoming Park did not have its own movie theater. The closest one was in nearby Galewood, but few Dutch went to movies, not even to see Clark Gable in the recently released *Gone with the Wind*. Young people were raised with parental admonitions that, "Christians don't buy tickets to movies that support the sinful lifestyles of people in Hollywood." Radio was very popular, and families would gather around a large console most evenings to listen to such programs as *The Shadow, The Jack Benny Program, The Edgar Bergen and Charlie McCarthy Show*, and occasionally, the President of the United States, with one of his popular fireside talks. Beautiful new Packards and Hudsons were in the showrooms, although for most in Wyoming Park, Fords and Chevys were found in their single stall garages. The Andrews Sisters and Bing Crosby turned out hit after hit, and teens drank real malted milks at the soda fountain in Ganzel's Drug Store, where, if they had a nickel to spare (most didn't), they could listen to the sounds of Glen Miller and Bennie Goodman and their Big Bands on the jukebox. There, they also participated in root beer drinking contests and got free all-you-can-eat ice cream cones when Mr. Ganzel occasionally switched brands.

The joys of the summer of 1940, however, were tempered by an ominous, dark shadow being cast toward America by the fascist regimes of Europe. After the quick annihilation of Poland in September of 1939, the Nazi juggernaut swept over

Denmark, Norway, The Netherlands, Luxembourg, and Belgium. The fall of France in June, 1940, shocked the world. Most of Europe was now suffering under the Nazi terror. Hitler next turned his attention toward bringing Britain to her knees. He knew that invading the island would be difficult and thought that an indiscriminate bombing campaign, aimed not only at military and industrial targets but also at large population centers, would bring the British to the surrender table. The Battle of Britain was about to begin.

Winston Churchill became prime minister in May of 1940 and told his people that all he could offer was "blood, toil, tears and sweat." But as German bombs began obliterating English cities, the British Commonwealth responded to the plight of the mother country and thousands of troops and vast amounts of supplies began arriving in the Island Nation. They came from South Africa, Australia, New Zealand, India, Canada and dozens of other countries. At home, President Franklin Roosevelt walked a tightrope, trying to help Britain while promising to keep us out of war.

High school graduates were facing difficult and challenging circumstances. Times were scary that summer of 1940, especially for families with men of military age. There was a sense of approaching doom that most didn't want to think about. But it was the uncertainty of it all that made planning a life and career so difficult. For Robert Timmer, however, there was little doubt in his mind about his future; he knew for certain what he was going to do.

After graduation, he got a job loading trucks at the Nehi Beverage Co. in Grand Rapids, and he saw a lot of Eileen. They walked and biked through the neighborhoods, swam at Lamar Park, went roller skating, visited relatives, hung out with the gang at Ganzels, and went to church together. Sadly, as the idyllic summer of '40 drew to a close, Eileen went back to high school for her senior year, and Bob joined the freshman class at Michigan State College. The end of a fun, romantic summer together made parting difficult. They would miss each other very much.

~~~~~~~

Wells Hall was a men's dormitory and one of the older buildings on the Michigan State campus, which had been remodeled in the late 1930s. (Coed dorms did not exist in 1940.) Behind it was the Red Cedar River, which could be heard from the dorm as it flowed over the dam nearby. Across the river to the south there were only woods and fields where the howling of coyotes and the whistle of trains often interrupted the boys trying to concentrate on their studies.[28] The front of Wells faced campus, with its beautiful lawns, flower beds and buildings built in the old English style architecture, called "Collegiate Gothic." It was reminiscent of the buildings at Oxford University, England. Much of what was there in 1940 still survives, helping to make Michigan State one of the most beautiful major college campuses in the country. Unfortunately, Wells Hall is no longer part of it, having been razed in the 1960s after a fire. The MSU Library now stands in its place.

Bob was assigned to room A12 on the sixth floor. His roommate was fellow freshman Robert E. Donley, from Buchanan, Michigan, an engineering major. There was one black telephone on each floor which, no doubt, was used frequently by homesick freshman attempting to stay connected to their families and friends. There was hot and cold running water, most of the time, and mice could occasionally be heard running between the walls. The boys were required to eat all their meals in the dorm and could relax after dinner with a game of ping pong in Wells' basement rec room.

Bob chose Police Administration as his major. It seems a strange choice since there is no indication that he was ever interested in going into law enforcement. However, of all the choices he had, it seems to fit best with his desire to join the military. He was well aware that he had to get just one year of college in before going into the service, so it wasn't that important. Besides, the freshman curriculum consisted of many required courses with few electives, so it would likely be a year or two before he would take classes related to his major. Michigan State, in those days, divided the academic year into three terms, or trimesters, while most others had two semesters.

He took courses in chemistry and English composition all three of his freshman terms, as well as two terms of social studies, one of them being Geography 101. He also took speech, an elective carried over from one of his high school interests. He had three terms of anatomy and physiology, which may have been related to his major, because they certainly are not typical freshman course requirements. Physical education was required, but students had a variety of offerings within the department. Bob took Boxing and Wrestling, Life Saving, and Group Games as his three choices, a testament to his variety of interests.

Military Science (ROTC) was a required course, and every male at MSC, and other Land Grant Colleges, had to take it for two years or six terms. With war raging in Europe, it was possible that the United States would someday be in it, and it was important to have a well-trained officer corps. It was a big part of college life in those days. If the students passed the necessary physical and academic requirements, they were referred to as an "advanced officer" for the rest of their college careers. They received college credit for the course and were granted membership in a campus officer's club. In addition to class work, they also went on maneuvers, and every Tuesday the coeds would come out to watch them march in formation on the campus parade ground. It gave Robert Timmer a taste of what was to come, and he enjoyed it.[29]

He didn't exactly set any freshman academic records during his first term on campus. Going away to school had to be a big adjustment for a young man who, in his seventeen years, rarely left Wyoming Park. The shock of being an all-everything in high school to being a lowly college freshman has caused many good students to drop out before finishing their first year. Bob was from a large and close family. His brothers and sisters were each other's best friends, so leaving them, his parents, Major, and his own bedroom was not easy. Then, of course, there was Eileen and the difficulties of maintaining a relationship while being apart for long periods of time. Besides, the old black phone in the sixth floor hallway was not exactly conducive to private conversations seeking affirmation that feelings were still there. Whatever the cause, this student on scholarship received Cs in every course his first term, a 2.0 grade point, not exactly a scholarship performance. Then, for some reason, he kicked it in, perhaps after a good talk with himself. His grades the last two terms were all As and Bs with one exception: he got a C in Group Games! Despite his less than auspicious start, which was a real drag on his overall grade point, Robert Timmer pulled a 3.6 and a 3.4 his remaining two terms to finish his first year with a 2.7 overall, or a B minus, not bad for a freshman. The scholarship committee renewed his scholarship for another year, no doubt due to his two-term performance.

Bob and Eileen, Summer 1941

The summer of 1941 found Bob living at home and working in the shipping room at Grand Rapids Sash and Door, unloading box cars. Eileen had graduated from Wyoming in June, and they were spending as much time together as possible. Jay Van Sweden had also just graduated and was working at Paul Gezon's grocery store in Wyoming Park. Jay remembers that Bob came into the store that summer and proudly told his friend that he would soon be leaving for Windsor, Ontario, to join the Royal Canadian Air Force. While it was common knowledge among his friends that Bob would someday train to fly, Jay was surprised to learn that he was joining the service so soon. Most American boys, knowing that they would be called up if the U.S. became involved, were waiting until that happened and hoping that it wouldn't. His parents were very much against his going, but soon realized that he was committed to his goal and there would be no talking him out of it. It meant that the war would come early to the Timmer family of Avon Avenue, and his sister Grace remembers that her mother "cried and cried."

Robert notified Michigan State that he was dropping out and giving up his scholarship. In early August, he said good-bye to Eileen. With his friend Jim Evers, he boarded a bus headed for Windsor, Ontario, where he would officially become a member of the Canadian armed forces.

Why would a young man who seemed to have a very bright future in whatever field he chose, who was in love with his steady girlfriend, and who had a full college scholarship, give it all up and leave his family and friends to go into the military service of a foreign country?

While his desire to get into the fight in Europe was part of the reason Bob joined the Canadian forces, the main reason was that at that time, he needed two years of college to be accepted for U.S. Army flight school, but only one year for Canadian flight training. He'd had a plan all along; he had known that he would spend only one year in college before he ever went to Michigan State. His decision to enter the Canadian military had little to do with anything except the fact that Robert Timmer, scholarship or not, girlfriend or not, war or no war, just flat out wanted to fly airplanes.

Chapter IV Canada

The vast British Commonwealth of Nations had morphed from the remnants of the British Empire upon which "the sun never set." In the nineteenth century, the Empire began suffering from sporadic attempts, often accompanied by incredible violence, to throw off the British yoke. This resulted in efforts by the small mother nation to keep control of breakaway attempts, which, in turn, began putting impossible burdens on her men, money, and materials. Soon it became politically and economically impossible to maintain the colonial status of so many far-flung entities. Now, on the eve of yet another European war, many of the old colonies had become independent nations run by parliamentary democracies, based on the model of their mother country. (Indigenous people were not part of the process.) They still recognized the British royalty as their own, and English was their language. Some, like Ireland, wanted nothing to do with its former ruler; others, like India, were still in the throes of rebellion; but for those who made up the Commonwealth, there were economic and political benefits for maintaining close ties with Britain and each other. Those ties, however, came with a price because there were European wars to be fought. So boys from Australia, New Zealand, Canada and other far away nations died in the trenches of World War I beside their English cousins. The bonds of loyalty and brotherhood were not free.

No member of the Commonwealth was more tied to "good ole England" than Canada, at least, English-speaking Canada. It had a proud history of loyalty to the Crown going as far back as its refusal to join the American rebellion. When Hitler began rattling his Luftwaffe, threatening all of Europe during the 1930s, Canada was as much a part of the strategies of Nazi containment as were most western European countries. (Unfortunately one of the strategies was appeasement giving Hitler what he wanted in exchange for promises of peace which, to the lying Fuehrer, was a strategy that resulted in peaceful Nazi takeovers of Austria and Czechoslovakia.) In the mid '30s, as Churchill raged in Parliament over Britain's naïveté in dealing with Germany and her lack of preparations for a war that he knew was coming, the British military began to realize that they were woefully behind Germany's huge military rearmament program.

The leaders of the Royal Air Force were especially worried, given their knowledge of Germany's development and production of planes and the training of its airmen. It was commonly understood in both political and military circles that availability of training facilities and airmen could make the difference on whether the next war would be won or lost. The commander of the Royal Air Force was Air Commodore Arthur Tedder, who had on his staff a Scottish airman named Robert Leckie. In a memo to his boss, Commodore Tedder, Group Captain Leckie proposed a Flying Training School based in Canada.[30] His rationale included: flying schools in a country that would be far removed from a European war, parts and supplies that were available from good neighbor USA in the event of disruptions to an Atlantic supply line, and a ready supply of athletic, outdoor-type men who could make excellent airmen. He also pointed out that Canadians were some of the best flyers in the RAF during the Great War.[31]

Ultimately, Canadian officials were approached about the possibility of RAF flying schools in Canada. Negotiations between the two countries began. A host of concerns needed to be addressed before the planning process could start and most of them centered on issues of turf. Canadians were concerned that, if Britain controlled military training facilities in their county, it could have implications for Canadian sovereignty and become a political issue with voters. The British, on the other hand, believed that they needed to control the training of their own airmen. Financing the whole venture also became a stumbling block. As the talks dragged on and on, Hitler continued gobbling up the countries of Europe, and when war broke out in September of 1939, there was still no agreement in place. Finally, later that month, after shockingly observing how the German Luftwaffe went about destroying Poland, the two leaders, Neville Chamberlain of Britain and MacKenzie King of Canada, agreed, in principle, to a proposal for training airmen. Eventually approved by the leaders of Britain, Canada, Australia, and New Zealand, it was called the British Commonwealth Air Training Plan and went into effect in December of 1939.

The BCATP was not just for training pilots. In the beginning, three types of air crew went through training: pilots, air observers, and wireless operators/gunners. With the eventual introduction of the four-engine bomber and the need for additional crewmen, the Plan was training men in eight different categories by the end of the war.[32] However, most recruits wanted to be pilots or a flyer of some kind, but not all of them were able to pass the rigorous physical and academic requirements that pilot training required. Therefore, the program became a process for sorting the recruits into appropriate areas of need for the Canadian Air Force.

The need for instructors was critical. There were few experienced military pilots due to prewar cutbacks and the present need for them in the growing conflict in Europe. The

RCAF addressed the problem by recruiting experienced civilian pilots to fill the void. Many were bush pilots from the northern Canadian wilderness and Alaska. Hundreds also came from the United States. Many of the early (and often the best) graduates under the Plan, to their great disappointment, were frequently made instructors instead of being sent overseas.

Finding instructors was only part of the urgency. Training facilities had to be built; planes, equipment and mechanics had to be procured; and, although there were disagreements over finances and who the airmen would fly for once they were trained, the need was so urgent that they eventually worked out the details and soon thousands of potential airmen came to Canada from all over the world. They came from the ranks of the unemployed, who were suffering under the Great Depression; they came because they thought this could be the greatest of adventures; they came out of a sense of duty and loyalty to their country; they came because the images of the bloodied infantry in the trenches of WWI were still fresh in their minds, and they wanted no part of it. But, most of all, they flocked to the recruiting offices across the land because they had a chance to fly airplanes a chance to become the hero of heroes, an airman. The Plan would ultimately produce 131,553 trained air crewmen, and the Royal Canadian Air Force would be in charge.[33] Canada was about to become the flight training capital of the world.

~~~~~~~

Flight Lieutenant William D. Stroud of the Royal Canadian Air Force sat behind his small wooden desk and lit a cigarette as he waited for the next recruit to be ushered into his office. It was August 8, 1941, and hot outside the RCAF Recruiting Centre in Windsor, Ontario. It was hot inside, as well, and a small fan lazily blew in front of the one open window, creating a slight breeze, which helped spread the smoke (and ashes) around the small room. Stroud liked his job, even though he rarely got a break due to a constant stream of hopeful young men waiting to see him. He was well aware of the importance of his work because of the critical need of sending young men up the training pipeline to become airmen in the service of the King. He met men, teenagers most, from every walk of life and from far-flung countries of the world. Lt. Stroud had a crucial role to play in Canada's flight training procedure. He had to make the initial determination on whether or not the raw recruit had the potential to become an airman.

Eighteen-year-old Robert Timmer, an American, entered the room and shook hands with the Lieutenant. At 6'1" and 190 pounds, he looked good; his clothes crisp, despite the fact that he had walked in the heat from where he was staying at the YMCA several blocks away. He was invited to sit in the room's only chair for guests. On his desk, Lt. Stroud had a typed copy of a personal information form, called an "Attestation Paper," that had previously been filled out by the recruit, listing the usual: name, birth date, etc. He also had a copy of Robert's birth certificate and a blank interview form. He began by reviewing the Attestation Paper. From the information in front of him, Lt. Stroud asked Robert questions about his background, his education, his activities, his job history, whether he was in debt or had ever been convicted of a crime.

One of the questions on the form asked the recruits what their training choices would be upon entering the service as an airman. Bob had crossed all of them out except for pilot. The fact that he listed approximately 200 hours in the air as a passenger impressed Stroud, as well as the fact that he had worked as an "apprentice mechanic" at the Kent County

Airport. Next, his references were reviewed. On the top of Bob's list was his pastor at Grandville First Reformed, Jacob Blaauw. Also listed were Herman Weirenga, the supervisor of Wyoming Township; Stephen Partington, the "head of the school" (superintendent) at Wyoming Schools; Hugh Gander, who taught business subjects at the high school; and George Vanderwal of Vanderwal and Depuit, "Dealers in Groceries & Gen. Merchandise," on Porter Street, who Bob identified as a shopkeeper. (George's store was across Avon from the Timmer Meat Market, and he had known Bob from birth.) It was quite a list of local VIPs.

After about half an hour, the interview ended and Bob was asked to sign the typed form. He signed Robert J. Timmer, thought a second, and then crossed out the "J." (After that he never used the J. He was probably tired of the question, "What does the J stand for?") Once the recruit left his office, Lt. Stroud filled out his evaluation form. Under the column "Approach," he noted that Bob was "easy" rather than confident or nervous. His manner was "sincere" not reserved or overbearing. His speech was "clear" and his responses were "quick," not slow or hesitant. Overall, he wrote, "Good average type, alert, husky, good training material." Then, he added the words that set Bob on the course for which he had long dreamed. At the end of the evaluation form, under the heading "Best Suited For. . . ," Lt. Stroud wrote, "Pilot Training."

Having passed his physical on the 6th of August, Robert Timmer was photographed, given air force number R126533, and assigned to the No. 2 Manning Depot at Brandon, Manitoba. Before he left Windsor, however, there was one other task to perform. Instead of taking an oath of loyalty to King George VI, which would have annulled his American citizenship, he had to raise his right hand and make a

"Declaration" which stated, in part, "I, Robert Timmer, do solemnly declare that the forgoing particulars are true, and I hereby engage to serve on active service anywhere in Canada, and also beyond Canada and overseas, in the Royal Canadian Air Force, for the duration of the present war and for the period of demobilization thereafter. . ."[34] "For the duration of the present war!" There was no "tour of duty" in those days. One was in until it was over, no matter how long it took.

His Windsor tasks completed, Bob headed home for a few days to say good-by to his family and friends, and spend his last civilian days with Eileen. It was an uncommon event to have boys leave for the service in the days before America's entry into the war. But after a few days of making the rounds to the homes of his brothers and sisters, he left Wyoming Park for a long train ride to Manitoba, Canada, where the first phase of his new military career would take place. His parents and siblings were still trying to understand, and there was a lot of sadness in the home on Avon. His distressed mother wrote a note, "My Bobbie left me, Aug. 12, 1941."

For an airman to become a pilot in the RCAF, he had to progress through four distinct phases of training. At each phase he was evaluated as to his fitness, academic and physical, before going on to the next. Pilot training was extremely rigorous and also dangerous, as accidents were common among the students. Instructors at each phase were tough on their charges, expecting them to meet high standards which were, for obvious reasons, not compromised. It was tough to become a pilot by going through the BCATP, but those who made it were among the best-trained flyers in the world. At this point in Robert Timmer's fledgling military career, flying an airplane was not even in the near future. This was the military, and for every recruit there was basic training.

In Canada, the complexes where they put their new recruits through basics were called "Manning Depots." There were five of them scattered throughout the country. "Manning Depots served a twofold purpose. They prepared recruits for military careers, which would require precision in every aspect of their lives, from ironing their clothes to piloting an aircraft. Simultaneously, it provided the Air Force with men who were mature, physically fit and disciplined."[35] These were the places where the recruits became acquainted with military discipline by exercising and drilling endlessly with their ancient Lee-Enfield rifles. When they weren't drilling, they were attending classes, studying the basics of aviation history, regulations, and navigation. Men who had escaped the Nazi takeovers of their countries, Poles, Free French, Danes, and Dutch, were also given English classes—important because English was the language of air traffic controllers.

On the corner of Victoria Avenue and 11th Street, not far from downtown Brandon, Manitoba, is a shabby, defunct strip mall with a spacious, empty parking lot. On that spot, in the fall of 1941, stood a huge, yellow brick edifice with a rounded roof, lots of windows, and a large overhang sheltering six front doors. The Wheat City Arena, the largest building in the area, had been used, primarily, as an ice arena by the citizens of Brandon. When commandeered by the Canadian military in 1940, it was renamed Manning Depot # 2.

The new owners moved quickly, gutting the inside and leaving a vast open space with the main room seemingly large enough to house several blimps. Crammed into that space were hundreds of bunks, only a few feet apart: the only space that each trainee could call his own for the next several weeks. It was so vast that a recruit who was unlucky enough to have to get up at night to use the facilities was faced with the difficult task of finding his way through the cavernous space in the dark. More daunting, perhaps, was the challenge of finding his own bunk after finishing his business.[36]

And there were noises. With hundreds of men in the same room, the large assortment of sounds that men make while sleeping - snorts, grunts, snores, whimpers, and groans - combined with the sharp rips of flatulence, blended into a constant low decibel hum.[37] Sleeping was difficult. Manning Depot #2 was an uncomfortable and intimidating place for young men far from home. There was no privacy. Recruits slept, drilled, exercised, studied and ate together with the purpose, like basic training everywhere, of making them identical. Lines of men snaked through the complex. There were lines for food, haircuts, bedding, shots, for a basin to wash and shave in, and for their pay of $1.30 a day.[38] Individualism was out and uniformity was in, and if all went well, perhaps in a few weeks they would begin to resemble airmen.

Robert Timmer was given the rank of Aircraftsman 2nd class, the lowest of the low (untrained private) in the Royal Canadian Air Force, and he, along with several other Windsor AC2s, arrived at Brandon on August 14, 1941, after a two-day train ride. Still in civilian clothes, they were met by a corporal who marched them from the train station to the #2 Depot. (Here Bob's college ROTC training may have come in handy.) At the Depot, they were first led to a room with piles of varicolored hair covering the floor to have their heads shaved by "barbers." Actually, head barber Jack Taylor took his job very seriously (probably more so than his airmen helpers) and in a caring gesture he asked the recruits as they came through the line if they would each sign their name and indicate their hometown in a loose-leaf notebook. By the end of his time at #2, Jack had collected 22,000 signatures of young men from around the world. "AC2 Timmer Robert R126533 Grand Rapids Mich." is distinguishable from the other signatures on the page, not only because of his bold strokes, but also because his fountain pen leaked causing a large blot over the "ob."

After his head shave, Bob was assigned to a bunk and got into another line to pick up his uniform and supplies. The blue/gray uniform of an AC2 consisted of boots, tunic, fatigue pants, wedge cap, three pair of socks, two sets of underwear, four shirts, and a large kit bag which, when stuffed properly, held everything he owned. Supplies consisted of a shaving set, shoe polish and brush, tooth brush, Brasso for polishing buttons, and a device called a "button stick" which, when slipped under a button, prevented the Brasso from soiling his tunic. In addition, there was an item referred to as "the housewife." It was a gray canvas folding "wallet" with three pockets containing sewing equipment: thread, needles, pins, and extra uniform buttons. After collecting his necessities, Bob was given the evening to move in, eat, and introduce himself to those around him.

Early the next morning the new recruits ate a meal and reported to a marching field called a "drill square." The corporal ordered them to form up. They shuffled into position. "It took far too long. The corporal's features darkened, lips and nostrils a-twitch. He glowered at the untidy lines before him that wriggled like fidgety-serpents. He glanced heaven-ward, as if seeking divine assistance, then informed the recruits that they were without question the sloppiest, stupidest bunch of deadbeats it had been his misfortune to encounter in his twenty-four years of faithful service, and if even one of them managed to become a member of an air crew in the Royal Canadian Air Force it would be one of the miracles of our time and he personally would pass on the glad news to Rome."[39] He could have notified Rome right then, for as the corporal already knew, many of these fidgety young men standing in front of him would soon become heroes in the skies over Europe.

Among them stood eighteen-year-old Robert Timmer, a dreamer in the company of dreamers, hundreds of miles from those he loved. Alone in a world of strangers, who often didn't look like him, didn't speak like him, and surely didn't treat him the way people treated him in his homogeneous community of Wyoming Park, Michigan. Basic training would be a tremendous adjustment, but there were new friends to meet and confide in and a determination that if anyone made it through this, it was going to be him.

And so it began. Seemingly endless days filled with activities designed to turn out-of-shape civilians into fighting men and instill in them the discipline they would need when they climbed into their planes and headed into combat. An hour or two of calisthenics each day, along with running and marching, got the men in shape quickly. They learned to march in British precision, with their chests puffed-up and their arms swinging high from their shoulders. When they were not pounding around in their heavy boots out on the drill square, they were going to lectures, getting shots, cleaning, peeling, polishing and painting. They also pulled guard duty. AC2 Timmer, bayonet firmly fixed on his Enfield, was photographed standing in front of a guard shack about the size of a small outhouse. He is wearing his government issued clothing with a white scarf around his neck neatly tucked into his shirt collar. With the grin on his face and his loose-fitting outfit, he is not exactly Mr. Spit and Polish, and if it was not for the bayonet, it is doubtful anyone would have obeyed his order to "halt."

AC2 Timmer

The need to inoculate seemed endless. The procedure consisted of shirtless recruits shuffling along between rows of swabbers, shot givers and catchers. The stabbing took place in both arms sometimes simultaneously until as many as seven shots were received. There were many hearty souls, warriors-to-be, who didn't make it to the end of the line, and fell into the arms of the catchers. Others who queasily remained vertical to the end wobbled to the nearest chair or bench to recover.[40] Given the temptations encountered by young men far from the restrictions of home, members of the clergy held morning lectures on the wages of sin and on the earthly and heavenly consequences of sex, while in the afternoon medical personnel told them how to do it safely.[41]

At the Manning Depots, the air force made each man feel like the number he was. They were there only to take orders. All decisions were made for them. "Life narrowed to its essentials: sleeping eating and surviving getting through the next unpleasantness, so you would be ready to face the one after that."[42] However, there were also things at the Depot to occupy rare moments of leisure time such as reading books from the library, playing cards, and watching free movies. The time moved quickly and after weeks of marching, inspections, and discipline, the recruits began to feel more comfortable and were confident they were on their way to becoming airmen.

Unfortunately, the assembly line that was to produce flyers for the Commonwealth had become clogged. So many would-be airmen had jammed the recruiting offices throughout Canada that the training system could not process them fast enough. Those completing the six-week basic training at the Depots had to wait until slots opened up ahead of them in the training regimen.[43] Joyfully, the corporals found plenty for the lowly AC2s to do while they waited for their slot. Recruits were available for anything that the NCOs (non-commissioned officers) in charge could dream up, and there was a variety of boring, non-essential tasks that needed doing. One of their favorites was assigning recruits guard duty, both on and off the base. They were told to guard everything from buildings to birds and to take their old Enfield rifles with them, which would have been quite useless if they ever had to use them.

During WWII the Canadian military had some unfamiliar (to Americans) terminology when recording an individual's comings and goings from one training or combat unit to another. When a person joined a unit he was recorded as "Taken on Strength," or TOS, and when he transferred out he was said to have "Struck of Strength," or SOS. On October 10, 1941, Robert Timmer was SOS from the Brandon Manning Depot after about eight weeks of basic training. It appears he may have stayed past the typical time frame, but, because of the lack of spots up the ladder, it was difficult to define a typical time frame. Some were likely to have spent less time at Manning Depots and others more. Bob, however, received a surprise assignment, which was atypical for someone who was in the pilot training pipeline.

On October 11, he was TOS at #5 Bombing and Gunnery School in Defoe, Saskatchewan. He may have been lucky to get out of the Manning Depot as soon as he did, sooner than others, perhaps, and he probably welcomed the opportunity to learn about other facets of flying. However, if some of his fellow AC2s moved on into pilot training positions, then he would have been bitterly disappointed. Major Mathew Joost of the Canadian Directorate of History and Heritage, who reviewed Bob's records, stated that the assignment occurred because there were still no slots available. The Major also pointed out that, for a person who wanted to become a pilot, the jobs Bob was assigned to at Defoe were "menial."

The B&GSs were established to train observers/navigators

and wireless operators/air gunners who, basically, learned to drop bombs and fire machine guns during a six-week course. With the rudimentary bombing equipment of 1941—it would become much more sophisticated later in the war observers had a difficult time getting their bombs, which were filled with a chemical that emitted a puff of smoke when they hit, within fifty yards of the target. It was a cause for celebration if the observer, defying all odds, actually did hit the target, a makeshift wooden structure. This momentous, but rare, event led to a round of beer for the house, compliments of the proud student.[44]

It is doubtful that AC2 Timmer ever participated in the actual hands-on portion of the B&GS program. Even though he never had to drop a bomb or fire a machine gun in his brief experience at Defoe, it did give him an appreciation for the challenges members of his crew would later face, especially when operating in combat conditions. And while he also appreciated the fact that he was finally around flying again, he knew from talking to the pilots, graduates of the BCATP, that he wanted no part of flying training missions pulling dummy targets for neophyte bombers and gunners.

AC2 Robert Timmer ended his stay in Defoe in an unexpected way. Around the 24th or 25th of October, about two weeks after he'd arrived, he began experiencing severe abdominal pain. He checked into sick quarters and was diagnosed with appendicitis. He was immediately rushed into surgery for an emergency appendectomy. On November 6, while recovering, his pastor, Jacob Blaauw, wrote him a letter. Rev. Blaauw pointed out that he knew other servicemen who had "appendix troubles" and it was apparently "common to men in the service." He realized that it was easy for young men, far from home, to become homesick when in the hospital, but he hoped that it would not be the case for Bob, and he wished that he could visit "and cheer you up a bit." He said that he talked to "Ma" on the phone that day and that she was worried about him and had heard that he was having surgery, but would like to hear directly from him. "No news is good news," she had told him, "but I would like to hear from him." He told Bob that "Ma" was well but, "she is concerned about you and a card from you can easily straighten that out." Then, the pastoral conclusion: "I want to wish you God's blessing and a speedy recovery. Keep looking up. In this world real friends are few and far between but with Christ as your friend you will have ONE who sticketh closer than a brother. Let us give Him our hearts for he gave us His life." From what is known about Robert Timmer, the letter was appreciated, and he would soon be in contact with his mother and family, because he was coming home.

[Note: The Timmer children never called Effie "Ma." She was "Mother" or "Mom" and Nick was "Dad."]

It was standard procedure to grant servicemen a leave after each phase of training. This one was for fourteen days. It was a long way from Defoe, Saskatchewan, to Grand Rapids, Michigan, especially for one recovering from recent surgery, so Bob's dad cobbled together about $100 to fly him home—a lot of money in those days. While there, he received some needed TLC from his mother, visited his friends and his married siblings, and spent as much time as he could with Eileen.

~~~~~~~

After basic training at one of the Manning Depots, potential pilots and observers were sent to one of seven Initial Training Schools (ITS) across Canada, which was the next step in their training process. Bob was assigned to #2 at Regina, Saskatchewan, the capital and largest city of the province, just a few miles from Defoe. So it was back out west, this time by train. Interestingly, Bob was TOS in Regina on December 7, 1941, the day Pearl Harbor was bombed. He might have had some second guesses about signing up with Canada now that the United States was in the war. On the other hand, he was probably still convinced that he would be flying sooner in his current venue than if he had to start over in the States.

The old Normal School buildings just north of the parliament buildings in Regina housed the men of #2 ITS. That wasn't all that it housed. Huge cockroaches had taken up residence there as well. It was so bad that the men ate with one hand and stabbed the roaches with their knives in the other. A treat for the men was pie, baked once a month in large tins and cut into square pieces. It was a wise airman who remembered to check his dessert by peeling back the crust to see if the plump bugs were part of the filling, as they often were.[45]

At the ITS the sorting continued. This training regimen would separate potential pilots from those who would be assigned to another flying position, such as navigator or observer. The students would spend ten weeks of intensive study in algebra and trigonometry, aircraft recognition, armament, Air Force law, radio, and a variety of other subjects. All but the very brightest had to "hit the books" because the RCAF never let up in what the AC2s had to endure. The men's approach to math was often calculated: their thinking was that if one performed too well in the subject, they could be slotted to be trained as an observer (navigator) which, for pilot wannabes, was unacceptable.

A typical day began at 6:00 A.M. with reveille. The recruits would then have to wash up, shave, fold up blankets and sheets, polish boots and buttons, clean and dust their space, hustle to breakfast, return and pick up books, and march to the gymnasium in time for parade at 7:15.[46] Their day continued until about 5:00 p.m. After supper most studied until about midnight. They rarely made time for recreation because of the fear of washing out of the program.

In addition to the tough coursework, each ITS was equipped with a few machines that would definitely separate those who were ready to be pilots from those who weren't. One of them was the famous Link Trainer, often referred to as a "claustrophobic torture chamber."[47] A 1940s era flight simulator, it was a small aircraft-like machine, made of wood and mounted in the center of a circular room often with walls painted like the scenery a pilot would see in flight. It operated on a system of air bellows that moved it around on its sockets. It moved up, down, sideways and around, giving the "rider" a feeling of being in flight. Its controls were extremely sensitive, and the rider had to work the stick and rudder constantly to keep it "flying," all the while listening to the instructor yelling orders into the intercom.[48] It could, realistically, spin and dive and even crash, but what it did with saddening regularity was create a bunch of violently sick airmen, which usually spelled doom for their dreams of becoming pilots. Once the initial phase was completed, a hood was dropped over the thing and the rider had to rely on instruments to keep it under control. Failure in the Link meant failure in the course, with little hope of a second chance. It is likely that the Link washed out more guys than any other phase of training.

The decompression chamber was another sorting machine in use by the BCATP during the initial training phase. It would test the student's airworthiness by simulating a flight into the stratosphere. At various levels of altitude, the students were tested to determine how they would handle actual flight conditions. At 17,000 feet, when fingertips began to turn blue from lack of oxygen, respirators were made available.[49] With various monitoring contraptions wired to their bodies, the airmen were subjected to another device called the altitude chamber. This simulated a two hour trip to the sub-stratosphere. As the simulator took them through power dives and steep climbs, with and without oxygen, their body and brain reactions to flying conditions were measured and recorded.[50] AC2 Timmer did very well in both chambers. When subjected to the maximum stresses, his symptoms were recorded as "nil."

The AC2s fate in the RCAF was being decided, but the instructors seemed to be in no hurry to make up their minds about them. The testing was unrelenting, as if they were determined to find something wrong. They probed, picked, and pricked, testing knowledge, fitness, reactions, math skills, coordination and mental toughness. The medical exam was a four-hour ordeal. The final selection was based on academic standing, physical fitness and psychological factors. At the conclusion of all this training and examination, there was the nerve-wracking interview with two or three officers of the Aircrew Selection Board. The students rehearsed their answers to the anticipated questions, but often forgot a poignant phrase under the stress of the interview.

As the end of the time at the Initial Training School drew near, the results of all the class work and testing were posted on a bulletin board. Given the fact that nine out of ten wanted to go on to flight training, the posted list was approached with much trepidation. There were tears of both joy and sadness among some tough and talented young men as they found their names under columns labeled either "Pilot" or "Observer."

Robert Timmer excitedly noticed that he was recommended for training as a pilot. He did well at #2 ITS. His ratings for various aspects of the course were detailed in his military records dated January 28, 1942. He finished 65th in a class of 132 with an overall rating of 81 percent. His best grades were in signals, aircraft recognition and general studies. Math was about average, as were armament, drill and law. The commanding officer stated on his report, "This airman from the U.S.A. is surprisingly well matured for his age 19. He has courage, tenacity and ambition. Applies himself well and appears to have a fair sense of responsibility. Leadership qualities may develop as he grows older." Interesting word, "courage," a quality most common in the "Greatest Generation." Courage often leads to selfless acts of bravery, and acts of bravery create heroes— which Bob's generation had in abundance.

Robert Timmer had overcome the first hurdle in his quest, but there was a long way to go. The pressures and challenges were just beginning. Nearly one in three who found their names under the "Pilot" column at ITS would wash out before they accomplished their goal.[51] Successful completion of the ITS meant a promotion to a leading aircraftman (LAC) and a move to the next training phase. But for now, Robert Timmer proudly sewed the propeller insignia of a LAC on his sleeve, placed a white flash in his cap designating an airman in training, and looked forward to his $1.50 a day raise and another leave.

Chapter V Wings

After his home leave Bob was TOS at #5 Elementary Flight Training School (EFTS) in Ft. William, Ontario, on March 1, 1942. Ft. William, now called Thunder Bay, is located on the north side of Lake Superior. Here he would begin to train for what he had dreamed about most of his life–flying an airplane. The leading aircraftman uniform that he wore can only be described as "dorky." A photograph of him in that uniform shows that the jacket has large flapped pockets just below the brass buckled belt with equally large flapped pockets on either side of his chest held down by small brass buttons. On each sleeve he has the one stripe of rank and a USA patch on each shoulder. (All foreign airmen in the RCAF wore shoulder patches designating their country of origin.) The belt flares the bottom of the jacket, making it look like Bob is wearing a corset. Four large brass buttons tightly hold the jacket topped by a small collar. His tie is wide and what is showing of his shirt looks uncomfortably stiff. The uniform gives this handsome and proud young man a wrinkled and frumpy look. In his wedge cap, also adorned with brass buttons, he beamingly placed his white flash. He was very fond of that uniform, especially the white flash, even though ground personnel and army and navy men spread rumors among local girls, that the white flashes identified VD cases.[52]

Things were different from life in the Depots for the teenaged airmen (the vast majority of whom were eighteen or nineteen) at the twenty-two Elementary Flight Training Schools scattered throughout Canada. They immediately noticed the difference in the food. Good stuff, not the institutional slop they had received at the Manning Depots or the ITS. They were also treated differently. They were, after all, a big part of the future of the Commonwealth war effort and the goal, now, was to help them succeed rather than to sort them. Still, it was not going to be easy. There were real planes out there on that field, not Link Trainers. Instructors had to insist on excellence from their students, as anything less would not have served the military or the student and could be downright dangerous. Mess up and the best thing that could happen to you would be to wash out and be sent to train for a non-pilot position. None of them wanted to think about the worst things that could happen.

Upon arrival in Ft. William, Bob was given the standard flying suit, consisting of a leather helmet with goggles, a two-piece flight suit with lots of zippered pockets and a fur collar, fleece-lined flight boots, and gauntlet gloves. Optional equipment, worn under certain conditions, were a fuzzy undergarment called a "Teddy Bear" and an inflatable vest worn on the chest called a "Mae West," named after the 1930's movie star whose real "vest" was not of the inflatable type. He may have struggled to get himself into these garments and to learn their complexities, but his mirror showed him that, at long last, he at least looked like a pilot. The next step would be to become one.

Surprisingly, for many Canadian LACs of that day, an airplane would be the first vehicle they would have the opportunity to ride in, their families having never owned a car. (Some had never even ridden a bicycle.) Thus, the first job of the instructor was to introduce his newly arrived students to an airplane. He would point to the wings and remind them that there had to be at least one of them on each side before it would fly; that the cockpit did not have a steering wheel but a stick; and that the tail of the thing, like that of dogs, was in the back of the beast. He made them promise they would not try to take off without an engine, which could be found in the front of the plane. He reminded them that the wooden blade that protruded from the engine was a propeller, and when the engine was running (making noise) it was best not to get too close to it.[53]

The BCATP employed two basic air planes for its elementary flight training program, the de Havilland Tiger Moth and the Fleet Finch, both made in Canada. The planes at #2 EFTS in Ft. William were Tiger Moths. The Tiger Moth was a biplane that, at first glance, appeared to be a rather flimsy machine. Skinny bracing wires crisscrossed between the upper and lower wings made of tightly stretched fabric. Among the wires were four struts which, seemingly, held the double wings apart. It had two non-retractable struts jutting out from the fuselage on an angle, holding small wheels with large puffy black tires. Under the tail was a small wheel that would swivel as the plane maneuvered on the tarmac. The fuselage had two cockpits, one in front of the other, and they were covered by a movable transparent top. Except for the black metal enclosing the engine, it was bright yellow, making it easy to see when in the air and for searchers to spot in the event it went down.[54] The tips of the bottom wings and each side of the fuselage carried the red, white, and blue roundel insignia of the Royal Air Force, while the tail had a flag, striped with the same colors.

It was powered by a 145 horsepower gravity-fed Gypsy Moth engine, which moved it through the air at a maximum speed of a little over 100 mph. The fuel tank was located in the middle of the upper wing. Because gravity fed the fuel to the motor, and because aerobatics were part of the training syllabus, it was important that the plane not stay upside down very long or it would be starved for gas and stall — a fact neophyte flyers quickly had to learn. It was a rugged little thing. Pilot Murray Peden said that in the early stages of training the novices "bounced them all over the aerodrome like rubber balls; but they kept coming back for more."[55] It was a perfect plane for what it had to do: train prospective airmen to fly.

The instructors were an interesting lot. Many were civilians, including Americans, who had learned to fly before the war began. There were a few former military flyers, even some who had flown in World War I. The youngest instructors had recently graduated from BCATP and, having finished at the top of their class, were assigned to spend the war teaching others to fly.[56] What disappointment for men who dreamed of flying Spitfires in dogfights over Europe being relegated to flying small trainers with inexperienced boys who had their hands on the controls of the airplane. Most were not happy with their situation and did all they could to get an overseas assignment, which rarely happened, for they were sorely needed as instructors. Protest too much, however, and they could find themselves towing targets for gunnery practice at places like Defoe.[57] Despite the disappointment, most became good instructors, committed to teaching young men to fly. The best ones were attentive to their students' needs and realized that their students were all different, with varying abilities and aptitudes, and that it would take some longer than others to learn to fly.

Archie W. Londry, a farm boy from the western plains of Canada, used to climb a tree near his home, sit on a branch, pull and push small sticks around, and pretend he was flying an airplane. When he joined the RCAF, Archie and other boys from the farm were quickly labeled "plow jockeys" by other recruits. After he and his buddy, also a farmer, finished first and second in their class, the labeling ended. But, sure enough, against his wishes, Archie was fingered to be an instructor. So, after completing SFTS and getting his wings, instead of going to fight in Europe like most others in his class, he was ordered to attend what was called the "University of the Air" for additional training as an instructor.

Each instructor had four students. In the morning two would be flying while the other two were in class. They switched places in the afternoon. With that schedule, the airspace around communities like Brandon was crowded with planes, most flown by inexperienced pilots. There could be as many as twenty in the air and three landing at the same time, all of this without radio communication. Flares were fired when pilots needed to be alerted to a problem, as it was the only way to communicate with the planes.

Instructing could be dangerous. Student mistakes were often fatal and many took their instructors into the ground with them, More than nine hundred students, instructors and ground crew were killed while training in Canada.[58] Split-second timing on the instructor's part was essential in order to avoid tragedy. Archie stated that the instructors purposely got the trainee into a "mess," a spin for example, and expected the student to get out of it and stabilize the aircraft. Act too quickly to take the controls and risk losing a teachable moment and a student's confidence. Let the student have control for too long without pulling out of the spin and the plane could be unrecoverable. The Brandon Municipal Cemetery has more than a few side-by-side grave markers with the same date of death — one with the name of an LAC and next to it the name of his flying instructor.

LAC Timmer – note white flash in cap

Ground school was also a very important component of the EFTS. The LACs took classes in airmanship, navigation, theory of flight, and aircraft recognition. It was as necessary to pass ground school courses as it was to meet the standards of elementary flying.

Flying Instructor Harry Sideen leaned against the fuselage of the little yellow plane as he greeted Leading Aircraftsman Timmer. Bob was all decked out in his flying regalia and ready for his first lesson. It was February, 1942, and it was cold on the northern shore of Lake Superior. Generally, instructors started off being a little standoffish with their students, sort of an, "I can't get too close to this guy, I might have to fail him," attitude. But, most often, they began to get closer to each other as training proceeded and the instructor became vested in his student's success. Sideen was no exception; he was friendly but all-business. He and Bob took their obligatory walk around the plane, checking the propeller, wings, struts, fuel, and tires. Bob's bulky flight suit consisted of a leather helmet, goggles, boots, and gloves—but now, added to the heavy assemblage of clothing, was a parachute hanging from his rear end with long straps crisscrossing his chest and disappearing around his waist and between his legs. Unlike some of his fellow LACs, he had flown before, lots of times as a passenger while hanging out at the Kent County Airport, but this was different and he was nervous.

He climbed onto the wing and squeezed into the tiny front cockpit, carefully trying not to touch anything or catch his flight suit on an important switch. He was surprised to find that the wooden instrument panel held only five dials: a tachometer, a compass, a turn and bank indicator, an altimeter and an engine temperature gage. Sideen climbed into the cockpit behind him and pulled the canopy over them. They communicated with each other using a device called a Gosport, which was basically a system of speaking and listening tubes between the cockpits; crude, but an improvement over gestures and written notes that had preceded it. Sideen took him through the preflight countdown and, as there was no electric starter, a mechanic gave the wooden prop a spin. The engine caught on the second try and as it coughed and sputtered to life the plane started vibrating and shaking. The little airplane, which had seemed so innocuous a few minutes ago, had turned into a snarling beast, belching smoke as it came to life, popping and pulsating amid the sickening smell of oil and exhaust. Soon they were slowly bumping over the grass field, toward the dirt runway. Once there, the engine roared as Sideen pushed the throttle forward and the tiny plane bounced and lurched into the air. Finally it had happened — flight lessons at last.

It was an exciting time: the culmination of hopes and dreams. The days and years of anticipation were over, and it was time to fly airplanes. Sadly, however, it did not take long for many to realize that what they wished for wasn't what they wanted. As tough as the Link Trainer had been, one knew that it was still on the ground. The ground beneath the Tiger Moth was, in a matter of seconds, hundreds of feet below. Quickly, the neophyte was high in the sky in a frail, vibrating, roaring, cloth-covered machine that, no doubt, was soon going to disintegrate around him. His stomach was doing flips, his hearing was uncomfortably impaired, and his eyes often felt like they would pop out of their sockets.[59] And then, if the instructor decided to get a little cute with the controls and do a few roller-coaster moves, up came breakfast. And the rule was—you heave it up, you clean it up.

Flying really did take a strong stomach and many like Robert, who had dreamed of flying since they were kids and who had done well at Manning Depot and ITS, could not keep the contents of their stomachs under control. That fact alone led to the demise of many a dream.[60] There were more than a few who decided flying was not for them and never would be, and they quickly transferred out of pilot training. Others had wanted it so badly and had dreamed about it for so long, that they tried to keep at it, despite the grave realization that their desire to fly had evaporated. Fear of flying was not a quality that the RCAF looked for in a pilot, so they were quickly sent elsewhere. Some, though, who had bad first experiences, stuck it out and became lifelong flyers. Robert Timmer was one of many, however, who loved everything about it, but it would have been unusual if he did not have a queasy stomach now and then.

The goal of flying with an instructor in EFTS was to learn to handle the plane unaided and eventually fly solo. Gradually, as the student gained confidence and became more comfortable with the controls, the instructor gave him more time flying the plane on his own, with the instructor ready to assume control immediately if he messed up. Success did depend a lot on the instructor. Early in their training, students were absolutely dependent on them. There are stories, however, of hotdog instructors who, when taking up new trainees, would pretend they were on a strafing run and roll the little plane into a steep dive at a speeding train and then pull up at the last moment, scaring the pants off both the white-faced trainee and the people on the train.[61] Thankfully, those guys were not the norm, for most took their jobs seriously, doing their best to send good pilots to the RCAF.

Nervous students, when given control, often gripped the stick too tightly and moved it too quickly, forcefully sending the machine into a flight pattern that looked from the ground like a wounded duck, alternately slamming instructor and student alike backward and forward in their seats. "Students discovered that contradictions abounded in the air. They also discovered how persistently old habits kept intruding. If a landing approach seemed to be too fast, many a student pilot instinctively pressed on the rudder pedals as if they were the brake pedals in a car, just as, in an earlier era, student automobile drivers going too fast were known to pull back on the steering wheel as if they were holding reins."[62] Students admired the skill of their instructors who, when they assumed control, smoothly dropped the plane onto the runway.

Landing was the most difficult skill for students to acquire and the most common problem was coming in with too much speed. There were many instructors, who, having given up control in order for the student to learn the technique, were thumped down hard as the wheels slammed into ground and then thumped again as the plane bounced into the air and again slammed back to earth. It took a lot of willpower to refrain from grabbing the controls away from the rookie.[63] Some students were natural flyers, of course, and handling a plane came easily to them, but most had to work hard and spend even more time in the Link Trainer to rehearse their flying requirements. All of this trial and error, teaching and learning, was to get them ready for an approaching event to which all flyers aspire: flying solo. It remains the greatest thrill of every pilot's career.

When the big day arrived, LAC Robert Timmer excitedly listened to the final instructions from Sideen and climbed into the cockpit for the first time by himself. It would be difficult to determine who was more nervous, the instructor with his reputation on the line and with no control over his student or his plane, or the trainee who was about to attempt to fulfill the dream of a lifetime. For Robert Timmer, this was it. After those many years of hanging around the Kent County Airport, working on planes, talking about planes, and riding in planes, all the while hoping for "solo day," the day was finally here. As Sideen stood by, Bob confidently crawled into the tight cockpit, studied his dials and adjusted the switches. He pulled his goggles down over his eyes and signaled the mechanic that he was ready.

The little plane started with one spin of the propeller and began bumping through the grass as it approached takeoff. Bob throttled up, and as the Tiger Moth gained the required speed, he pulled back on the stick and within seconds launched the yellow bird into the air. Sideen and those observing on the ground became smaller and smaller as Bob soared. He did his required routine and then he just flew the thing enjoying the euphoria of having total control over *his* airplane. Then came the tough part— landing. He dropped the little plane to 500 feet, circled into the wind, and began easing the stick back gently as he approached the runway. He focused on a point 70 yards ahead and began talking himself down as he had been taught, "Steady now, right stick, back, back, easy now, gently, gently—down!" and he felt the thump as the wheels engaged the ground. The plane did a few short hops before it relaxed onto its three wheels.[64] As he turned and taxied towards the hanger, he could see the smiles on the faces of his instructor and the other observers and exited the plane to receive the back slaps, "atta boys" and "it was swell" from those waiting. It was often hard for observers, watching these neophytes fly, to determine which was the bumpiest: the takeoff, the flight itself, or the landing. It didn't matter; the flyer's unrestrained joy that followed a successful solo affected the entire school.

De Havilland Tiger Moth

Soloing, however, was not the end of the training cycle. It was only the beginning. The first hurdle came after about twenty solo hours and was appropriately called "the twenty-hour check." If all went well, it was followed a few weeks later by "the sixty hour check." In both, the student flew with a testing officer (not his instructor) and was required to pass the rigorous requirements that he had been taught up to each of those points in his training. It was very stressful for young airmen who had just learned to fly. One either met every standard or was sent elsewhere.

Archie Londry's specialty was teaching instrument flying, one of the most difficult segments of the training plan for students to master. Flying in zero visibility was the best way to learn instruments but fog was not a common occurrence in Brandon, where Archie spent most of his career. Therefore, the student pilot's visibility was stunted by means of a cockpit covering called "the hood," which forced the student to fly by instruments. According to Archie, once the hood was on, it could not be taken off, and if the student messed up to the point of needing rescue by his instructor, the lesson started over until it was done right.

The sixty-hour check involved an initial assessment of a trainee's first attempt at instrument flying. When the hood was pulled over and outside vision cut off, the neophytes really struggled to keep the plane level and on course. Ground observers would know when the hood was pulled because a smooth flight suddenly began looking like a roller coaster bumping through the sky, all and sliding from right to left, as the rookie, without success, tried to read his instruments quickly enough to maintain control.[65] Many said that learning to fly with instruments was the most difficult part of EFTS training while aerobatics was the most fun. Even though flying upside down, hanging from their straps with gravity pulling them in the opposite direction, made accessing the controls difficult, loops and rolls, stalls and dives gave young men exhilarating sensations they had never before felt.

On May 22, 1942, Robert Timmer received his evaluations for his time at #2 EFTS in Ft. William, Ontario. He passed his ground school classes with an overall score of 83.5%, which was eleventh in a class of forty-three. In his remarks, Bob's instructor said that he was "careful and conscientious," and "Pulls himself up by his bootstraps." In flying training, Bob had forty-one solo hours in the Tiger Moth and thirty-five hours of dual control flight. He also had several hours on instruments and night flying. He was given an "A" in the course with AA being the highest rating. Instructors could recommend a student for continued training in either multi-engine (bombers) or single engine aircraft (fighters). Bob was delighted to be recommended to train in single engine planes, which meant that he was on his way to becoming a fighter pilot.

Sideen remarked, "General progress and ability very good." One had to be good. Approximately 25% of airmen who entered the Elementary Flying Training Schools did not make it to the next level.[66] Instructor Londry, a cattleman after the war, in commenting on what distinguished a good pilot from an average one stated, "the good ones were part of the horse."

~~~~~~~

A few months after Pearl Harbor, about the time LAC Timmer was finishing EFTS, American and Canadian officials traveled together to the various air training programs across Canada in order to facilitate the transfer of American airmen from the RCAF to the American army air force, the navy, or the marines. Almost half of the American trainees they interviewed decided to transfer. Bob was not one of them.

He was going back to Brandon, Manitoba, where he had undergone his basic training at the Manning Depot, familiar territory. Only this time, he would get to see more of the area than the drill square. He knew as soon as he received his assignment that there probably would not be fighter planes in his future. The Service Flying Training School at Brandon was #12 and it trained men to be bomber pilots. The purpose of the SFTS program, scattered throughout Canada, was to teach airmen to fly larger and faster trainers and to learn the basics of combat flying and navigation, therefore gradually getting them prepared for flying combat aircraft. The majority assigned to bomber training were disappointed, because it was the dream of most aspiring pilots to fly fighter planes. For those whose dreams were of soaring alone in the sky, with total control of their own aircraft and destiny, a fighter is where they wanted to be. Hatch gives another reason, "…most students, inspired by Canadian aces of the First World War and the heroes of the Battle of Britain, opted for the fighter role…"[67]

Bob, too, was disappointed with his assignment to multi-engine planes, especially after being recommended by his instructors for single engine training. However, he was proud that he had come this far through a difficult training scheme, had accumulated a goodly number of solo hours, and had new, exciting challenges in front of him. His disappointment also was tempered by the joy he felt as he boarded a train headed for Grand Rapids and a fourteen-day leave. He missed his family, Mother, Dad, his brothers and sisters, and a growing crop of nieces and nephews, but most of all he missed Eileen. It was the end of May, 1942.

Bob and Eileen had a lot to talk about. Now, chances were very good that he would be going into combat. There was still a possibility that he could be assigned as an instructor and avoid going overseas, but the odds were against that happening. If he did well at #12 SFTS, he would probably be in Europe before the end of the year. What kind of plans did two teenagers in love make at times like those? At nineteen and eighteen, they had an abundance of hormones cruising through their bodies and months of separation only made things worse. In their culture, sex before marriage was certainly not condoned and often condemned. They were brought up that way and, if nothing else, were sensitive to that standard. They probably discussed marriage, but knew that, at their age, their parents would never approve. Elope? Again, their culture got in the way. But those were special times, and they were facing what thousands of other service couples had to face, attempting to find their way in a world falling apart. There would be no easy answers.

On June 7, 1942, Robert Timmer arrived back in Brandon to begin training on twin-engine planes. It is difficult to determine exactly how the airmen were separated into single engine or multi-engine training. Certainly the qualities that airmen demonstrated, both in the air and on the ground, at the Elementary Flying Schools had something to do with the decision. Bomber pilot training, for example, emphasized professionalism and precision flying, while fighter training would better suit the freewheeling pilot more adaptable to quick changes in circumstances. However, Hatch states that, "service requirements became the overriding determinate," on whether a pilot was assigned to single or multi-engine aircraft.[68] So the current needs of the military were the overriding factor in the decision. At the time Bob finished EFTS, there was a shortage of fighter planes needed for training and also a pressing need for bomber pilots. Whatever the reason, they seemed to have made a good decision in sending Bob to bomber school. He definitely came into his own flying the twin-engine planes at #12.

They lived in barracks that were called "H huts," two rectangular living spaces set side-by-side with an attachment between them housing showers and toilets. All buildings in the complex at Brandon were painted a dark green with white trim. Life was not bad. There were dances every Tuesday night with local girls for partners. (The "jitterbug" was the popular dance of the day, but very few men would or could dance it.) Two or three movies a week were shown, and one could buy ten cigarettes for ten cents. They were even served real butter. Social events were held at the Canteen which had large paintings of both King George VI and his wife Queen Elizabeth hanging where they could best watch over the festivities.

The ten-week course at the SFTS, like previous training, was part flying and part ground school, only with more advanced requirements. Flying exercises included night and instrument flying, while ground school included advanced courses in navigation, engines, airframe, airmanship, meteorology, armament, and photography.[69] What little spare time an airman had was spent studying or polishing buttons for the almost constant inspections.

The Leading Aircraftsman became an all-hours and all-weather flyer, often being rousted out of bed at 0200 on a rainy night to go flying. If learning to land the Tiger Moth was challenging, the next step was to master all manner of landings: forced, power, gliding, and rough ground. One had to pass navigation tests, flying ninety miles on a straight heading, then changing course to fly strictly on instruments with the cockpit hooded for a number of miles before flying back to base using maps to follow rivers and roads.[70]

Here, they were also introduced to formation flying, which was an even more dangerous exercise among inexperienced flyers than takeoffs and landings. It was mandatory that the LAC log one hundred hours of flight at the SFTS, with forty of them solo - a lot of flying in ten weeks.

Cessna Crane

There were two types of twin-engine trainers at Brandon, the Avro Anson and the Cessna Crane. Robert Timmer was assigned to the Crane, the less popular of the two because it had a reputation of being "flimsy." Made in Wichita, Kansas, out of wood, metal tubing, and fabric, it was dubbed "the

Bamboo Bomber" or the "Wichita Wobbler" by its pilots. However, both the Anson and the Crane were among the safest of trainers. A converted prewar transport, the Crane had five seats, but in training, the maximum on board was two students and an instructor. It had an enclosed, dual control-cockpit with side-by-side seating, no more yelling in the Gosport to communicate between instructor and student. There was no radio in an ordinary Crane.

It might have seemed flimsy, but it was a classy looking plane, with the cockpit set back from its bulbous nose and plenty of windows all around, heralding its passenger plane roots. Each of its twin Jacobs 7-cylinder 245hp radial engines was spliced into its own wing and were located close to the cockpit. They could push the plane to 22,000 feet and reach a maximum 195 mph. It had retractable landing wheels with a small swiveling wheel under the tail. Interestingly, the fuselage had no undercarriage. A person could duck under the lower frame, stand up inside the empty space, and observe a few cables running from the cockpit to the rudder. Like the Tiger Moth, it was painted bright yellow (perhaps for the same reasons) with the red, white and blue roundel on each side of the fuselage. The vertical tail markings also had the same red, white, and blue stripes (which looked very much like the flag of the Netherlands).

On June 17, just ten days after arriving in Brandon, Bob cabled his parents to wish his mother a happy birthday and a happy Father's Day to his dad. In the telegram, he mentioned that he had soloed "last Saturday" (June 13) and was the second in his class to do so. Not bad for someone who had met a Crane for the first time that week. Even in his quick note to his mother and father, his pride was showing.

At about the same time, fellow nineteen-year-old LAC Len Morgan entered SFTS as a fighter pilot trainee. Years later, he described what flyers like himself and Bob were feeling. He wrote, "19 is an impressionable age. Put a boy who has never wanted to do anything but fly in a big, hefty, bulky…airplane and he soaks up his new world like a sponge. The heady aroma of gasoline and dope, the spine-tingling sound of aircraft engines coming to life at sunrise, the utterly indescribable sensation at the top of a loop, the talk of those who speak your language, the snug feel of parachute straps, the entire over-whelming atmosphere. I remember it all. That was living."[71]

Life at the Service Flying Training Schools was challenging. While the EFTS were operated by civilians under the auspices of the military, the SFTS belonged to the Royal Canadian Air Force and military standards were rigidly enforced. In addition, students found themselves flying powerful airplanes that were far more demanding than those at the Elementary Flying Schools. Surprisingly, many airmen who had come this far, through some very rigorous training, and who had survived with joy the various stages of the sorting out process, could not adjust to the advanced aircraft and washed out.[72] Most, however, with the additional flying hours at the SFTS, adjusted quickly, and to them flying was becoming second nature. Their hands and feet coordinated without thinking and without effort, and flying became as natural as driving a car. With that, of course, training took a step up, both in the air and on the ground.

The air force was well aware that putting a cocky, fearless, nineteen-year-old in a fast, powerful airplane, with a teenager's penchant for showing off, was often a recipe for disaster. Therefore, most schools kept the crumpled, blackened, blood-spattered remains of a former flying machine that had met its demise at the hands of an over confident and brash student pilot in a place at the hanger where newly arriving airmen could not miss seeing it. In 1941, the year Bob started his military career, 170 students and instructors died in accidents due to low flying, aerobatics, stalls, collisions, and mechanical failures.[73]

As before, one could be great in the air, but if he did not pass the requirements of ground school, he was going no further. Passing ground school was not based on a grade point average where a B or two could offset a couple of Es, as in, "keep a 2.0 and you'll be eligible for football." Here, you had to pass every class and meet every standard in order to move on. Each course had a maximum point value and a minimum value. If you scored above the minimum you were deemed to be proficient in that discipline and you passed. You were not going to fly in the RCAF if you were not proficient in every aspect of training: a flunk one, flunk all policy.

In *Aerodrome of Democracy*, F. J. Hatch points out that in the beginning of the Plan, instructors tended to be too lenient with their students to the point that Air Marshall Leckie had to get involved. He reminded his training commands that seventy and eighty year-olds can be taught to fly elementary aircraft, but they needed these airmen to fly Spitfires and Sterlings. A student was not to be carried on because he was a "nice fellow." Weaker pilots who were sent overseas were the first to become casualties. If they were not good pilot material they had to be weeded out.[74]

In ground school, there were courses in airmanship, armament, navigation, meteorology, and signals. In the air, flying in big machines that were one level removed from actual combat aircraft, they practiced formation flying, night flying, instrument flying, navigation and bombing. Here, the advanced students at bomber schools often flew with each other without an instructor in the plane. Soloing at night was also part of the training at the SFTS. Solo night flying was part scary and part exhilarating. On clear nights, alone in the plane, the sights of lights glimmering from the ground with the bright moon and endless stars above gave a beauty to flying that was long remembered. On the other hand, there was a lot of insecurity among inexperienced pilots when leaving the friendly lights of the home airfield and venturing alone into the blackness of the night.

In early September, 1942, nearing the end of ten weeks of training and a year and a month after he entered the Royal Canadian Air Force, Leading Aircraftman Robert Timmer began receiving the ratings for his time at #12 SFTS. In his twin-engine Crane, he had accumulated almost seventy-four hours of solo flight, with seven hours and forty-five minutes flown at night. He ranked high in his class, and his flying instructor called him, "A good natural pilot." He also did well in ground school with an overall rating in his seven classes of 87%. The chief ground instructor remarked that he was "Distinguished An Energetic and Thoroughly Capable Student Worked hard and Consistently." But nice as all of that was, there was one defining trial before he could receive his wings. He had to take at least one flight, and maybe several, with the chief flight instructor, who would assess him and every other student pilot on every aspect of training. The tension must have been high before and during the flight, but when the CFI noted Bob's "very satisfactory progress," and when he "CERTIFIED THAT PUPIL PILOT HAS PASSED ALL TESTS REQUIRED FOR PILOT'S BADGE," Bob felt the joy and relief that he had so long sought. He had earned his wings at last.

At last, it was party time! All the pent-up stress over months of relentlessly seeking a difficult goal resulted in a lot of over-exuberance and over-indulgence. Airmen, most of whom were not old enough to drink alcohol back home, chipped in for a private party of celebration at which many tried liquor for the first time. They began by toasting the king, followed by toasts to their many instructors. This frivolity resulted in some very sick new pilots who, if they could walk, staggered back to their huts.[75] Fortunately, security kept them away from the airplanes.

The Prince Edward Hotel in downtown Brandon, Manitoba, was described as "an elegant gathering place." In mid-September, Nick and Effie Timmer received the following professionally printed invitation from the Royal Canadian Air Force:

> *No. 12 S.F.T.S., Brandon requests the pleasure*
> *of your company at their Graduation Dinner*
> *to be held at the Prince Edward Hotel at 1900 hours*
> *on Wednesday, September 23rd, 1942*

Unfortunately for Bob's proud parents, Brandon was just too far away for them to attend.

Prior to the dinner, there was a uniquely Canadian ceremony called a Wings Parade, which was the highlight of the training regimen. The students spent days rehearsing the entire ceremony. Planes were arranged on the tarmac so that they formed a parade square, and bleachers were set up for visiting families and friends. When the big day arrived, the students looked immaculate in their perfectly pressed, crisp air force blues. With flags flying and bands playing, the candidates marched smartly in ramrod straight columns from the hangar where they had assembled, to stand in formation while their hard-earned wings were pinned to their bursting chests.[76]

It was usually the commanding officer who had the honor of conducting the pinning, but occasionally a VIP, like World War I flying ace Billy Bishop, showed up to do the job. At #12, Brandon's Mayor Young was often was given the honor and proudly offered words of congratulations and encouragement to those who would soon depart his city and go off to war.[77] (One time there was a member of the military brass, who was given the honor. In front of parents, wives, and girlfriends, he reminded the new pilots that they were taught to fly and fly properly, so that now it was time to go out there and kill ruthlessly, because in this business, it is kill or be killed not the kind of sendoff that proud families were wanting to hear. He was not invited back.)[78] After the pinning ceremony they were dismissed to the joyful shouts of visitors and hugs from their families, and then it was off to the Prince Edward for a feast of celebration. It was a day they would never forget.

The British Royal Air Force, of which the Canadians were a part, had a strange and controversial policy of determining the rank of recent pilot graduates. In the United States, when receiving wings, students were automatically promoted to the officer rank of second lieutenant. In Canada, only the top students in each class were recommended for the rank of pilot officer, equivalent to a second lieutenant in the U.S. The others, who had completed the exact same requirements, were given the noncommissioned rank of sergeant pilot. The few that did make officer rank were given additional perks, a sharp new uniform and a raise in pay to $6.25 a day, while the noncoms made $3.95 for performing the same tasks. It was grossly unfair and led to a lot of resentment among the men. Canada fought the policy, but the Royal Air Force belonged to the British and they would not budge.[79] Eventually, Canada did their own thing and commissioned who they wanted to commission. That, of course, infuriated the RAF and led to some difficulties in attempting to administer different standards.[80] Be that as it may, after receiving their wings and being designated sergeant pilots, students anxiously awaited word on whether or not they would receive the "King's Commission."

On September 27, four days after the wings ceremony, the commanding officer of #12 SFTS at Brandon notified his superiors that, as of September 25, Robert Timmer had been commissioned as a Pilot Officer in the Royal Canadian Air Force. Major Mathew Joost of the Canadian Directorate of History and Heritage stated, "When LAC Timmer completed his service flight training he was automatically promoted to sergeant and commissioned as a pilot officer. The latter indicates that he was an excellent pilot, as only the top three or four students would be commissioned."[81] Bob also had a new assignment: the No. 1 "Y" Depot in Halifax, Nova Scotia. With that assignment, he now knew he would be going overseas. But first, Pilot Officer Timmer, proud and cocky with his wings firmly in place on the left chest of his jacket and with his cap minus the white flash of a trainee, headed home for a ten-day leave.

Eileen – with wings.

Soon after he arrived in Grand Rapids, he was interviewed by a reporter from *The Grand Rapids Press*. With a headline over his photograph entitled "Too Young for US Force, Wins Wings in Canada," Bob pointed out that he joined the Canadians because he was too young for American pilot training. It also states that he recently turned down a chance to transfer to the US Army Air Corps because he believed that he would get overseas (i.e., combat) sooner with the RCAF. Naturally enthused about his achievement, Bob stated his belief that pilot training in Canada is "about the best in the world." At the Brandon SFTS, he went through training with a group of Australians and remarked in the interview that "they were the smartest class there is, holding the highest average of any group up there."[82]

The statistics for those going through pilot training and active service with the RCAF are startling. Of every one hundred who requested airman training, ninety-eight of them wanted to be pilots, but only twenty percent of that number received their wings.[83] Once the new pilots were assigned to an RAF combat squadron, sixty out of every one hundred would become a casualty before completing their mandatory missions.[84] Understandably, veterans of World War II still talk about the urgency of the times. Everything, especially relationships, was on fast forward. For them, tomorrow may not come, so why not do today what you may not have a chance to do tomorrow?

"Minister of the Gospel" Jacob Blaaw pronounced Robert Timmer and Eileen Donna Koopman husband and wife on October 1, 1942, in the First Reformed Church of Grandville, Michigan. He was nineteen and she eighteen. Only a few members of their immediate family attended the ceremony. They were married despite the concerns of their parents who thought they were too young to understand what they were doing, too young to make a marriage work given the anticipated period of long separation, and too young to make a good decision. In addition, they were reminded that Bob was going off to war, a very nasty war, with a distinct possibility of getting hurt or killed. Eileen's parents pointed out that, with Bob's "for the duration of the war" pledge, even if he did return sound in body and mind, it could be years before she saw him again, and that was not a good situation for a teenager.

Bob was raised to understand that, in his culture, the man in the marriage union was expected to be the provider, protector, and spiritual leader for his wife and their children. His parents argued that fulfilling those roles was not going to happen while half a world apart. Why not just wait, they asked? After all, they knew several dating couples from church who were going to wait until the soldier returned, why couldn't he?

It was not easy for either of these "good kids" to act against the advice of their parents, but they argued that they knew what they were doing; after all they had been dating for over two years and couldn't be more in love. They also knew that over the months and years of separation things could happen to affect a relationship, but marriage would create a legal bond that would help ease their insecurities of being apart for so long. As far as going off to war was concerned, it was all the more reason to get married. At least if something did happen, they had experienced married life. Obviously, whatever arguments were made against them marrying had no effect, and could have had no effect, for simply put, these kids just wanted each other.

They didn't have each other for long. Bob had to leave on October 6 in order to get to Halifax, his next posting. That equated to about five and a half days of wedded life. They made the most of the time they had, by taking their honeymoon in the master bedroom at the Koopmans, which the folks graciously loaned to them. Then, on a bright, sunny October day, Bob and Eileen, accompanied by his mother and most of his brothers, sisters, and their spouses, gathered at the Grand Rapids train station to see him off. Photographs of the occasion show his siblings smiling, his mother on the verge of tears, and Eileen with a rather dazzled look in her eyes. After hugs all around, the newlyweds had a lingering kiss, and then a wave good-bye as Bob stepped into the train. From the platform, they could see him waving through the window of the train as it pulled out of the station. They would never see him again.

The Final Good-by

Chapter VI The RAF

At the time Bob graduated from flight school in September of 1942, war had permeated the very fabric of our nation. Millions of men and women were already in uniform and millions more were pouring into recruiting offices. Earlier that year, Japanese forces, with most of the American Pacific Fleet freshly resting on the muddy bottom of Pearl Harbor, were cruelly occupying the vast reaches of the Pacific, while German armies, followed by their death squads, were driving deep into the Soviet Union. The United States was said to be on a "wartime footing" as our factories stopped producing automobiles and began churning out planes, tanks, and ships for the Allied cause.

But as the year progressed, there were signs that the tide might be turning. In June, the vaunted Japanese navy was stopped at the Battle of Midway and that summer, the marines were heroically refusing to give Guadalcanal Island back to the Japanese, despite suicidal attacks on their lines. Our Soviet allies stopped the German invasion at Stalingrad, though it would be months before its fate was decided. Allied leaders were preparing an American invasion of North Africa in November to relieve pressure on the British who, in October, had pushed the Germans back from El Alemein. As potentially positive as these events were, Winston Churchill put it all into perspective when, in a London speech late that year, he reminded the world that the events of 1942 were not the beginning of the end, but perhaps the end of the beginning. There was a whole lot of war yet to be fought.

Pier 21 in Halifax, Nova Scotia, was the Ellis Island of Canada. Here, beginning in 1928, thousands of immigrants from countries around the world were processed for entry into their new land of Canada. Obviously located on the waterfront where large passenger ships could dock, Pier 21 was a large red warehouse-type building with a huge internal open space surrounded by offices, baggage rooms, a detention center and dormitories. It was perfectly suited to handle the long line of immigrants who patiently waited their turn with the next official, shuffling their meager belongings along the floor, often while tending to crying babies and bored, overactive children. Very much like the scene in today's international airports.

When Canada entered World War II in 1939, the situation reversed. With armies marching and planes bombing, desperate people were trapped in Europe; immigration to North America slowed to a trickle. At the same time, thousands and thousands of soldiers and airmen needed to leave Canada for the battlefields across the Atlantic. When Canada declared war, the Canadian Department of Defense took over Pier 21 and called it "No. 1 Y Depot," for the purpose of facilitating the removal of troops to Europe. It had the capacity to process thousands of troops quickly and became a critical lifeline to Britain. Its seawall could accommodate large passenger ships, and the secure, deep-water harbor was perfect for assembling the navy convoys necessary to protect the troop ships during the crossing. Magnificent passenger ships like the Queen Mary and Queen Elizabeth, now converted into drab troop carriers with their names and markings obliterated to hide their identity, could carry four to five thousand troops at a time to Europe. During the duration of the war, approximately 495,000 troops boarded ships for the battlefields from Pier 21 – 50,000 did not return.[85]

Pilot Officer Robert Timmer, after a train ride of several days, arrived in Halifax on October 10, 1942, and was Taken on Strength at the Y Depot. Along with hundreds of other military personnel, he began an indeterminate wait for a ship to take him to England. As an officer, Bob was billeted in downtown Halifax, which was a short walk to the depot. Many enlisted men were housed in the main hall of the Pier where there was no privacy, reminiscent of the days at the Brandon Manning Depot. The waiting airmen spent their time boning up on their skills in the Link Trainer, parading, and getting more shots. Most were ready to board a ship and get over there, but after the recent good-byes to family, there was loneliness, apprehension, and anxiety coupled with the excitement of going to England. They were facing the unknown, and there would be no more home leaves. They knew that even if all went well, it could be years before they returned.

Pilot Officer in the RCAF

In the early afternoon of October 23, 1942, after waiting in Halifax for almost two weeks (the average stay was four days), Pilot Officer Timmer's unit was suddenly ordered to pack up and report to the nearby square where trucks were waiting to take them to the docks. Once there, they hauled everything they owned up the gangplank, settled into their cramped quarters (even small men had trouble fitting in the bunks) and soon heard the troop carrier's humming engines pull it clear of her mooring. A convoy of approximately 50 ships was waiting in the bay to form up and sail to England. There were ships of every size and description, all of which had another life prior to being converted to carry troops. Unfortunately, the convoy could move only as fast as its slowest member, and that made all of them vulnerable. Lurking along the convoy route were German U-boats, anxious to deposit a torpedo or two into a troop-laden ship. It happened often, and the men knew it. Bob apparently sailed at a particularly vulnerable time. "The pitfalls of North Atlantic travel in wartime were not lost on airmen about to make the trip, particularly in November 1942, one of the most successful periods of the whole war for the German U-boats."[86]

On board, the men crowded into bunks stacked so close together that rolling over while sleeping was almost impossible. Meal times were regulated by assigning times and tables. It was recommended that they wear lifebelts at all times but few did. Deck activities at that time of year were limited due to the rough seas and cold winds of late October and early November in the North Atlantic. Bridge was the game of choice, but it was played with special rules that permitted signals among partners; "convoy bridge" they called it. With limited space and little fresh air, the stomachs of many airmen, toughened by the loops and dives of their profession, were no match for the rolling, pitching and rocking of the troop ship. There was little relief for those who suffered from severe sea-sickness during their miserable journey. Of the few who could function, meal times were special because they could enjoy extra helpings in the near empty mess area. Hours were spent talking, speculating on what lie ahead, and telling stories of their training experiences. They already longed for their wives, kids and sweethearts, their feelings enhanced by popular tunes such as *I'll Be Seeing You In All The Old Familiar Places*, and *You'll Never Know Just How Much I Miss You*.

After about two weeks, the convoy came into the range of Folke-Wulf Condors launched from occupied France. They were made to hunt ships, and when they found them, they not only attacked with their load of bombs but also called in the U-boats. Because of the threat, airmen were required to stand watch on deck beside the sailors. The flyers, inappropriately dressed in their cloth greatcoats, were often soaked by the freezing airborne spray created by the ship as it blasted into huge waves. The wet, slippery decks rocked and rolled, and to keep from falling into the sea, they clung to any immovable object with their frigid fingers.[87] Experienced seamen, appropriately dressed, were unsympathetic to their struggles. Robert Timmer's convoy took seventeen days to cross the Atlantic. It was a long ride due to the slow pace and the zigzag course ships had to follow to avoid sub patrols. Most airmen were relieved to see the shores of England but Bob wrote his mother that the trip was "wonderful and exciting."

In late 1942, the English people were suffering. Because of the mighty effort needed by the Germans to subjugate the USSR, their nightly bombing raids had lessened somewhat from the attacks in 1940 and `41. Still, hundreds of German planes, using occupied France for bases, quickly crossed the English Channel regularly to bomb British targets and terrorize her citizens. Besides enduring constant fear, they were also hungry. Wartime England was a land of shortages. Everything was rationed, and ration books were needed to purchase everything from a can of beans, to a piece of cloth, to a loaf of what was referred to as "National Bread," made with ingredients unknown to the people who swallowed it. It was grayish brown in color and tasted like it looked. Eaten without butter, which was scarce, it was not a good substitute for people accustomed to soft white bread and fresh scones. Gasoline for private vehicles was almost impossible to obtain, and meat, when available, was limited to a few ounces per person, per week. Because of the shortages, prices were high even with price controls. Price-gouging was severely punished.

Pam Stacy was eight years old when the war came to her town near London. Her mother refused to let her be evacuated with the rest of the area children, and with her father and older siblings involved in the war effort, she was alone with her mother. She had few playmates in the mostly deserted town and schools were closed. She was allowed one egg a week and one half pound of sugar a month, but often the store shelves were empty. The meat ration was only enough to make a couple of small hamburgers a week. Frequently, when bread and potatoes where rationed, she was "really, really hungry." She wore cast off clothes from a fifty-five year old aunt and carried her smelly gas mask wherever she went. As they were on the main route for German bombers attacking London, sirens went off several times a night. They also bore the brunt of stray bombs and risked fiery planes plummeting to earth. Through it all Pam remembers, "Life was unbelievably boring: no school, no friends, no birthdays, no Christmas celebrations, decorations or gifts—nothing. And, back in those days, no TV, no radio."[88]

The beautiful English landscape was almost unrecognizable. The famous English flower gardens were replaced with vegetable gardens, and once graceful trees were shattered and broken from the frequent blasts. In the cities, there were vast stretches of rubble and craters, and homes, half blown away, revealed to passersby their smashed furniture, ripped wallpaper, torn curtains, broken china, and framed family photos, some still hanging askew on the walls. The acrid smell of explosions seeped from soot-laden buildings, churches and monuments. Air-raid shelters dotted the pocked landscape, and the ruins of thousands of once proud apartments, movie theaters, schools, office buildings, and even the famed British Parliament, littered the streets, blocking traffic and keeping essential emergency vehicles from quickly reaching fires and bombing victims. A third of London's streets were impassible, and at one point almost a million people were without gas, water and electricity.[89]

For buildings still standing, sandbags laid in doorways and windows with boards for glass gave a ghost-town look to once beautiful neighborhoods. Everything that could be used for the war effort was used. Metal fences, lamp posts, and railings were removed, melted down, and sent to factories making machines of war. In the country, farmers struggled to grow enough food to keep the nation from starving, working around the burned-out hulks of hundreds of German and British planes which fell regularly from the skies, staining their fields with gas, oil and blood. North Americans, fresh from the glittering lights of their cities and towns, had difficulty finding their way around the unfamiliar blacked out cities and were shocked by what they saw, heard, and smelled.

There was, of course, a thriving black market that provided goods to people unconcerned with costs. Some hotels and bars in London that catered to wealthy Americans, for example, were never lacking the finer things of life. ". . . the American notables in Britain lived in a walled-off world of cocktail parties and black-market restaurants, with virtually no idea of what life was like outside their comfortable cocoons."[90] Mary Settle, an American in the WAAF (Woman's Army Air Force), who worked at an RAF base, made some observations about the London gang of non-combatant Americans. She wrote, "Even the uniforms they wore were like costumes– well-cut, no grease marks, no ground-in dirt, no fading. . . Most of them had no experience of the strictures we lived by . . . no inkling of what it was like to live on rationing or of scrounging unrationed food, of standing in queues hour after hour, gray-faced with fatigue."[91]

The English, undaunted after three years of war, were weary but resolute. They wore shabby, threadbare clothing and were hungry and tired. The relentless bombing had killed so many that few were not suffering from the loss of a friend or loved one. Many bore the burdens without the joy of being with their children, because thousands of kids had been removed from the larger cities to "safe areas," which included Canada and the United States. Stooped and bent, but not broken, with their legendary "stiff upper lips" firmly in place on their stressed and drawn faces, they were stirred by the words of their prime minister who requested, "Let us therefore brace ourselves to our duties, and so bear ourselves that, if the British Empire and its Commonwealth last for a thousand years men will still say, 'This was their finest hour.'"[92] They found courage amid the devastation, and put their hope both in the victory he promised and in the arrival of the thousands of troops flooding their island from around the world.

~~~~~~~

Bournemouth was a resort city located on the English Channel. Its fine beaches (now covered in rusting barbed wire), nestled among the high cliffs which overlooked the Channel, were some of the best in England. Prior to the war, fine resort hotels were located both in the city and along the coast. Here, beginning in July of 1941, troops primarily from Canada disembarked from their ships to be processed at the No.3 Personnel Reception Center. It was a huge operation, taking in hundreds of men each week. Many of the new arrivals were billeted at area hotels, once the pride of the coast, but now government-issue drab, with their faded elegance stripped of everything worthwhile. They lacked both staff and services and featured Spartan rooms with nothing but a bed. Communal toilets were down the hall. Others found their accommodations decent with almost as many toilets as rooms.[93] Arriving airmen, after going through the necessary paperwork, waited for the next posting in their continuing training regimen. It was during this wait that Canadians were introduced to English life — a life that was different from what they were used to in the Canadian military, and different from the ruins and rubble further north.

Evidence of the war was here as well, though, with rationing, air raid shelters, sirens, and fearful people. Perhaps the first challenge for the uninitiated was learning the unique and frustrating British monetary system with its pounds, shillings and pence. It was difficult to mentally translate the system into dollars and cents. The system was epitomized by the strange, multi-sided three pence coin called, in the vernacular, a "thrup'ance." If a clerk said that she needed 2 and 5 for a cup of tea and a biscuit, for example, the airman's only choice was to pull the change from his pocket and let the clerk take the coins from his palm, not having a clue that she removed two shillings, a thrup'ance and two pence, or about thirty cents. If he received a compliment about his fine looking "wellies," he had no idea they were talking about his boots. When told to board the back of a "lorry" for a ride into town, he bewilderingly but correctly hopped into a nearby truck. Some embarrassingly failed to find the men's room when given directions. They then learned (and never forgot) that the large WC on the door meant "water closet" and that is where one did his business. The long trip over the sea caused many to rush to the nearest public house to quench their thirst with a famous British "pint," only to find that it was warm and bitter-tasting, nothing like the cold Labatt they drank at home.

The airmen loved to walk through the streets of Bournemouth, proudly showing off their fresh wings to the locals, and, for the most part, mingling with the townies quite well. The Canadians were not there long, however, before they heard the drone of approaching planes and watched as hundreds of German bombers came toward them out of the mist over the English Channel, heading north to inflict their dirty deeds on London, Birmingham, or Coventry. They were occasionally treated to the sight of British fighter pilots (Canadians among them), in their Hurricanes and Spitfires, rising to engage the invaders in aerial combat, and cheered when the enemy planes began belching fire and smoke.[94] There was also joy in seeing German bombers return from their raids, struggling to get back to their bases in Europe with feathered engines trailing smoke.

It wasn't only the northern cities, however, that the Germans marked for targets. The Nazi command was fully aware that the Bournemouth hotels were plump with hundreds of future fighters, a far too juicy target to pass up. ME109s and Focke-

Wulf fighter planes, operating out of northern France and carrying 300 kg bombs under their fuselage, paid regular visits to the city, especially at lunch or tea time when men would be gathered in groups.[95] Also, their 20 mm cannons could shoot up a town with impunity, and few hotels escaped damage.

Once Pilot Officer Timmer arrived and checked in at No. 3 PRC in Bournemouth, he came under the auspices of Britain's Royal Air Force and was officially assigned to the Royal Air Force Trainees Pool. He and other Canadian pilots, although still in the Royal Canadian Air Force, would have their future pilot training determined by the RAF. They flew RAF planes from RAF bases with RAF instructors. Ground personnel were all in the Royal Air Force. During advance flight training, there would be no separate RCAF with its own planes, bases, ground operations, and officer hierarchy.

On January 1, 1943, however, 6 Group was activated. It would become a RCAF operation where, eventually, fourteen Canadian squadrons would fly from their own bases commanded by Canadian officers. "This significant number of squadrons helped Canada ensure the autonomy of its national air force."[96] "Although 6 Group was RCAF, it was controlled at the top by the RAF as part of the overall Bomber Command."[97] Still, the majority of Canadian, New Zealander, and Australian airmen, when finished with training, would be interspersed among RAF squadrons,[98] even though they would continue to wear the uniforms of their respective countries.

At the same time, airmen from the United States were arriving in Britain in vast numbers. They, in contrast, would have their own command structure, bases and planes. That contrast could also be seen in their uniforms. Instead of the various shades of blue favored by their Allied colleagues, American airmen, as army officers, wore brown and tan.

After Bob left for England, Eileen continued living at home and working as a secretary. She had hopes of someday going to college, but money was tight and she really wanted to move forward in life with Bob by her side. She would wait for him, and then together they would determine the next steps. She wrote him several times a week and he her. Unfortunately, the mail was not often timely, especially mail going overseas, so there would be days, even weeks, with no mail and then piles of it would arrive all at once.

Bob liked England. He commented that the English people were treating them very well and, ever the optimist, said that the food was "alright" and the accommodations "perfect." He missed his mother's cooking, however. "I'm thinking of you and your cooking," was a frequent remark. In one note he asked his mother to, "Give Eileen a few tips on it (cooking) will you? She probably can use them. Only don't tell her I said that or she will shoot me."

To him, everything around him was different and interesting. There was a lot to see and he especially enjoyed the English countryside. His wonder was tempered, however, by how much he missed Eileen. He yearned for her. There was something about having an ocean between them that made his longing more painful. He wrote her often and even when he wrote his family, he couldn't resist referring to her. "Take good care of Eileen" was a frequent plea in his letters and telegrams.

Another wait began for Robert Timmer and his RCAF comrades. Instead of the training pipeline being clogged, as had previously been the case, this plug was due primarily to the lack of airplanes. In 1942, with the arrival of American bomb squadrons, Allied bombing of Germany's Europe began in earnest. With the British bombing at night and the Americans during the day, the loss of planes and crews was appalling. Because of the great numbers of airmen now being turned out by the BCATP, replacing crews was not the main issue — replacing planes was. The average wait for a training slot while assigned to the Personnel Reception Center was about a month.

So Bob, now resplendent in the snappy blue uniform of a Canadian pilot officer, filled his days with walking, reading, writing letters, and sharing flying stories with his fellow airmen. He may have been staying at the doomed Hotel Metropole in downtown Bournemouth, which was totally destroyed by German bombs a few months after he left. Food was served in a former luxury hotel near the beach, a few minutes' walk from where most men were billeted. There, Bob was introduced to the airmen's breakfast, served, ad infinitum, everywhere they went: powdered eggs and Spam fried in grease.[99]

> *[Note: The Hormel Foods Corporation perfected the process for preserving meat in a can. Their main product, made primarily of chopped pork shoulder with a dash of ham is called Spam, and it became a staple for fighting men all over the world, where access to fresh meat was often impossible. It was portable, easy to use, loaded with protein, and cheap. It was carried on to the battlefield, and served, ad nauseam, in British and American military mess halls. At first appreciated, it eventually was loathed by most servicemen who rarely considered that the meat alternative, depending on where they were in the world, could have been lizard, donkey, camel or monkey.]*

The men paraded twice a day to stay military sharp and had recreational activities like archery, golf, and cricket available. Bob took advantage of the large indoor pool at the Linden Hall Hydro to enjoy some leisurely swimming. Despite the amenities, he missed the converted gravel pit at Lamar Park back home in Wyoming, where he frequently cooled off after ending his summer shift of unloading boxcars. He also began smoking a pipe. Bob's father smoked one and that may be why he chose a pipe rather than the cigarettes favored by most military men and his older brothers, Ty and Nick. For men in the service, tobacco was cheap and plentiful, and smoking was popular.

Money (the lack of it) was a problem for the Canadian airmen. By the time they arrived in England, most were due back-pay from their SFTS days, which for most, was delayed in the bureaucracy of transitioning from the RCAF to the RAF. For twenty-somethings, turned loose in a foreign country, lack of cash was a real issue. Even if they had some when they boarded the ship for Europe, many quickly were parted from it by foolishly getting involved in games of chance. Those who ran the onboard crap games or other gambling devices were now in demand as lenders by those they had plucked. And when it was announced that airmen were to be given a Christmas leave, those who had cash were besieged by those who didn't. Pay from the Royal Air Force was received after a month of service, so many new arrivals, that Christmas of '42, unfortunately had to wait until after the holidays, and their leave, to get paid.

The RAF had a policy of depositing most of an airman's pay directly into his bank account, thus limiting the airman from getting a pocketful of cash from the paymaster each month. The policy likely had something to do with an awareness of how fast young men could blow it on frivolous pursuits. But it also made sense in other ways, because men in combat often went missing in action, and, therefore, a direct deposit system would ensure that they would continue to be paid until their fate was ultimately determined. Lt. Timmer opened his checking account in December with the Bournemouth branch of the Bank of Canada. Each month thereafter, twenty-two pounds, and ten shillings was deposited into his account. At the exchange rate of 1942, he was earning a little over $100 a month, which included an extra stipend for "war pay," even though he was not yet in combat. To obtain cash, an airman would have to write a check against his account. (In Bob's papers there is a copy of a canceled check made out to "Self" for £5.)

~~~~~~~

The next step in the seemingly unending pilot training process was assignment to an Advanced Flying Unit (AFU). The purpose of these units was to improve flying skills, especially on instruments, so there was a lot of night and bad weather flying. It was also important for the trainee to get the feel of heavier aircraft, since their only multi-engine experience was in the "Bamboo Bomber." It was the final training placement before learning to fly actual combat aircraft.

There were a number of AFUs scattered around England, all under the control of the Royal Air Force. Flying under the banner of the RAF presented some difficulties for the non-English flyers. There seemed to be a look-down-one's-nose attitude toward "the ruddy Colonials" among, not only the British command but also the rank and file, and it did not matter from what "colony" they came — including North America. "Many RAF 'brass hats' disapproved of the

Canadians, regarding them as rowdy cowboys who knew nothing of the subtler points of military discipline. In short, they were not the 'officers and gentleman' of legend."[100] This attitude affected pilot evaluations, which affected promotions. There was the perception among the British that flight training other than that done in the RAF did not quite measure up. F. J. Hatch notes in *Aerodrome of Democracy*, "It was hardly to be expected that the operational training units in the United Kingdom, whose job it was to prepare the BCATP graduates for operational flying, would be completely satisfied with the Canadian-trained pilots."[101]

Finally, Pilot Officer Robert Timmer received his orders to report to Number 15 (Pilot) Advanced Flying Unit (#15 (P)AFU) at an aerodrome called Tatenhill, near Burton-upon-Trent, in Staffordshire, England. The village of Tatenhill was about three hours driving time north of London, and the aerodrome was one of dozens and dozens littering the landscape in southern England. Not only were there separate air training facilities for the AFUs and the Operational Training Units (OTUs, the last step in the regimen), but also for British combat aircraft, both fighters and bombers. In addition to the British facilities, the Americans were arriving in droves, bringing thousands of fighters and bombers with them. Bulldozers, which once chewed up good English farmland for the Royal Air Force, were again pressed into action, scraping away precious topsoil to accommodate the Americans. Because it was necessary to keep these planes in the air as much as possible for both combat operations and training, and because Hitler's Luftwaffe frequently took their share of British airspace, thousands of planes at a time could be in the air over a small section of a small country. Mid-air collisions were not a rare event in the skies over war-time England.

The airfield at Tatenhill, located in a picturesque rolling countryside, was completed in 1941. The first flying group to use the new facilities was #27 OTU, training on Wellington bombers, but it was found to be unsuitable for them and #27 soon left. The field was turned over to a maintenance crew until #15 (P) AFU occupied it in November, 1942, about a month before Bob arrived.[102] There was nothing unusual or different about it to distinguish it from the many other aerodromes in that area. The men were housed in metal Nissen huts with bump-out dormers down each side holding rows of windows. Most other buildings in the complex were built of brick with a white stucco finish and a corrugated steel roof. There was a large rectangular mess hall, guard posts, latrines, a gym, a canteen for socializing, and a small control tower. There were several hangers for storing and maintaining planes and a separate building for the Link Trainer. All buildings had small windows because they were easier to black out at night.

Pilot Officer Timmer arrived at his new station before Christmas 1942. Soon he was inundated with letters and parcels from home which contained many needed gifts, including gum and candy which he shared with the "fellows." Seems they were limited to one candy bar a week. He sent an airgraph home thanking everyone for the "swell" gifts that he was "lucky" to get because there was a fire in Halifax which destroyed many Christmas packages for Canadian overseas service men. Ever a tease, he told his chubby mother, "Don't worry about me and keep your chin up—all three of them in fact." On January 1, 1943, Airman Timmer turned twenty and sent his parents a Happy New Year card embossed with the Royal Canadian Air Force symbol.

[Note: An airgraph enabled a person in the service to send a quick note home. The note had to fit in a space so small that in order to send more than a few words, the writer had to reduce the size of his handwriting to such a degree that they were hard to read. They served a vital purpose, however, as regular letters sometimes took weeks to reach their destination, if they arrived at all.]

Airspeed Oxford

At Tatenhill, Bob was quickly introduced to his next challenge: the Airspeed Oxford. It was the most common trainer used in the Advanced Flying Units and was called the "Ox Box" by those who knew and loved her. No wire and canvas was holding this plane together. It was solidly framed in wood and plywood covered. It was an advanced trainer, the closest thing to the "real thing." The new arrivals immediately began preparations for flying solo in the Ox Box and did so within a few days of coming to Tatenhill. They expected to fly and fly they did. They spent hours in the air, sometimes as many as seven or eight a day, with few breaks between flights. PO Timmer loved the flying, liked his new airplane and had a sense of accomplishment in stretching his flying skills.

In addition to pilots, the Ox Box could, with minor changes, be adapted to train navigators, radio operators, bombardiers and gunners. British made, it had two 370 hp Cheetah engines capable of 185 mph with a cruising speed of 140. It had a fifty-three-foot wingspan and was capable of having a dorsal gun turret installed for gunnery practice. It had retractable wheels and windows that wrapped around the cockpit, including one overhead. The Oxford was a demanding but reliable flyer. Although the coloring varied, most were painted an army green or gray green with the familiar British red, white and blue roundel on each side of the fuselage and a similarly colored rectangular flag on its tail. Most had yellow markings. The wing tips were yellow, and it had a yellow strip around the fuselage. Interestingly, it had yellow triangles on its large nose and fuselage. These were warning signals to other aircraft to recognize it as a trainer and to stay clear, because the pilot could be flying on instruments while sightless due to covered windows.[103]

Despite its design advantages, the Oxford had a troublesome characteristic: it had to be started by turning a crank inserted into an opening in the wing above each engine. Fit young men had to climb onto the wing (at times wet from rain or covered by frost), get on their knees, insert the crank into the appropriate opening and heave it round and round until the starter began a high pitched whine. At that point, they would have to signal the pilot in the cockpit to engage the engine, often to have the obstinate thing sputter, cough and die. Whereupon, the whole process had to be repeated, sometimes as many as four times, before it would catch and roar into action. Exhausted, the "starter" then had to climb down and cross to the other wing and do the entire procedure over again for the second engine. Good, upstanding, Christian boys could get through maybe three unsuccessful attempts before hurling profanities down the crank hole, while those with fewer language restrictions, knowing what lie ahead, cussed the engine through the orifice before even starting the process.[104]

While at Bournemouth, many of the pilots (in training to fly bombers) still hoped that their next assignment would be to a fighter training facility, and, although that was rare, it did happen from time to time. It is likely that Robert Timmer still hoped for such an assignment. The timing for that to happen couldn't have been worse. In early 1943, Britain began stepping up the air war over Europe and soon would be flying each mission with hundreds of four-engine heavy bombers, Lancasters and Halifaxes. Without adequate protection, due to the short range of fighters, the losses were deplorable. It was not unusual to lose twenty to thirty crews per mission. Hundreds of replacements were needed daily, not just for the pilot seats but for every position on the aircraft. With the knowledge of that need, wannabe fighter pilots began to accept the inevitability that they were going to be bomber pilots.[105] The disappointment was somewhat mollified by reasoning that anyone can fly a plane with one engine, but it took real men to fly planes with four.

On a quiet, chilly Sunday in January, 1943, sitting on his bunk in the hut at Tatenhill, Bob wrote home to tell his folks that he missed them and "their new daughter-in-law." He told them he was not exactly homesick, but when he saw "fish!" on the table he really missed his mother's mince pie and coffee. He commented that it was frustrating because there was so little that he could say, but he told them he had a cold, "which is unusual," and that he had made a good landing yesterday, "which is even more unusual." He promised his Dad that as soon as he got to Berlin, he would bring him back plenty of German beer. He must have been feeling a little down because life there was "alright," which did not reflect his usual upbeat attitude.

Eileen – Spring 1943

The coursework for the AFU training was divided into three segments. The first was to familiarize the pilots with the Oxford and to teach them its characteristics. They began a series of two-to-three-hundred-mile cross-country segments to brush up on their navigation skills, frequently flying on instruments with the windows covered or with a device on their heads which screened out everything but the glow of the instruments. Much of the flying was solo, although flying with an instructor from time to time was essential as the young pilots were still trying to hone their skills. Perhaps the toughest evaluators were their classmates, who flew in the second seat and were often more bluntly critical than the instructors. While the instructors could be counted on to maintain some semblance of teacher-student privacy, the classmate "judges" had no such compulsions and would blab to others over a drink in the officer's club about the skills (or lack thereof) of the person they flew with that day.[106]

In the early afternoon of January 21, 1943, near the end of the first phase of AFU, Bob climbed alone into his Oxford to practice takeoffs and landings. With both engines at full throttle, he roared down the Tatenhill runway, but as he approached takeoff speed, the starboard tire blew. Fortunately, as it turned out, he was able to get the plane into the air. Feeling the bump, he had an inkling of what had happened, and he made three passes over the field to get confirmation from tower personnel, who also confirmed that there was no other damage to the plane. While Bob circled, flying control huddled on how to get both pilot and plane to the ground in as few pieces as possible. They ruled out landing on one wheel because of the dangerous possibility that the plane could tip one wing into the ground and either spin or cartwheel down the runway or go off the runway and flip on its nose.

It took about half an hour to make the decision, and Bob, still circling, received the signal to bring it in on its belly. He watched as a fire truck and a specially equipped vehicle called a "crash tender" hustled from their garages toward the landing strip. He circled wide, lined up with the main runway and, with wheels retracted, began his approach. A short distance from the landing area, he cut gasoline to both engines and, seconds before touchdown, switched them off. The propeller blades crunched as the plane softly eased onto its plywood belly, shedding pieces of plane and propeller as it skidded down the runway. Rescue vehicles raced toward the sliding aircraft. As it came to a stop, Bob was out of his belts and on the ground, totally intact without even a scratch or bruise, as rescue personnel arrived. There was no fire.

The Royal Air Force report to the Air Ministry stated that the "burst tyre" was "due to foreign matter penetrating the outer cover" on takeoff. The landing was good but there was damage to both propellers, and both engines were "shock loaded." The report mentioned that there was minor damage to the bottom of the fuselage and that Pilot Officer R. Timmer, an American, was unhurt in this "unavoidable accident."

The first sequence at AFU ended with a test that consisted of flying on one engine, landing on one engine, map reading, turns, climbs, etc., some of it done "under the hood." Bob passed his tests and left Tatenhill for Spittlegate and the second phase of advanced flying, which he would find to be most challenging.

It was called BAT (Beam Approach Training) which, according to Instructor Londry, was difficult for many pilots to grasp. Basically, BAT was a navigation system that allowed pilots to find their way to an aerodrome runway when visibility was greatly restricted by fog or low cloud cover. With English weather being what it is, that happened often, so it was a system that could really save lives. Trainees were no longer just flying back and forth over the aerodrome, as in the Tiger Moth days, but were taking their Oxfords on substantial cross-country jaunts. As was often the case, planes would take off in bright sunlight but be totally socked-in a few hours later when it was time to land. Even with all the landing facilities dotting the landscape, they were very difficult to find, given the instrumentation of that day. Landing without good visual contact was extremely dangerous and was attempted only in a dire emergency, thus the Beam system.

Through the use of radio signals, cast in a variety of frequencies, a pilot proficient in the use of the beam could nail a landing even in thick fog. Murray Peden describes the basic layout "as an intersecting pair of aerial highways crossing over the aerodrome and dividing the territory for 30 or 40 miles around into four quadrants."[107] Find the beam, find the quadrant, find the runway, was the simplified version of how it worked. Once a pilot picked up the beam it became louder if the plane was going in the right direction. If not, the beam became fainter. Different aerodromes had different frequencies, and once a plane entered its beam field, Morse call letters were sent to confirm that the pilot was, in fact, on the correct radio range. There were also vertical beams on the approach to the runway that would give the pilot an altitude read by radio signal. A good share of the program was devoted to approaches and landings using the vertical markers.

If the famous English fog was not present, trainees flew "under the hood." Peden states, "It was always a thrill to snatch it [the hood] up and find the aircraft speeding above the runway like some huge bird, particularly after having sweated for 15 minutes seeing and hearing nothing but the demanding wavering instruments, and the monotonous theme of the untiring beam."[108] Most pilots did not look forward to their BAT training but recognized its lifesaving potential as an essential component of their experience. Instructors, for their part, had to breed confidence in their students for the beam, as well as confidence in their ability to use it.

Robert Timmer's instructor, Flight Lieutenant Patrick Friend, who administered his flying test at the end of the course, noted that Bob attained an "average standard." He also noted that he needed more practice on instrument flying. Of the various components to the test, Bob's lowest score was in cloud and night flying, exactly what the third phase of the AFU training was going to emphasize. Happy to finally be able to fly visually again, after eighteen hours of flying with fog and hood, P/O Timmer headed back to Tatenhill with new challenges for himself and his Ox Box.

The first two flights at "night school" were in a dual mode with an instructor. After that, it was mostly solo, with an occasional dual flight to work on a specific task. The main feature of this training phase was what the men called "pundit crawling." Each aerodrome had a device that emitted a tiny beam of red light, called a pundit, which was activated each night at dusk. Students were given an assignment where, using the pundit, they had to find several different aerodromes, land, and then quickly take off for the next location, repeating the process four or five times before finally returning to Tatenhill; i.e., "pundit crawling."

In addition to the pundit, each aerodrome had its own Morse signal. Knowing that signal for each airport along the route was important to the assignment, because a pilot could not land at just any field. He had to follow a predetermined order to complete the task successfully. Trainees tried to memorize the call signs for the various aerodromes but found that under pressure they often forgot them; just as they often forgot to take along a written list. The recommended technique was to write the codes on the back of their hand, but some hands came with more hair than others, which made seeing them in a dark cockpit difficult. Palms were no good either, as nervous perspiration accompanied the task of finding the right pundit or of making a difficult landing, thus smearing the ink into an unreadable blur.[109] Imagine a flyer, still inexperienced, alone in a powerful noisy machine, with only the glow of instruments and the red and green lights from the port and starboard wing tips keeping him company, attempting, under pressure, to locate landing fields in the dark. Pundits were not easy to see and the relief at finding one was sometimes tempered by the fact that the call sign indicated that he was approaching the wrong aerodrome. Once the pundit technique began to become somewhat familiar, the trainees were then told to fly a pundit course on one engine. Even though they had practiced one engine night landings at Tatenhill, doing it at strange landing fields was especially demanding. So with fog, hoods, BAT, and pundits bouncing around in their navigational heads, the dazed students really looked forward to their next assignment.

Although training at 15 (P) AFU was intensive and night flying challenging, by now, the British air fleet was launching its raids to Nazi Europe almost exclusively at night. Because the young men at Tatenhill were just one step removed from joining that fleet, they knew that quickly learning night flying techniques was essential. Near the end of February, 1943, those who had mastered the standards required of them in the Advanced Flying Unit at Tatenhill awaited assignments to Operational Training Units (OTUs) located in various parts of England.

The purpose of the OTUs was to train the men on the big four engine bombers they would actually fly in combat - Halifax's, Stirlings, and Lancaster - planes that the RAF was using to bomb Germany almost every night. Here at the OTU, the airmen from separate trades would gather to form into crews. It was hoped they would come together informally, but because pilots did not know many gunners, nor did bombardiers know radio operators, etc., most were assigned their spot on a crew. Once together, the crews began training in yet another plane, attempting to form a smooth working team. Gradually, as they progressed, they were worked into operational missions, perhaps flying diversions at first, then finally the real thing.

Pilot Officer Robert Timmer never made it to an Operational Training Unit. In February, 1943, in spite of making a normal progression through RAF training, Bob began to think more and more about transferring to the American Army Air Force. It was not an unusual event. Many Americans had trained in Canada and most had transferred once the United States was fully involved in the war. He had previously turned down the chance to transfer, thinking he would get into the war faster with the RCAF. Now, with that no longer an issue (the final phase of training on heavy bombers was about the same for both services), he began to consider the move. He reasoned that, as long as he was about to be trained on a British heavy bomber, why not an American one? Patriotism played a part in his thinking, along with talks he had with American flyers he encountered in England. Before making the final decision, he considered the difficulty of leaving his flying buddies, as well as the possibility that the learning curve could be slightly longer, given his need to "learn the ropes" in the American army. After weighing the pros and cons for some time, Bob made the decision to request transfer and, in late February, approached his commanding officer.

Canada had invested an incredible amount of time and resources in training this young man to fly. It was not easy for the RAF to grant permission for one of their flyers to go over to the Americans, but their policy was to release them; after all, they did have a common enemy. The paperwork was begun; Bob was pulled out of the training routine and, on March 4, was sent to RAF processing center in Cosford, England, where he waited for the paperwork to be finalized. In the meantime, he started working on procedures with the Americans to join their ranks. The Canadian experience officially came to an end when he resigned his pilot officer's commission on March 23, 1943. It had been a little over one year since Instructor Sideen watched him take his first solo flight in the little Tiger Moth.

Chapter VII The Circus

By the spring of 1943, the year-old Ninety-third Bombardment Group was already legendary. Military orders from the War Department had brought it to life on March 1, 1942, just three months after the bombing of Pearl Harbor. That was a time when America was scrambling to "get up to speed" with its war effort. Even though thousands of men and women were signing up for the service and our factories were beginning to produce the millions of tons of supplies that would be needed for an all-out effort, we were still woefully behind our primary enemies, Germany and Japan. Forming and equipping bomb groups would be essential to our war effort. By March of 1943, the 93rd was certainly not what it would later become, but its accomplishments in one year of existence were a testimony not only to the 93rd itself but also to what America could achieve in such a short time.

Under the auspices of the Eighth Air Force, the 93rd began its existence at Barksdale Field, an army air base near Shreveport, Louisiana. The first contingent of personnel numbered six, an officer and five enlisted men, but by the end of March, 1942, approximately six hundred men were transferred from the 98th Bomb Group to the new unit.[110] Initially, the 93rd had three squadrons, the 328th, the 329th, and the 330th. In May, the 409th was transferred to the fledgling bomb group. Soon, recruiting offices around the land were pouring men into Barksdale, and wooden huts began sprouting like swamp lilies over the vast reaches of the airfield. Trouble was, there were very few essential materials available for men-in-training to use for training, including the main ingredient in any bomb group — bombers.

Insignia of the Ninety-third Bomb Group
"Strike for Liberty"

The Ninety-third was designated to fly the newest of America's heavy four-engine bombers, the B-24 model D, made by the Consolidated Company of San Diego. Unfortunately, this early in the war, there were not enough B-24s to go around. (The earliest bomb groups, most constituted before the war, were flying B-17s.) Each squadron could only be allotted three planes, with two held in reserve by the entire group as backup; far below the twelve each needed to be fully equipped. Even if they had a full supply, there were not many at Barksdale who were knowledgeable about flying or fixing the large new planes. Few pilots had been trained on military aircraft, most having learned to fly at private facilities before the war. If they had any military training at all, it was because they had joined the service before Pearl Harbor and gone through training on fighter planes or B-17s. The same could be said for ground personnel. The pilots' combined combat experience was nil, except for the few surviving flyers of World War I.

One of the best things that happened to the fledgling new unit was the appointment of Lt. Col. Edward J. (Ted) Timberlake as the commanding officer. Thirty-three years old and a West Point graduate, Timberlake was gifted with the rare combination of leadership and personality that endeared him to the men in his command. He had a great sense of humor, was a good listener, and was innovative in his approach to tactical issues. Instead of commanding from the ground and sending his men into dangerous skies, he led them on many of their most difficult missions. Early on, he surrounded himself with pilots such as Ramsay Potts, John Jerstad, George S. Brown, Addison Baker, John (Packy) Roche, Hugh Roper, Joe Avendano, Walt Stewart, Lew Brown, Jack Jones, Mort Macks and Keith K. Compton, who themselves would become legendary leaders in the Ninety-third. Many of the survivors of this early group would become prominent in the new United States Air Force following the war.

Lieutenant Colonel Timberlake was pleased that the B-24 was assigned to his group, even though he did not know much about it - nobody did. To help, Consolidated sent out one of its test pilots to assist with training the men on the new plane, and soon, by rotating among their minuscule fleet, they began chalking up the necessary pre-combat hours. There was a critical need for navigators and bombardiers, and very few had those skills when they joined the service, so raw recruits had to be trained for those positions. A comprehensive ground school was begun, teaching skills such as bombardier techniques, engineering, weather, communications, and parachute rigging. But, typical of military efficiency everywhere, the men of the Ninety-third no sooner began to get their act together at Barksdale, than they were ordered to move to Fort Myers, Florida.

On May 15, the entire operation headed for its new home; the flyers by air and the ground crews by train. It was very hot, and the trains were often delayed, making for a longer than usual trip and for some irate mechanics on arrival in Ft. Myers. Their new base was created south of the city on sandy soil with the requisite alligators and snakes from area wetlands lurking around the enlisted men's tent city. Officers were billeted in area apartments and hotels, and soon wives and sweethearts (and women who were not wives and sweethearts) began descending upon little Fort Myers. Strict military discipline was in force, and MPs roamed the complex (and the city) enforcing it.

Home leaves and furloughs were frequent and often men used a B-24 to get home, even flying cross-country to do it.[111] Of course, once they were near the old hometown, they had to announce that they were back. They called it "buzzing" — just a little treetop show for the folks, girlfriends, and buddies in a huge machine with four thunderous engines, shaking buildings, rattling windows, and sending dishes crashing to the floor.[112]

In training, planes began to roam around the Gulf of Mexico from Key West to Cuba, to Mexico. Formation flying in combat was essential, and it took a lot of practice. And while they were at it, they began to look for German U-boats patrolling off the coast of Florida. Carrying depth charges in the bomb bay, they looked down from on high for long thin shapes in the water beneath them. Heavy bombers were not necessarily designed for sub patrol, but they got a couple-one for sure and two probable. It was the first time an air unit was engaged in combat without going overseas, and the incidents gave the Ninety-third its first national publicity. There would be a lot more.

In July, they called off maneuvers in Fort Myers and began preparing for a trip to Europe. On August 2, the aircrews left for Grenier Field, New Hampshire, as the ground personnel boarded a train for Fort Dix, New Jersey, where they would be processed for their trip to England. While in New Hampshire, each of the four squadrons was given nine brand-new B-24s, all painted a dull greenish brown. The aircrews spent a few weeks equipping and checking out the new planes before beginning their trip across the Atlantic. They began by flying to Gander Bay, Newfoundland, while their ground crews headed across on the *Queen Elizabeth*, sailing with very few remaining vestiges of her former glory.

The weather in Newfoundland was awful, far from a pleasant accompaniment for anxious crews who were to make their first crossing of the intimidating North Atlantic. Anxious or not, the inexperienced pilots of the 93rd began their crossing in the cold and rainy weather of early September. Most had little training in instrument flying, a casualty of the rush to put together a bomb group from scratch. Pilot Llewellyn (Lew) Brown recalls "sweating it out" as he lifted his B-24 off the runway in Gander Bay. Visibility was about zero, and all knew the unforgiving sea lurked beneath them. As they tried to rise above the weather, ice began to form on their wings, resulting in the need to drop to 2000 feet where the air was warmer. Finally, after eight hours through a steady, foggy mist, a coastline appeared, and Lew "was never so glad to see land."

One plane was lost in the crossing, but the rest, after refueling in Prestwick, Scotland, went on to a base at Alconbury, England-in Europe at last. It was the first time American bombers had flown nonstop across the Atlantic, and the first B-24 bomb group to arrive in England.

Alconbury Aerodrome was in Huntingdonshire, near Cambridge. It was a former Royal Air Force base carved out of the quiet, beautiful English countryside. The once productive farmland was now crisscrossed with runways, which launched and retrieved huge noisy machines. The small village of Alconbury stood nearby, filling the skyline with the spires of its many churches and gabled houses. It seemed to bear up well under the weight of all these foreign men and their odd-looking airplanes.

The Americans settled in quickly and didn't waste any time getting back to work. Work consisted of hours of formation flying at high altitude, gunnery practice in low temperatures, ground school, navigational practice, and bombing simulated targets. Practice they needed, because just a few months before, most had never even seen the inside of a bomber, much less flown one. Even with all the practice, these courageous young men and their flying machines were hopelessly under-trained for combat. They lacked experience flying the new bombers and the "esprit de corps" that develops from being together under fire had yet to be developed. But they were sent to Europe to bomb the enemy, and that is precisely what they were going to do - ready or not.

On October 8, 1942, just one month after arriving in England and only seven months after being formed, aircrews ate an early-morning breakfast and gathered in the briefing room to hear operations officer Major Keith Compton give details on their first mission. They were going to bomb the Fives-Lille Steel & Locomotive works near the town of Lille on the Franco-Belgian border in occupied France. Compton told them that, even though they were not going deep into "Fortress Europe," it was going to be rough. They would, however, have an escort of British fighters. The German Luftwaffe was formidable and operating at maximum strength, having not yet experienced the incredible losses that awaited them later in the war. Col. Timberlake gave a short pep talk, and men began leaving to don their heavy flight suits, made bulkier with their Mae West life preservers and parachutes. On the way out of the meeting, the chaplains gave spiritual blessings, and many men knelt around a communion table.

While the world waited and watched for news of the first combat performance of the new bombers, *Teggie Ann,* flagship of the Ninety-third Bomb Group, with Col. Ted in the pilot's seat and Captain John (Jerk) Jerstad flying copilot, lumbered down the runway and into the air with twenty-three anxious crews launching behind them. They formed up over England, and once they crossed the Channel and entered French airspace, the sky was filled with flak from the big German guns. *Big Eagle,* piloted by Alexander Simpson, took a direct hit and fell from the sky with the loss of most of its crew — the first 93rd ship to go down in combat.[113] As the Liberators approached the target, their neophyte crews watched in awe as the air around them filled with enemy and friendly fighters engaged in a classic aerial dogfight - there were planes everywhere. Trouble was, many of them were firing at the bombers. Badly shot up, they dropped their bombs, made a left turn, and headed back to Alconbury.

The returning formations, slowed by attempts to protect the struggling cripples, were overdue back at the base. Stressed-out ground crews began counting as the first specks appeared in the sky above them and soon knew that a plane was missing. Finally, when the planes were close enough to read the nose art, they realized that it was *Big Eagle*. (In contrast to today's emotional "fly-overs" honoring fallen servicemen with the missing plane formation, this plane really was missing!) For the first time, 93rd ground personnel experienced the wrenching feelings of those that wait; joy at having their crew and plane back on base versus the trauma of losing comrades. For most, battle damage was heavy. The crew of *Boomerang* counted more than 200 holes in their plane. Later evidence showed that few of the bombs hit the target, but a number of German planes had been shot down. The publicity about the raid (although censored) was positive. The 93rd was credited with six German planes shot down and five probable. Captain Jerstad enthusiastically told reporters that he had never seen such heavy flak.[114] He was not exaggerating–it was the first flak he had ever seen! All in all, the fledgling 93rd had done well in their baptism of fire. There would be more. They were just getting started.

In late October, the 330th Squadron was detached from the rest of the group and attached to RAF Coastal Command to go submarine hunting. The men wondered why and were not pleased to be separated; besides, this was not what they were trained to do. They did not know, however, that preparations were underway for the invasion of Africa by American forces, and it was essential to protect the convoys of men and materials heading to Africa from sub attacks. They patrolled coastlines from Northern Ireland to Algiers with ten-hour flights the routine. Although the Florida luck in finding subs didn't hold, Ramsay Potts and the crew of *The Duchess* achieved some notoriety by shooting down two, and damaging a third, of five German Junkers that jumped them while on patrol. The other two fled the scene. The 330th was proud of their unique role in supporting the African invasion. Meanwhile, the rest of the group joined B-17s in flying November missions to Brest, St. Nazaire, Lorient and Le Havre, without losing any planes.

On the 13th of November, the Ninety-Third Bomb Group recorded another first when His Royal Highness King George VI came to see them. It was also a first for the king as it was his initial visit to an American Bomb Group. His visit, known only to a few, began when his private limousine, followed by an entourage of British and American generals, pulled through the gate and was greeted by Colonel Timberlake and several of his staff. The king was there to see the new bombers, but first took tea in the colonel's office where introductions were made. Then, perched in the rear of Timberlake's jeep, but protected against the English chill by a royal blue overcoat, he was driven out to *Teggie Ann,* where he hopped aboard and was shown the business side of a B-24. Climbing down, he talked with the ground crew before "jeeping" around the base, waving at the men gathered to see him and smiling at the humor of the nose art. News of the king's visit was flashed around the world, and even though the place and the bomb group could not be revealed, word soon got out about the Ninety-third's latest coup.

In early December, 1942, Timberlake was ordered to take three of his squadrons, the 328th, 330th, and the 409th, to Africa. The 329th was to stay in England. Those leaving were told that it would be a ten-day job. Green American troops, under the command of General Eisenhower, were having a tough time of it against the experienced German Afrika Korps, commanded by the "Desert Fox," General Erwin Rommel. It was hoped that the "Heavies" could soften Rommel's rear supply lines, thus giving our embattled troops a break from the relentless Germans. On December 7, the first anniversary of Pearl Harbor, the three squadrons, left their ground crews and most of their personal items behind and flew out of Alconbury, headed for Tafaroui, Algeria, in North Africa.

They expected sun and sand but instead got rain and mud. They tried to fly, but when the first ship, *Geronimo*, attempted takeoff, it buried its nose in the mud, so operations were suspended until the weather cleared. They bombed the fine harbor at Bizerte, Tunisia on successive days in December and then unexpectedly received orders to fly to a new base in Libya on the eastern side of North Africa—so much for the ten-day mission. They set up their tents and began to experience life in the desert, with its harsh blowing sand. Christmas dinner was the usual: Spam, beans, and dehydrated cabbage cooked in alkali water. Fresh fruit and vegetables were unheard of. The desert was hard on men and machines, and the group was now down to twenty-one planes. But they were there to fly missions, and that they did, with strikes against Tunis, Sousse and Tripoli. When not bombing cities and harbors, they went after ammo and petrol storage areas as well as shipping and rail facilities.

As 1942 drew to a close, the Germans were finally on the run in Africa, and the Allies began preparing for the invasion of Italy, which would start with the island of Sicily. The "Boot" needed some softening up, so during January and February, 1943, traveling from their bases in Africa, the 93rd rained bombs down on Naples, Palermo, and Crotone. Abruptly, they were ordered back to England. Their ten-day, quick-hitter had turned into a ten-week desert sojourn, and they were glad to be headed back "home."

Meanwhile, back at Alconbury, the 329th Squadron was put on sub patrol and assigned the task of helping British contractors ready the Ninety-third's new airfield for bomber operations. That assignment was made uncomfortable by the harsh winter weather. They were also involved in experimental missions using newly developed radio-guided navigational equipment called Gee. In early December, they packed up their stuff, which included planes and things that fixed them, and took up residence at Hardwick Aerodrome in Norfolk County. It was to be their home for the rest of the war.

On January 2, four B-24s of the 329th, set out (carrying bombs) to test the new electronic gear. Purposely flying in bad weather to help avoid detection, they penetrated German airspace before turning back because of clearing weather. (They could not afford to have the secret equipment fall into German hands.) Disappointed that they did not at least set off some air raid sirens, they were happy to chalk up another first for the 93rd. It was the first combat flight of heavy bombers into Germany.[115] In February, they went as tagalongs to B-17s on several rough bombing missions in Europe, including one to Wilhelmshaven, a port and industrial complex in northern Germany. They were roughed up, but the raid was deemed a success.

When the three African squadrons arrived at their new home in late February, there was a great celebration. A host of war correspondents and photographers, including some from *Life, The New York Herald Tribune, Colliers,* and *Newsweek,* along with soon-to-be-famous, Walter Cronkite of the *United Press* and Andy Rooney of *Stars and Stripes,* were there to welcome them back.[116] Finally, after many weeks apart, the Ninety-third was together again.

Cpl. Carroll (Cal) Stewart was a former Nebraska newspaper man who joined the 93rd in August of 1942 as a radio operator. With publishing in his blood, he soon began an unofficial weekly called the *Liberator*. It was the first overseas, frontline newspaper in military history, and, of course, featured the exploits of the Ninety-third Bomb Group.[117] When the 93rd returned from Africa, the censors forbade any reference to the designation of the group and to where they had been, even though, with their tan skin, long sun-bleached hair, beards, and general scraggly appearance, it was quite obvious. So Cal Stewart, now the Group's public relations "officer" (even though he was a corporal), expeditiously began referring to the 93rd as "Ted's Travelling Circus." Press conferences and news releases sent directly to U.S. newspapers made the Circus famous and gained the ire of B-17 units, who jealously wanted the same publicity for their groups.[118] Thus, the incredible, legendary legacy of the Ninety-third Bombardment Group is due, not only to the acts of its heroes, but also to the significant gifts of their own Cal Stewart in telling their story.

~~~~~~~

East Anglia is the part of eastern England that bulges into the North Sea, and its Norfolk County, a short distance across the North Sea from European targets, had, during WWII, an astonishing amount of aerodromes in its small space. It had thirteen bases just for B-24s— not to mention bases for B-17s, British bombers, and Allied fighters.[119] The largest city in the area is Norwich, which was then, as now, a thriving commercial city and one of the finest examples of a medieval town in Europe. It was, that is, until April, 1942, when German attacks, specifically planned to bomb cities of cultural and historical distinction, obliterated the central city.[120] As a result, when the 329th arrived in December at Hardwick, about fifteen miles south of Norwich, signs of war were everywhere.

There was nothing unusual about Hardwick; it was typical of airfields being built all over England. It had three concrete runways and a concrete control tower two- to three-stories high, with a second-story balcony stretching halfway around the tower. There, men would gather, protected by iron railings, to anxiously scan the sky for planes returning from a mission. The roof of the tower was adorned with antennae for communicating with various headquarters and aircrews. Below, fire trucks, ambulances, jeeps, lorries, and a Red Cross mobile canteen lined up between the barracks. The men with the vehicles, having less of a view, listened to hear the sounds of their returning planes. As soon as the planes were more than specks in the sky, the counting began to determine if any were missing. In coming planes with wounded aboard would fire flares to alert medical personnel of their situation. Once landed, emergency vehicles raced to those planes where medics hopped aboard to attend to the wounded. The remaining crew members boarded the lorries and headed to debriefing huts where interrogation officers were waiting to interview them about the mission.

Life at the Hardwick Aerodrome wasn't bad. The men lived in Nissen huts (slightly smaller than the Quonset huts used in the Pacific) which were tucked under trees whenever possible, not only to shelter them from the sun but also to hide them from air attacks. Near the barracks were the mess halls, showers, the PX, and social clubs, which were separate for officers and enlisted men. There was an all-faith chapel, a theater, and a fitness center. Also on site (it was the size of a small city), were administration buildings, ammunition dumps, a quartermaster, weather experts, finance experts, military police, and a post office. Buildings located near the runways were for repair and supplies.

Similar to the accommodations at RAF Tatenhill, Hardwick's Nissen huts were corrugated metal edifices shaped like a half barrel set on cement slabs. On one end they had a door with two small windows flanking either side A few bulbs giving off dim light dangled from above. The small cots were lined up along either wall leaving an aisle down the middle. Shelves were hung from the ceiling where men could put their belongings and from which they could hang their uniforms. In the center of the hut was a potbellied coal stove. Coal trucks would dump their load in a pile near the compounds and a designee from each hut would scramble to fill a bucket or box of the precious stuff, caring little about the time it took later to get coal black out of clothes and off of body.

Occasionally, the stoves would be used to prepare food different from the humdrum served at the mess hut. Fried rabbit was a treat at Ray Eck's hut. Brought to them live by local lorry drivers, all the flyers had to do was kill it and cook it for a delicious departure from the routine. Some enterprising young men found a wire fan guard and fashioned it into a grille which balanced on the stove. They "borrowed" some real eggs from a local chicken coop, tossed them in a skillet, and delighted in their freshly scrambled eggs. One of the gunners got so enthused that he quickly inhaled about six of them just before he left on his mission. Once his plane reached altitude, however, he virtually exploded.

The cots they slept on varied in size and each had a canvas mattress. Airmen were each given a pillow and three blankets. At the foot of their cots were footlockers that held all their belongings. Generally, there were three topics of conversation among the men in the huts, girls, girls, and girls. Their on-base social events consisted of movies and dances, with music provided by men of the base or by scratchy 78 rpm records, and with local girls invited in for partnering. The Red Cross ran the clubs—one for the sergeants and one for officers—but only the officers' clubs had liquor. They were equipped with pool, Ping Pong and card tables. Parked outside the living quarters were dozens and dozens of bicycles, the vehicle of choice for the men. They were needed to get from place to place on and off the base. At some bases bikes were government issue particularly to the ground crews, but if purchased, they could cost up to 50 pounds - a lot of money for low paid airmen.

Dotted around the base, within biking or walking distance, were many fine examples of a uniquely British institution called a public house, pub for short. One of the closest to the base was the Three Horseshoes where the men from Hardwick soon grew accustomed to their "pints" of warm beer and became very proficient at another British institution: pub darts. Flyers say that the English patrons always bought the rounds even though they most likely couldn't afford it. To buy back, the Americans had to lose at darts something that was not hard to do against the experienced English throwers. The pubs not only occupied a good share of the airmen's time, but also took a lot of their money. No matter, most didn't have anything else to spend it on anyway.

With the narrow, shoulder-less roads in the area, getting to and from anywhere on a bike was dangerous. Tail gunner Carl Grigg remembered that on many occasions, despite warnings, young men well "into their cups" would attempt to wobble back to the base from the pubs on their cycles in the blackout.

Many were hurt, some severely, as they ran into curbs, walls, buildings, and each other. Some of the injured even thought they should be given Purple Hearts for their "war wounds," but the higher-ups would have none of it.

Lorries used to transport crews to and from their planes, made liberty runs to Norwich every night for those with permission to leave the base. Norwich was a large city with a lot to do: hotel bars, theaters, the Samson and Hercules Ballroom and, of course, girls. American young men were good looking, gregarious, boisterous, outgoing, impulsive, and naughty, in contrast to their rather staid, more serious British counterparts. They also were paid more. That, along with their innate Yankee charm, swept many an English lass off her feet. Children in the area loved them. Of course, candy and gum handouts went a long way in gaining and keeping that affection. Kids commonly greeted the Yanks by saying, "Any gum, chum?" Which often drew the retort, "Got a sister, mister?"[121]

Robert Timmer, no slouch and no prude when it came to having fun, joined his buddies on their forays into Norwich. Although he was not a big drinker, he loved the competition that games like darts supplied, and would have quaffed a pint or two while engaging in the joys of a trip to town. Girls were off-limits however, and he and other married men who shared the same values about wedding vows hung out together.

With all the airfields in the area, Norwich was often jammed with servicemen. American and British, although fighting on the same side, frequently took umbrage with each other, usually over a girl, and fisticuffs were often the result. Competition over girls was not restricted to Brit vs. Yank however. The Americans were masters at it, and it too frequently disintegrated into a good old American bar brawl which the English delightedly referred to as a "punch-up." MPs had many busy nights patrolling the Norwich night scene, and kept the brig back at the base fully occupied. Perhaps Norwich was where the famous English observation about American servicemen originated: The only thing I don't like about Americans is that they are "overpaid, over fed, over sexed and over here."[122]

For long leaves, London, about a four-hour train ride from Norwich, was the favorite destination. Everyone took a leave in London, and Bob was no exception. Although appalled by the rubble, Big Ben (standing above the ruins of Parliament), the Tower, Westminster Abby, Buckingham Palace and a boat ride down the Thames attracted thousands of American servicemen to the big city. For war-battered airmen, however, it was far from tranquil. In the spring of 1943, the German bombers paid regular visits to the city. Streets blocked with rubble and the strictly enforced blackout made it difficult to move around the city and put a real damper on evening activities.

If rooms were available, the men stayed at either the Salvation Army or the Red Cross, who both ran several facilities for housing servicemen. The Salvation Army was preferred over the American Red Cross because the rooms and the cigarettes at the SA were without cost, while the ARC charged for cigarettes (which they received free) and $2 for a room. Many WWII veterans wanted nothing to do with the Red Cross after the war because of their London policies, especially on cigarettes. Later in the war, when Hitler's guided bombs started landing on London (Londoners called the deadly things "doodle bugs"), men from Hardwick began going to Edinburgh, Scotland for their leaves.

~~~~~~~

With all four squadrons of the 93rd back together, March brought new attempts to cripple the German war machine by almost constant daylight bombing. On several occasions, the Circus flew diversionary missions in an attempt to draw the German fighter planes away from the main missions flown by B-17s. The Circus got some licks in, however, when, on March 18, they attacked submarine pens and shipbuilding works at Vegesack. Clouds of fighters came up to greet them, and the .50s of the Circus claimed nine of them with another seven probable. Unfortunately, they lost their lead ship, *Hot Freight,* and its popular crew, later learning that most of them were killed. March also brought a continuing stream of VIP visitors to Hardwick, anxious to horn in on the Circus's fame.

With the coming of April, 1943, the Ninety-third, celebrated its first birthday, a new home, and a new nickname. It had received an inordinate amount of publicity, due to its extraordinary exploits. It also had a new pilot.

The young American in the cool blue uniform of a Royal Canadian Air Force officer entered Colonel Timberlake's small office and snapped a salute to his new commanding officer. He stood at attention while Timberlake glanced at the man's papers on his desk in front of him. Col. Ted asked some questions, primarily about his service with the RCAF, and told him that his own experience with Canadian trained pilots was a positive one. He told the new guy to be at ease, and they talked a little about the 93rd, then a handshake welcomed him into the United States Army. He was advised to report to the office of the leader of the 330th Squadron, Major Ramsay Potts, to, among other things, get the correct uniform.

At the quartermaster's hut, he was outfitted in his new army officer's dress uniform, consisting of dark brown jacket with tan pants, shirt and tie. On the top of each shoulder, he wore the single gold bar of a second lieutenant, and on his left chest were the new silver wings of an American pilot. The round patch of blue with golden wings and white star with a red center, emblem of the Army Air Force, was on the sleeve of his left shoulder. His officer's cap, with the golden eagle on the crown, was also dark brown. As yet, there were no campaign ribbons or medals to be affixed to his uniform; they would come later. He did have permission, however, to have his cloth wings of the RCAF sewn on the right chest of his American jacket. He was pleased with that policy, because he had spent a lot of time and effort to earn them. There would be a lot more processing to come, including an introduction to his new plane: the B-24 Liberator. (His Canadian wings can be seen in the photo on the book's cover.)

Robert Timmer's assignment to the Ninety-third Bombardment Group was a matter of sorting men into slots where they were needed. It was not a choice. In April, several pilots came from the RCAF and Timberlake was glad to have them. Their training gap was short. For the Circus, waging winter war both in Europe and Africa was unprecedented and put a lot of stress on men and machines. "The Circus was becoming richer in battle wisdom but poorer in number. Attrition inexorably depleted the number of fliers and B-24s available. No replacements, except for a dribble, were in sight during those disheartening months. The case for high-level daylight bombing still hung in the balance due to unacceptably high loses."[123] In addition to the high loss rate, many of the original surviving flight crews had more than their twenty-five required combat missions and were due for reassignment. Replacements like Bob were desperately needed, and they had to be trained on their new planes quickly.

Chapter VIII The Liberator

Sitting on the tarmac outside the hangers at Hardwick were some serious airplanes — fully equipped and ready to do the deadly business of war. Numerous patches adorned their torn hides, and little bomb icons, one for each mission, were plastered under their cockpit windows. And every time a German plane met its demise at the expense of its .50 calibers, a little swastika was pasted next to the little bombs, vivid testimony to the fact that these muscle ships were not in the business of ferrying VIPs around Europe.

Painted on the nose of each plane was its name, which was often accompanied by a cartoon-like caricature of that name. Nose Art, it was called, and it spoke to the creativity of the crews in coming up with names and pictures and to the artists who did the painting. Names and art were generally humorous, often profane, sometimes downright risqué, and always interesting. The art had the effect of taking away some of the cold metallic nature of these deadly weapons, making them seem more personal and human, and attesting to the fact that men were involved with these things.

It seems there were as many varieties of paint schemes on the planes as there were squadrons. Colors ranged from metallic (no paint) to pink. Many were multi-colored, even polka-dotted. In contrast to the colorful images conjured up by the name "Circus," the planes of the 93rd were drab compared to some of their more brightly painted sisters in other bomb groups. Their color could be called olive brown, a decorative scheme that unintentionally blended well with their many forays from the Sahara Desert. Only the nose art, the white star in a circle of blue on the waist, and the call letters on the tail broke the monotony of the drabness. Planes damaged to the point of being sent to the scrap heap were often ravished for parts by enterprising ground crews. It was not unusual to see a green plane with a pink wing. No one cared; fashion was not what they were about.

They were called "Liberators," or "Libs," for short, an apt name for a bomber that flew in every theater of World War II, helping to stamp out the enslaving, fascist, militarist governments of Germany and Japan and their friends. Officially, it was a B-24, the largest and fastest of WWII heavy bombers until the B-29 came along near war's end. American made and several years in development and testing, the first combat models rolled off the assembly line at the Consolidated plant in San Diego, California, in early 1941, months before Pearl Harbor and America's entry into the war. The nickname was chosen in a contest conducted at the Consolidated plant, which was won by Mrs. Dorothy Fleet, wife of the company's founder, who anonymously submitted her entry.[124]

B-24 Liberator Bomber

Consolidated was the first to produce the B-24, but other companies soon adapted their production facilities to make them. By the end of the war, Liberators were rolling off assembly lines in five plants throughout the United States. The plant that received the most attention, however, for its sheer size and production capability, was the Ford plant in Willow Run, Michigan. Construction of the massive factory began in April, 1941, and was completed in late 1942. The plant was a mile long and a quarter mile wide and covered 3.7 million square feet in area.[125] The assembly line was the longest ever built at 3.5 million feet —that's 662 miles![126] It was accompanied by Willow Village, containing homes and dormitories, which housed many of its 42,000 employees. The village had schools, police and fire departments.[127] There were two nine-hour shifts. When full production capacity was reached, the plant was producing a B-24 every hour, and the

Ford plant was only one of five!

Big factories were needed to produce big planes, and the B-24 was a big plane, even by today's standards. It was almost 70 feet long, 18 feet high, and had a wingspan of 110 feet. It was powered by four huge Pratt & Whitney 14-cylinder engines, each with 1200 horsepower. Its cruising speed was 225 mph at 25,000 feet, but its maximum speed was 303 mph, with a maximum ceiling of 32,000 feet. The engines had 3,614 gallons of gas to suck, giving it a maximum range of 3,500 miles; but a full bomb load cut that range to 2,300 miles, still the longest in the business. It was also lethal, carrying up to eight 1000 pound bombs and, depending on the model, had anywhere from eight to eleven .50 caliber machine guns onboard.

The Liberator had some unusual design features. The plane had a tricycle landing gear, with the third wheel under its snout instead of under the tail like the B-17. The fuselage hung from its top mounted wings. The most distinctive feature, however, which made the Liberator unique among heavy bombers and, therefore, easily recognizable, was its tail, with twin vertical rudders. The crew entered and exited through the main entrance hatch which was below the waist gunner's windows. They could also use the bomb bay opening. A camera for recording bomb strikes was mounted above a small opening near the main hatch. A catwalk, eight inches wide and crossing above the two bomb bay doors, separated the front from the rear of the aircraft. The bombs were mounted vertically on both sides of the catwalk. During flights, the crew, while working in their bulky flight suits, routinely crossed from fore to aft using the catwalk, even when the bomb doors were open!

While the bomb bay was the bailout exit of choice, other openings like the waist openings and the hatch were also used. Actually, men inside a falling plane jumped out of any hole they could get to and through. Though thousands successfully bailed out of crippled B-24s, thousands more died because, burdened with their heavy outerwear and parachutes, they could not move quickly enough to get to an opening.

The designers of the B-24 did not give crew comfort even a passing thought. The plane was not built for comfort or ease. It was designed to carry the largest payload the longest distance, faster than any other heavy bomber made. It achieved that purpose remarkably well. Standing on the tarmac and looking up at the inside through the bomb bay, one would see a tube-like structure similar to the inside of a submarine. Wires, cables, pipes, vents, handles, levers, belts, pulleys, hoses, and straps, all colored in drab army olive/brown, were coming and going from front to back and side to side. Looking up at the cockpit, one would see hundreds of dials, gauges, switches and levers above, beside, and below the hard, straight-back, adjustable seats of the pilot and copilot. There were no drink holders, arm rests or padded seats. (Their bums were cushioned by their parachutes.) Looking aft, one would see a bulkhead with an opening through which the waist and tail gunners would crawl to get to their positions.

Life inside a B-24 was difficult, to say the least, even without being the object of enemy fire. There was no heat, and the plane was neither insulated nor pressurized. Oxygen masks made of rubber, malodorous from repeated use, had to be worn when reaching 10,000 feet. With temperatures plunging to 40 or 50 below zero at cruising altitude, they often clogged with ice or froze to the men's faces. Bare skin would quickly freeze to metal at those temperatures, and frostbite was a major problem, grounding an inordinate number of crewmen. Adding to the misery, 200 mile-an-hour winds blew through open gun ports and doors. The ride one got in a Liberator was far from passenger jet quality. Climbing to 36,000 feet and catching the jet stream for a smooth ride was not an option. The B-24 jumped and bounced, bumped and slid through the skies, often with another at its wingtip doing the same thing. The constant but comforting thrumming and droning of the four huge engines was tempered somewhat by the headsets worn by the crew. However, without sound abatement systems, there was a constant roar inside the plane, to the point that many WWII flyers had early hearing loss. One vet even named his double hearing aids "Pratt and Whitney."

Crewmen were equipped with electrically heated flight gear, worn over long woolen underwear. They wore the original "bomber jacket": fleece-lined leather with a large fleece collar and fleece showing at the wrists and waist. Insulated flight pants were adorned with zippers and flaps and tucked into huge leather flight boots pulled tight by buckles at the top and bottom. Difficulty in performing delicate tasks was increased by heavy three-fingered gloves constructed with individual receptacles for thumb and forefinger. Without them, a crewman would experience frostbite within minutes at higher altitudes. Their leather helmet was imbedded with ear phones and had a chin strap which was rarely buckled. Tinted goggles were strapped around their heads with a thick elastic band and were generally worn pushed up on the forehead until needed. The rest of their face was covered by the oxygen mask and its rubber hose which dangled from their faces, tethering them to the inboard oxygen source. Mobile oxygen was available when it was necessary to move about inside the aircraft. Draped around their necks, with a strap around their back to hold it in place, was the inflatable Mae West life jacket. Finally, their parachute, with straps crisscrossing their bodies, hung from their lower back or chest, depending on the type. All that paraphernalia encasing each crew member was cumbersome and limiting; yet, life and death jobs had to be performed while wearing it.

One might think the military would have devised some method for feeding and hydrating their flight crews as they went into combat. It would seem that young men under extreme stress would perform better if they had more to eat and drink than the eggs and coffee they were given for breakfast. Needless to say, they were not sent off with box lunches, compliments of the cooks. The reality was that there was no place to carry food or even a cup of coffee on a B-24. Besides, liquids would freeze at high altitude, so the insulated canteen of water they carried was all they had for the duration of the mission. Another reality was that many didn't feel like eating; the anxiety of combat, coupled with the rough ride of a B-24, made keeping down food problematic. Crew members may have stuffed a candy bar or two into one of the pockets of their flight gear, but with flights lasting up to twelve hours, there were some hungry and thirsty young men returning from missions.

The bulky flight suits encased in the many straps of parachutes and Mae Wests presented the men with another problem: that of relieving themselves. There were, of course, no toilets. Two little tubes were located forward and aft to catch urine. They were difficult to hit while wrestling with heavy clothing and auxiliary oxygen connections, along with the bumping of the plane. The small amount the tubes did catch often froze, jamming the system. This task had to be accomplished quickly, as the men were well aware that exposed skin was vulnerable to frostbite. As for the other function, imagine dropping several pair of pants and exposing one's bottom in that kind of cold. The job was performed in a mechanism that was lined with a wax paper bag which, when the task was completed, was carefully tossed out one of the plane's openings to shouts of, "bombs away!"[128] The men dreaded having to use either fixture but, with missions of at least six hours, even the best "holders" had no choice.

Flying a B-24 demanded extreme physical exertion. Crewmen were strapped into adjustable but uncomfortable and unpadded seats, or were curled into the small bubbles of turret guns, sometimes for hours. That, combined with the cold, subjected their bodies, especially their limbs, to numbness and tingling, which, in turn, made performing their tasks difficult. Flying the plane was like wrestling a gorilla and taxed the strength of the men, even though most were in great physical shape. In his book, *The Wild Blue*, author Stephen Ambrose tells of a B-24 flyer, pilot Guyon Phillips, who recalled that he never knew a pilot who would choose to fly a Liberator. There were so many other planes that were more preferable to fly. Flying in formation for several hours, using his left arm to steer and his right for the throttles and switches, gave his left arm a workout and enabled Phillips to win arm wrestling contests but only with his left arm. He had no chance with his right.[129] Pilot William Carigan Jr. related, "Whatever else the B-24 was, [it was] a man's airplane, sternly unforgiving and demanding sometimes super strength, always requiring considerable muscle. Heavy on the controls, the airplane tires the strongest teams of pilots on long missions. The wearer of the silver wings wonders why he ever took up flying."[130]

There was at least one Liberator that was quite comfortable, however. Modified with sleeping accommodations, heating components, and even a small stove, it was the personal plane of the British prime minister. Painted matte black for secret night flying, it had its name, *Commando,* painted neatly on its nose.[131] In it, Dutch-American pilot Capt. Bill Vanderkloot, with Winston Churchill frequently in the copilot's seat, flew WSC and his entourage on several of their longest wartime journeys.[132]

Most Libs flew with a crew of ten. The pilot and copilot seats were located on the cramped flight deck, which was accessed by climbing up from the main hatch. The glass canopy was over and around them, offering views forward, above, and to the sides. The forward view however was restricted by the massive control panel looming in front and above them. The pilot sat on the left and was the ship's commander. In training, he had to learn the job description of each of his men and be knowledgeable enough to perform each of the tasks, if necessary. His job was to fly the plane to the target by maintaining the tight formations necessary in high-level bombing. As the commander, he was also responsible for making the required split-second decisions when leading men into combat. The copilot was second in command and was trained to do everything the pilot did. He was fully capable of taking over command in the event something happened to the pilot and was equally adept at formation flying. He was as skillful in navigating the plane as the navigator and could take over that job, as well. Most bomber pilots were once copilots and were promoted based on experience and leadership qualities.

The Liberator's substantial nose was home to the nose gunner, bombardier, and navigator, who were located below and in front of the flight deck. The nose gunner, in his glass enclosed power turret, had the "best seat in the house" for observing the stunning views from his perch high along the flight path. Once the action started, however, he was most vulnerable, as he was often targeted by oncoming enemy fighters, who preferred a frontal assault on the heavily armed Libs. He fought back with two or three machine guns, depending on the model of B-24 he was in. Crawling into the nose bubble took a special brand of courage because the gunner knew that, in the event of a crash landing, he would be the first to meet the ground.

Bombers were designed for one purpose: to deliver high explosives to a target. That being the case, the bombardier had the most important job in the airplane. Without his skills, the plane was useless. He had much in common with the pilot, for when the bombing run began, it was he, via the autopilot, who flew the plane over the target.[133] Also a man of courage, his task was so important that total concentration was critical. While performing his job, which required precise mathematical calculations, he relied heavily on his training to ignore enemy fighters, flak bursts, damaged planes, and personal wounds to achieve his mission. Fortunately, as the war progressed, advancements in technology gave the bombardier more useful tools, which made his work easier and more effective.

Highly trained navigators were responsible for getting the plane and crew from their base to the target and back. Their tools of the trade were compasses, sextants, drift recorders, graphs, tables and charts. In guiding a huge plane to where it had to go, variables such as air speed, altitude, compass bearing, wind speed, and direction had to be considered. A navigator could not make mistakes. His skills were especially critical if the plane experienced difficulties through breakdowns or combat damage and had to drop out of formation and out of sight of the main group; he then had to direct a crippled plane, and its ten men, back to base on his own.

Generally, navigators and bombardiers were officers who sometimes outranked their pilots. Be that as it may, the pilot and the copilot after him were, without question, in command of the airplane. This set up an interesting situation, whereas a lower ranked officer like copilot 2d Lt. Robert Timmer, according to protocol, would have to salute his bombardier, Capt. Claude Culpepper, on the ground, but Claude would have to take orders from Bob in the air. In reality, they operated as a team of equals, and acknowledgement of rank among the team was ignored, even on the ground.[134]

The top or dorsal turret gunner climbed into his bubble at the top of the fuselage from right behind the cockpit. He had a 360 degree view from his revolving Plexiglas perch, and, therefore, the best firing arc compared to the other gunners on the plane. He could see enemy fighters coming from every direction, except beneath him, and was equipped with two .50 caliber machine guns. His parachute could not be worn in the turret, so he climbed into his position with the straps of his chute dangling about his body. He left his chute on the floor under him, so if it was needed, he would have to hook himself up before bailing out. He was also trained to serve as the plane's engineer, functioning as its onboard mechanic. He was an expert in fixing blast-shattered wires and cables; many crews owed their lives to engineers who could "patch up" a wounded plane well enough to get it home.

The radio man was responsible for maintaining contact with

ground operations, communicating with other planes, reporting the plane's current situation, and communicating with headquarters. He was also responsible for keeping a log of all of the plane's pertinent actions. He received training as a gunner and could perform that task, if needed. He and his cubby hole, crammed with switches, dials, and wires, were located right behind the cockpit.

Each B-24 had two waist gunners, called the Right and Left. Closer to the tail than the cockpit, they each fired their single .50 caliber machine gun through "windows" in the side of the ship. Because of the limited angles in firing from that position, the gunners had to have excellent hand/eye coordination. Liberators had huge sides, and waist gunners suffered a high rate of casualties because enemy fighters loved to strafe the Lib's vulnerable profile. They were, however, closest to openings and, if able, were among the first to get out of a stricken plane. Gunners were trained to be gunners and often assumed any one of the gun positions on the plane. While they may have had their favorite gun position, they often took turns at a variety of gun stations.

It took a special kind of man to seek the tail gunner's position on a B-24. He fought from a glass "bump" sticking out between the Lib's two huge tail rudders. He and his two .50s were the only things back there. He was alone and liked it that way. His job was simple: to protect the rear end of the plane, which was particularly vulnerable, especially if the plane was crippled and slowing.

Some Liberator models had a ball turret, a bubble that hung below the fuselage behind the wings. Small men, without parachutes, had to so position themselves in their "seat" that they looked like they were in a tiny, cramped version of a modern recliner. It was cold in that bubble, and many ball gunners suffered from frostbite. The turret was raised and lowered for takeoffs and landings, and the gunner climbed into it and out of it accordingly, for when protruding from the bottom of the fuselage, it was not the place to be in the event of a belly landing.

The B-24 was a formidable fighting machine. Many a German fighter pilot underestimated, with dire consequences, the deluge of crossfire that the .50 caliber machine guns could throw at attacking Focke-Wulfs and Messerschmitt's. But the Libs had a weakness; they could not, even with all guns blazing, immerse the front of the aircraft with the withering crossfire that covered the rest of the plane. It was called the forward arc of fire and the Germans began exploiting its vulnerability with the most unnerving of all tactics: the head-on pass. With the increased use of this aggressive tactic, Liberator losses began to mount perceptibly.[135]

Despite depleted numbers, there was no relief for the flyers of the Circus who continued daylight bombing runs against German targets in Europe. While Lt. Timmer spent much of his first few weeks at Hardwick in ground school, his fellow airmen had a rough month, especially on the raid to bomb harbor facilities at Brest, where three planes went down. Most of the men were listed as KIA.

~~~~~~~

Captain Hugh Rawlin Roper from Oak City, Utah, was one of the first pilots of the 93rd, joining the group at Barksdale in early 1942. A star athlete in high school, Rawlin, (as he was known back home), played football and was the center on the basketball team. After graduation in 1933, he attended

Brigham Young University and graduated with a degree in secondary education. Prior to the war, he taught a year in a remote one-room school and then high school in Wellington, Utah. Tall, lanky and handsome, he was a devout Mormon. As storms of war gathered over Europe, Hugh decided to enlist in the Army Air Corps in hopes of being assigned to pilot training. After basics, he was sent to flight school, graduating as a second lieutenant just a few days after the bombing of Pearl Harbor. An outstanding pilot, he requested assignment to a bomber command and arrived in Louisiana with his new wife Abbie to begin training on B-24s. He commenced assembling his crew even though, at first, planes had to be shared among the squadrons. He noticed on a list of incoming airmen the name of Walt Stewart, also from Utah. He did not know Walt, but asked him to be the copilot on his crew. They became very close friends.

Prior to the trip to England, Hugh got his own plane and named it *Exterminator*. It had nose art of a skunk riding a bomb. In England, Hugh was transferred, temporarily, from the 329th to the 330th Bomb Squadron to fly sub-patrol off the coast of France and Spain. From his diaries, it is evident that Hugh and Abbie missed each other terribly, but they knew it could be years before they would be together again. Hugh remained in England with the 329th and, therefore, did not go to Africa during the winter of 1942-43 with the rest of the 93rd. In February and March, Hugh racked up significant combat experience as *Exterminator* flew several successful missions over Europe. In early March, his good friend Ramsay Potts was named the new commanding officer of the 330th and asked Hugh to transfer, permanently, to his squadron. Hugh accepted.[136] Walt and Hugh moved into a barracks at Hardwick with several other 330th pilots and copilots. Cribbage was the game, and so the barracks became known as "Cribbage Haven." In April, the Utah teacher was promoted to Captain.

On Good Friday, April 23, 1943, Robert Timmer climbed up through the hatch of *Exterminator* and strapped himself into the copilot's seat next to Captain Roper. It was his first training flight in a B-24. The flight lasted only forty-five minutes, but it was enough for Bob to get a first look at the cockpit with an experienced combat pilot doing the flying. That Sunday, Bob attended Easter sunrise services, which were held outdoors at Hardwick's athletic field at 0630. One of the officers, a former choir director, led the singing, and Father Murphy read the Scripture and offered prayers. Colonel Timberlake offered a review of the Ninety-third's activities during their year of existence and asked everyone to remember the fallen. Chappy Burris preached the sermon and conducted the memorial to those who gave the supreme sacrifice. The service ended with the "Star Spangled Banner." That afternoon, Captain Roper took Bob flying again. The last week in April, Bob flew with Hugh several more times, even getting time in the pilot's seat and chalking up four landings.

Early in May, another first for the Circus turned into a tragedy. Lt. Gen. Frank M. Andrews, a former World War I pilot, was chief of the European Theater of Operations, and as such, he was the highest ranking American serviceman in Europe. As overall commander, he was responsible for the initial planning for what would become the invasion of Normandy. During the 1930s he was an early proponent of strategic air warfare and foresaw, before many others, the role that bombers would play in the next conflict. On several occasions, from his London office, he visited Hardwick to review the airmen and visit with Colonel Timberlake. He liked the Ninety-third. In late April, Andrews arrived in Hardwick to make arrangements to fly back to the States for consultations with Washington officials.

Bob "Shine" Shannon, pilot of *Hot Stuff*, and his crew were selected for the honor of flying General Andrews home. Captain Shannon was an excellent pilot who, along with most of his crew, had completed his 25 combat missions. It would be the first time a battle-tested heavy bomber would be returning home. A heroes' welcome was planned, including ticker-tape parades, ceremonies, and press conferences. The popular Shine Shannon, with his charming Irish personality and battered Liberator, would be the perfect war hero to show off to the home front. It would also allow the spotlight to focus on the role of the B-24 and on the now famous Ted's Travelling Circus. The American public, suffering under tough rationing and negative war news, was in need of what Shine and his crew would bring.

General Andrews, however, brought along a larger-than-expected entourage, which made it necessary to leave several of the crew behind. Andrews also wanted to fly in the copilot's seat, thus robbing Captain Shannon of dependable and experienced Lt. John Lentz, who had to stay in England.[137] The group departed on May 3 and, given favorable weather reports in Iceland, decided to refuel there, by-passing the opportunity to refuel in Scotland. Thick fog greeted them in Iceland, however, and visibility was zero. With air traffic controllers trying to talk them down and running low on fuel, *Hot Stuff* attempted to land on an invisible runway several times before plowing into the side of a mountain. There were fourteen men on board, and all were killed except the tail gunner, who lived to tell the story.[138]

The world was in shock, and tributes poured forth. Bob

Shannon's father, a newspaperman from Iowa, wrote and published a moving tribute to his son; a tribute that many families who received the "dreaded telegram" found comforting. Andrews Air Force Base, outside of Washington D.C., made famous as the home of Air Force One, is named for General Andrews.

~~~~~~

His fellow 330th pilot, Walt Stewart, called him "Jonesy," but when he took 2d Lt. Timmer flying, he was "Captain Jones." One of the originals of the Ninety-third, Captain Jack S. Jones, was a southern boy from Franklinton, Louisiana. A sandy-haired man, slightly over five feet tall, he must have had great strength to muscle around the controls of a B-24. A tiny man from a tiny town, Jones was a crack Liberator pilot and a best buddy of Hugh Roper. They made quite a pair around the base, definitely the long and short of it. Jack probably appreciated having Bob in the copilot's seat as most pilots, regardless of stature, preferred partners with long, strong legs for extra strength on the rudders and ailerons, essential for controlling the aircraft especially under stress. His plane was called *Hot Freight*, and on the nose was a railroad car with wings speeding down a track. He loved to fly. From time to time there were visiting planes at Hardwick that were different from Libs: fighters, cargo planes, small bombers, etc. Jack delighted in taking those planes up for joy rides, buzz a few bases and towns and return the borrowed plane to Hardwick, mission accomplished.[139] By May of 1943, Jones had completed his mandatory combat missions and was moved behind a desk to squadron operations. That didn't stop him from taking an interest in teaching a newly arrived officer the intricacies of a B-24. Diminutive Captain Jones took Bob under his wing, even though he was small enough to fit under

Bob's.

During the month of May, 1943, Captain Jones and Lt. Timmer managed, despite the fickle English weather, to rack up a considerable amount of training hours. Most flights were of short duration, flying around Hardwick or from Hardwick to a nearby base, so there were a lot of flights. The emphasis was on takeoffs and landings, and Bob made fifty-eight landings while in control of the aircraft, many of them from the pilot's seat. They also practiced navigation and instruments, including night flying. Not only did they spend time together in the cockpit, but Jones spent time meeting with Bob before and after their flights, briefing and debriefing. Bob thought the world of Jones and appreciated the amount of time Jack put into his training.

~~~~~~~

The Circus stood down for most of the month of May, flying only one diversion and two combat missions. On May 17, the group took part in another first, that being part of an all Liberator raid, no B-17s included. The Circus provided fifteen planes and the 44th Bomb group nineteen. The target was the huge French port city of Bordeaux, which housed German U-boats and a series of critical locks that protected the harbor from the tides. Bombing was extremely accurate, destroying the locks and a large pier used by subs.

Shortly after, Colonel (soon to be General) Timberlake was promoted to command the 201st Bomb Wing, an umbrella command that included all the B-24 combat units in Europe. He turned over command of his Travelling Circus to the CO of the 328th Squadron, Lt. Col. Addison Baker. Timberlake had led the Circus since its beginning and through fifty-one combat missions, many of which he flew.

A few weeks later, in another all Lib effort with thirteen Circus bombers participating, the harbor at La Pallice, France, was pounded, with excellent results. Lt. Walt Stewart's copilot, Loren Koon, in *Utah Man,* was scratched just before the mission after badly cutting his finger in a fan. Walt flew the eight-hour mission by himself. B-24s are difficult to fly with two men in the cockpit, but after his ordeal, Walt was as peppy as ever.[140] It was the 25th and last required mission for Morton Macks, another early pilot of the 330th, who had recently been awarded the Distinguished Flying Cross. Meanwhile, back home, a B-17 named *Memphis Belle* was being showered by the attention that was supposed to have gone to Bob Shannon and *Hot Stuff.*

To call the competitiveness between the flyers of the B-17 (the Flying Fortress) and the flyers of the B-24 a rivalry would be an understatement. While not wishing each other any harm in the skies of Europe, they really didn't like each other very much. B-17s had been around since the late 1930s, while the B-24 was the new kid on the block that was designed to compensate for some of the 17s weaknesses. Because they had been in production longer, there were many more B-17s in combat than 24s, and more planes meant more of them on missions, and more on missions meant more publicity, and that was part of the rub. Cal Stewart speculated that some of the glamour reporting that the 17s received back home was due to the fact that their bases were closer to London, where most of the correspondents lived and worked.[141] Besides, the sleek 17s were much prettier than their lumpy, frumpy rivals. It looked like an airplane should look, with its high traditional tail assembly and rear wheel, very similar to modern passenger planes. B-24 crew members, especially when in the presence of men from the 17s, talked about how it took "real men" to fly a Liberator. The image of the B-24 took some hits, though, when Flying Fortress crews began referring to it as "the crate that ours came in."[142]

The B-24 could fly further, faster, and carry a bigger payload than its counterpart. That led to the observation among B-24 men that the "B-17 huffed and puffed, climbed to 30,000 feet and dropped a hand grenade."[143] Unfortunately, when the planes went on missions together, as was the case for most of the war, B-17 strategies prevailed to the detriment of the 24 and its crews. "Since there were more B-17 than B-24 groups in England, tactics in the Eighth Air Force were built around the Flying Fortress. Because the B-24s were so much faster, the Liberator pilots were forced to fly at reduced airspeeds and do a lot of jockeying to maintain the precise formations called for by Eighth Air Force policy. Consequently, the B-24 was underutilized in the strategic bombing role in Europe."[144]

After a particularly devastating mission, where B-24s followed B-17s to the target and took a shellacking, Ted Timberlake reported on the situation to his superiors at Eighth Air Force Headquarters. He commented, "Disorganization of formations, excessive fuel consumption, and a disproportionate number of failures due to excessive manifold pressure are inevitable if B-24 formations attempt to follow B-17 Combat Wings above 23,000 ft. closely enough to drop on the B-17 Pathfinders."[145] Apparently, the commanders of the Eighth Air Force never figured that out, and often put the crews of the 24s in the position of being the ugly step-sisters to the Fortress Cinderella's. It also put them in jeopardy.

June, 1943, was an interesting month for the Circus. Lt. Timmer was just getting the hang of flying his new plane when an unusual order came to his commanding officer, Col. Addison Baker. The 93rd was to begin practicing low-level flying, no reasons given. They were put on non-operational status, which meant there would be no combat until further notice. Obviously, there was a secret mission in the works somewhere, but no one at Hardwick knew what it was.

It was also obvious that, once again, the Ninety-third was being called upon to do another special job, this time, a job the planes they flew were not designed to do. No one involved in the design of the plane ever considered that they would be ordered to fly a mission at treetop level. The big old crates were difficult enough to handle at 20,000 feet, much less 50! Besides, the tight formations required for maximum protection from enemy fighters was virtually impossible at low-level. The curious crewmen began to grasp the gravity of the situation when their new Norden bombsites were removed, and old-fashioned ones, more suited to low-level bombing, were installed.

The officers at Hardwick had a new club called the Aero-Club. It was operated by the Red Cross, and the talk there was almost exclusively about the low-level stuff. Rumors abounded. They wondered what they were going to do - to whom - and where the whom was that they were going to do what to! Some thought they had it figured out, but no one did. They didn't like how they were flying; it was dangerous. Low-level formation flying was certainly not for the faint of heart, and the secret of it all put them on edge. But they were men of courage, who may have taken strength from a verse in the Book of Job, where God tells a fearful Job, "to gird up now thy loins like a man."[146] Like it or not, brave men did what they had to do.

When they were not flying, the men were attending lectures (required), drilling—lots of drilling (required), and shooting skeet (not required). The brass also instituted physical education classes (required). Hardwick had an excellent baseball team, with several college and professional players, which traveled around the area playing teams from other bases. Movies were shown every night, including *Holiday Inn* starring Bing Crosby, who introduced the song "White Christmas" in the film. For days after, men went around the base singing or humming the song, usually out of tune, quite appropriate for a summer day in England! Lines formed for everything, but they were especially long when the week's allotment of seven packs of cigarettes was given out. Even non-smokers patiently waited for a supply of fags. The "nons" used them to obtain all kinds of valuable goodies from smokers who couldn't restrict themselves to a pack a day, and who, by the end of the week, would trade just about anything for more cigarettes.[147] They were also useful in purchasing favors from the heavily rationed Brits outside the base.

Lectures were a regular feature on the base and were given on a wide variety of topics, as long as the topic was military. The most memorable and most popular lecture that June was given by Lt. Harry Russell, an intelligence officer, who had been sent to a three-week seminar on tank identification. The combat crews were gathered to hear him present his new-found knowledge. Lt. Russell began, "Gentlemen, I've had an interesting three weeks and I have learned a lot about tanks. I'll pass it all on to you in one sentence–if it doesn't have a circle or a star on it blow it to Hell! Dismissed."[148]

While training at Hardwick, Lt. Timmer received word that his brother Gerald was now in the army and he could not resist some brotherly jabs. He wrote home that the army would do

Gerald "a lot of good." Then, "Wish I could be around when Ty goes in. They will have to salute me and call me sir if we were in the same camp together. The Rookies!" He again was frustrated by the censorship, but was having a swell time flying the big ones.

They began this new low-level training in three-ship elements (formations) but soon were flying in various configurations with sometimes as many as twelve abreast. Then on June 15, after weeks of practice, and with Bob Timmer in one of the pilot seats, 24 Liberators took off with the mission of "bombing" their own airbase. The British had installed mobile radar controlled anti-aircraft guns at various locations around the airfield. As the B-24s roared out of the west to drop their water bombs on targets near the base, the guns filled the sky with simulated flack that took readings on their effectiveness. Prophetically, perhaps, the brass huddled as they studied the performance reports and concluded that, if real, an appalling number of planes would have been lost.[149]

It didn't take long for the locals to start complaining about the incredible noise and disruption that these low-level flocks of aircraft were having on their daily routines. They complained that bicycles were forced off the road, chickens quit laying, cows stopped producing milk, and bees would not make honey. Public relations officers, who heard their complaints, couldn't always console them with reminders of the sacrifices needed during war. Many villagers had suspected the Yanks were crazy, but now they knew for sure.[150] Then, as quickly as the Americans had come, they were gone; and, thankfully, quiet returned to the rural neighborhood.

Major Ramsay Potts was a battle-hardened veteran, one of the original pilots of the 93rd. By the time they began low-level practice out of Hardwick, he was the commanding officer of the 330th Squadron to which Bob was assigned. He also had completed his 25 mandatory missions but had no intention of finishing his tour of duty in the States. He was ambitious, fearless, a stickler for detail, easily angered, and, according to gunner John Sherman, "the best pilot in the Air Force." His long-time copilot, Delbert Hall, had flown 27 missions and returned home. Major Potts' need for someone to copilot his plane, *The Duchess,* coincided with Robert Timmer's readiness for a crew assignment. Twenty-year-old Timmer, without a mission under his belt, became the second in command of a seasoned aircrew that had fought together on many missions.

One might wonder how a man with Potts' experience and rank ended up with an inexperienced copilot fresh out of training. Sergeant Louis Smith, nose gunner on *The Duchess* who had flown with Potts on many of his missions, and who also thought that Ramsay was the best pilot in the business, stated that, "given Potts' record, rank and leadership in the 93rd, he could have had any copilot he wanted." According to Smith, Potts accepted Timmer because he was good. "Ramsey wanted someone good, and they said they had the best man for him, Bob Timmer. We all thought well of him. In fact, I looked at him as my younger brother, even though I was only twenty-three and he was an officer. He was a fantastic guy."

[Note: *The Duchess* was unique among B-24s because it had two names. Painted on the copilot's side of its nose was the name *Evelyn,* and on the other side was *The Duchess*. It is possible that, at some point, its name was changed and no one ever got around to making it uniform. Neither of the names was accompanied by nose art.]

In late June, there were signs that the long expected move was imminent. The first clue came on June 21 when all combat crews were given passes to leave the base. The next day, they were fed pancakes for breakfast and a rare treat of pork chops for dinner. Another indication was that on the 23rd, when General Jacob Devers (Andrews' successor) showed up to inspect the troops, he instead spoke words of encouragement and congratulated the crews on their ability to learn low-level flying. Meanwhile, ground personnel, called "ground pounders" by their admiring aircrews, hustled to prepare the planes for a long tour. Orders came to them to have equipment ready to go on a moment's notice, and on June 25, shortly after lunch, they were told to load up and launch.

The force left Hardwick in six plane formations, each taking off in thirty second intervals. They headed toward Portreath Aerodrome in southwest England, where they were to refuel and spend the night. Upon landing, they immediately had something to eat, then went to the operations center to be briefed. For the first time, they were told what many had suspected: they were going back to Africa. It would be the second tour of that continent for the Travelling Circus.

Their next day's destination would be La Senia Airport, a few miles from Oran, Algeria. In the morning they were up at 0500 for a weather briefing and breakfast, and the planes were on their way by 0830. Lt. Timmer, in the copilot's seat of *The Duchess*, with all his months of flying had rarely ventured far from his own air base. Now he was headed south to a different continent, and he enjoyed what he was seeing. The weather was beautiful, and they flew at about 2000 feet. They stayed off the coast of Portugal, but crossed the Mediterranean Sea at Gibraltar, where he thrilled to see the big rock in the bright blue shining sea below. "Old Gib" looked much more impressive in person than in the Prudential ads. All the planes were landed in Oran by 1400 and, after waiting more than an hour, the transport trucks arrived to take them to quarters that once housed French cadets. That evening they ate American chow, drank a few beers, and sang "Home on the Range" and "Yankee Doodle" to the accompaniment of an accordion.[151]

They were awakened at 0500 to the best bugler they had ever heard and were given their final destination, but they still were not told why. It was back to Libya, but to a different base from the one they had occupied the previous winter. Leaving Oran on June 27, they flew over the deserts of North Africa where, a short time ago, after months of brutal fighting, combined British and American forces had ousted German General Rommel, "the Desert Fox," and his Afrika Korps from the continent. At first, they looked down on beautiful beaches and villas tucked against the Atlas Mountains, but then the landscape changed. Mountain beauty gave way to desert devastation, and as Robert Timmer looked down from his cockpit window, he saw the broad scope of the incredible destruction of war.

Burned-out hulks of tanks, trucks, and trains littered the sand for as far as he could see. Skeletons of planes, burned-out hangers, broken control towers and cratered runways, gave evidence to the last visit of the Circus to Africa. Harbors and docks, once proud hosts to Mediterranean shipping, were savaged by numerous blasts and lay cratered and crumbled in the clear blue water. Ships from many nations and of all sizes and shapes lay twisted on the sea bottom, oozing fuel; some were showing their bottoms to the sky, others were in pieces, and most had parts of their broken bodies silently breaking the surface of the sea. Even veteran flyers were stunned by the scale of the devastation.

They landed at a place called Ras Caroura, about eighteen miles south of Benghazi, Libya, in a swirling sandstorm. The base was called Terria, and it was laid out on a barren desert plain just a few miles from the Mediterranean Sea. After landing, they again waited to board the dawdling trucks that dropped them off at various threadbare tents, where they dropped off their gear and headed for the mess hall for yet another meal of Spam. The next day they received their daily orders and, except for the bareness and the sand, they could have still been at Hardwick. Sand and wind permitting, it was low-level and more low-level.

So there was Robert Timmer, halfway around the world from Wyoming Park, Michigan and those he loved, without a clue that he was about a month away from one of the most epic battles in military history; a battle in which he would lose several of his new friends and witness unimaginable horror and bravery. Eileen and his family had no idea where he was.

Chapter IX The Approach

American Colonel Jacob Smart sat on the foot of Winston Churchill's bed while the prime minister, in his pajamas, slippers, and dressing gown, puffed a huge cigar and paced the floor, listening. A glass containing a small remnant of last night's toddy was on the table next to his disheveled bed. It was June, 1943, and they were in Churchill's private flat at the No. 10 Downing Street Annex located above the fortified subterranean shelter known as the Cabinet War Rooms. It was late morning, and it was not unusual for the P.M. to conduct business from his bedroom. He typically worked early into the morning, with a whiskey in one hand and cigar in the other, directing his far-flung armies. His schedule was due, in part, to British troops battling in every part of the world, generating round-the-clock dispatches that needed his attention. Colonel Smart had requested an appointment with the prime minister to review an American plan for an attack on the German held oil fields of Ploesti, Romania.[152] He expected that Churchill would be receptive to his project, because he had heard that Churchill loved surprise raids — and Smart had put together a beauty.

In January of 1943, Churchill and President Franklin Roosevelt, along with their top military aids, had met with General Dwight Eisenhower at Casablanca, Morocco, to plan the invasion of Sicily. At those meetings, the Allied leaders recognized the need to cripple the Nazis' ability to throw the invaders off that Italian island. The bombing of targets that produced the means to wage war was part of the strategic planning at the conference. If they could destroy the oil fields at Ploesti, it would hurt the German's ability to wage war not only in Sicily but throughout Europe. The fields were vital to the Nazi war effort.

During this time, the Russians were in a titanic struggle with the Nazi invaders of their country, and Premier Stalin was constantly calling for his western allies to open a second front to take pressure off his armies. While Churchill and Roosevelt were not yet in a position to strike at the coast of France, as Stalin kept urging, they hoped that the Sicilian campaign would get Stalin "off their backs," at least for a while. In addition, the destruction of the Ploesti fields would hurt the flow of oil to the German armies in the Soviet Union. Thus, the momentum for planning the raid was set in motion from the highest levels of the Allied command. Coming from the "top," this was unlike other major strategic missions of the war, to date, where commanders in the field usually developed the plans and submitted them for approval from the Allied war councils.[153]

The task of drawing up plans for the operation was handed over to General Henry "Hap" Arnold, Commander of the U.S. Army Air Force, and passed on to Colonel Smart of his inner office planning staff. Smart was faced with making a plan to destroy an oil complex that was 2,300 miles, round trip, from the new airbases in Libya, which were the closest to the target. This was outside the range of any Allied bomber. The only "Heavy" that had a chance was the American B-24, but only if it could be outfitted with additional fuel tanks. He had a near to impossible task. "The Allied chiefs had given Jacob Smart a strategic mandate without a known tactical solution."[154] It mattered not; he was handed a job, and it was going to be done.

Smart began by learning all he could about the oil complexes around Ploesti. He studied maps and aerial photos and interviewed allied personnel who knew the area, some of whom had even worked at the complex. He learned that the refineries were not a single complex, but a dozen of them ringing the city. They encompassed an area six miles in diameter with pipelines, pumping stations, marshaling yards and trenching depots. He did not have enough bombers to go after the entire dozen, so he decided that they would have to choose several of the most productive to destroy. He also had to plan an attack that would smash the outer ring but not touch the city of Ploesti, which was in the middle of it all. Low civilian casualties were still a part of American planning efforts. He knew, as did other military leaders, that a raid flown from such a distance, mostly over enemy territory, would be costly to men and planes and far more expensive than any mission yet flown. It would have to inflict major damage to justify such costs.

Colonel Smart was also faced with the task of making it a surprise. He assumed that German defenses would be formidable (but he would not know how formidable they really were) so that a surprise attack was necessary. He wondered how he could come up with a plan to take that many planes that far, mostly over enemy territory teaming with radar and ground spotters, without the Germans knowing that they were coming. While wrestling with all these seemingly impossible issues, Jacob Smart and his staff finally settled on a strategy-a low-level, sneak attack. A number of conflicting factors that Smart and his staff considered went into this unprecedented decision. Foremost among them was the fact that Allied forces did not have a heavy bomber suited to low-level attacks.

Bombers designed to fly that low did not have the range and could not carry enough of a payload to inflict maximum damage. B-24s could bring the necessary payload, but they didn't have the range, and they were not designed for effective low flying. However, they could be modified to carry extra fuel. As a combat pilot himself (he planned on flying the mission), he knew that the quality of the Liberator pilots was high, and he believed that they could be trained for a low altitude attack. So the B-24 was chosen. Smart and his staff considered other factors in their low-level scenario. They figured that there would be a lot of anti-aircraft guns around the complex and reasoned that at low altitude those guns would be less effective. The flak guns would also be vulnerable to machine gun fire from the attacking planes - impossible from 20,000 feet. They reasoned that bombs dropped from around fifty feet would be more accurate. Smart also knew that if a plane was shot down, it would have a chance to belly land, giving the crew a better chance of surviving than if they fell from high altitude. By flying low, under the radar, the task force would also have a chance to go undetected, and they would use less fuel, which was critical on a mission of this distance. With these factors in mind, he drew up his low-level plan and submitted it to his boss, Hap Arnold. They took it to Eisenhower and received a green light from him and the Joint Chiefs of Staff. There were many in high military positions, however, who objected to the plan. Brigadier General Uzal Ent (who would fly on the mission), for example, thought that the losses would be unbearable.

Churchill responded with enthusiasm to Smart's proposals. He even offered several Royal Air Force Lancaster bomber groups and crews to lead the Americans to the attack. (Insinuating, whether he realized it or not, that the Americans couldn't find their way to the target. As events later unfolded,

Smart probably should have taken him up on the proposal.) Smart thanked him but pointed out that with different types of aircraft and their varying performance standards, maintaining the tight formations necessary would be impossible. The prime minister understood and endorsed the plan.[155]

With the plan approved from the highest levels, Smart now had to find someone to carry it out. He approached Colonel Timberlake, who had recently brought his Travelling Circus back to England from their first round of African based missions. Timberlake welcomed the challenge of planning the operational portion of the strategy. To help with the thousand and one details such an operation involved, he chose Major John "Jerk" Jerstad one of his former squadron leaders, to head his planning staff. Jerstad, from Racine, Wisconsin, had flown so many missions with the Circus that he had lost track. The Major was pleased to be working with Colonels and Generals.[156]

Jerstad enlisted the help of Captain Leander Schmid, an expert on navigation and low-level flying, to help him devise the best routes to Ploesti. They spent weeks pouring over maps to find the best approaches to the target. They reasoned that the shortest route from the south would be the most heavily defended, so they opted to come in from the north, a longer but less hazardous approach.[157] They searched for some easily recognizable landmarks to help navigate the fleet to the target, realizing that with planes flying that low and that fast, most ground objects would be just a blur. They decided on a railroad line north of Ploesti, at the small town of Floresti, as their key navigational point. A turn there would take them into their target run to Ploesti. At that point, at the speeds they would be flying, they would have only a few minutes to get into attack formation, with the goal of bringing waves of B-24s over the targets.

The specific targets in the oil complex were chosen, assigned, and given code names. Target "White One" was given to the 376th Bomb Group, the "Liberandos." They would have the lead formation and the responsibility to navigate the entire fleet to the targets. Next to them was the Travelling Circus, the 93rd. They would split into two groups and attack "White Two" and "White Three." Target "White Four" was assigned to the 98th Bomb Group, called the "Pyramiders." The fifth target, called "White Five," was given to the "Flying Eight Balls" of the 44th Bomb Group. Two other targets were "Blue," which was about five miles south of the white targets and was to be attacked by another group from the 44th. The last was called "Red," and it was located about eighteen miles north of Ploesti. The "Sky Scorpions" of the 389th had that one.

Meanwhile, back at Ploesti, the Germans had plans of their own and were hard at work on them. Their commander, responsible for defense of the complex, was Colonel Alfred Gustenberg, a short man, single, with red hair and a scholarly air about him. He was a connoisseur of fine books and paintings. A host of Bucharest society, his dinner invitations were much sought after. He was a World War I flyer and a war comrade of Hermann Goering, Hitler's number one man. There was little doubt that his relationship with Goering enabled him to get men and materials for his defensive command, even though German forces were in a death battle with the Russians. Despite his connection to the German leadership, he was not a Nazi, and he refused to wear the swastika on his uniforms. He worked sixteen hours a day with one goal: "to make Ploesti too costly for the enemy to attack."[158]

His men built forty anti-aircraft gun batteries around the oil fields, each with six 88mm, four 37mm and four 2mm guns. Outside of these forty were hundreds of machine gun pits and towers. More guns were embedded in factories, bridge approaches, water towers, church steeples, and chicken coops. Some were even concealed in haystacks. They practiced regularly using old German planes as the "attackers." He also had 250 fighter planes nearby; all in all, Gustenberg had about 75,000 troops at his command to defend Ploesti. And if, by chance, some of the attackers got through, he had imported about 500 well-trained firefighters from Germany (sorely needed at home) and had detailed plans in place for becoming operational soon after a destructive attack. Dugan and Stewart state that, "Ploesti was a colossal land battleship, armored and gunned to withstand the heaviest aerial attack."[159]

German intelligence was very much aware that the build-up of American forces in the desert of Libya could only mean that an attack was imminent. They knew that Ploesti was a possible target, perhaps even the most likely one. They did not know for sure when it was coming but, when it did, they would be ready.

~~~~~~~

Long before dawn on Sunday, August 1, 1943, the desert started to come alive. Ground crews swarmed around their assigned planes and began making last minute preparations. Groggy aircrews crawled out of their cots, wiping the sleep from their eyes. Many were already awake, having not slept at all. Col. Addison Baker, boss of the Travelling Circus, had a short meeting with his men. He told them that this was going to be one of the biggest missions of the war, and that it was going to be rough, but that he had every confidence in them.

He was prepared to lead them to the target and, when asked what would happen if he didn't make it to the target area, Colonel Baker replied, "Nothing like that will happen. I'm going to take you to this one if my plane falls apart."[160] After their short meeting, the men headed for breakfast at around 0215. Some did not feel like eating, but for those who did, real eggs and bacon were on the menu.

The trucks arrived to take the crews to their planes. It was still dark outside, and the lights of the trucks bounced off the looming Liberators as they wended their way among the planes. The weather reports along the flight route were mostly positive, so the day that they had spent months training for had finally arrived. This was it. The day for "The Big One," "Hipper Dipper," and "Super-duper," had come, only now it was officially known as "Tidal Wave."

Seventeen thousand men of the "Greatest Generation" were getting ready to strike a blow for democracy, which would, as many believed, shorten the war. In the trucks, the men were silent, thinking, alone with their innermost thoughts. "Have courage," they told themselves, "do your job, don't let your country, your team, or yourself down." When they exited the trucks, the men who would fly began the preflight "walk around" of their aircraft. They checked the guns, the engines, spun the propellers a few times to clear the oil from the cylinders, and talked quietly with their crew chiefs with whom they had a special bond. The crew chiefs would also have a tough day "sweating out" the return of their planes and crew. It was not uncommon for a crew chief to climb onto the flight deck before takeoff to wish the crew good luck and remind them to "bring my damn plane back."

Second Lieutenant Robert Timmer climbed aboard *The*

Duchess and squeezed his way into the copilot's seat, adjusted his equipment, and began the preflight countdown to takeoff. Flying with him in *The Duchess* that day were Pilot Ramsey Potts, Navigator Claude A. Culpepper, Bombardier Julius A. Stormer, Tail-gunner John H. Sherman, Nose-gunner Louis Smith, Top Turret-gunner Herman C. Clay, Radio Operator Charles M. Huffman, and Waist-gunners Felton H. Croswell and Edward L. Bagby. Several of the crew had completed their twenty-five mandatory missions and could have opted out, but according to John Sherman, Potts, rather than risk taking a very inexperienced crew on this mission, had asked three of them if they would stay on. They agreed. One of them was Louis Smith, who crawled into the cramped glass bubble which made up the nose of a B-24. He had "the best seat in the house" for seeing the action. Rumor had it, however, that the Germans had installed a lot of barrage balloons in the target area, some rigged with explosives. If it were true, and knowing that he, at treetop level, would be flying among them, scared him to no end. John Sherman crawled into his equally cramped tail-gunner's position. At the "ass end" of the ship, he was pleased to be as far away from the cockpit as possible.

On the flight deck the long-serving crew chief of *The Duchess*, M/Sgt. Herbert "Pop" Hastings, told Major Potts that the plane was in tip-top shape so there could be no excuses for not completing the mission. After wishing his aircrew the best of luck, he hopped out of the bomb bay to nervously watch his "baby" takeoff. Pop knew what he was doing. *The Duchess* eventually flew 53 missions without an abort for mechanical malfunctions, a record in the Ninety-third.[161]

The Duchess and unidentified crew

In *Exterminator*, Capt. Hugh Roper watched from the cockpit as a jeep sped down the runway towards his plane. Bouncing around in the passenger seat was his little buddy, Jack Jones, in full flight gear. Jones, who had done far more combat flying than required, jumped from his jeep and climbed through the bomb bay doors to join Roper as an unauthorized passenger.[162] He thus fulfilled the predictions of his betting buddies that he would never sit out the Big One.

At last the signal was given to start the engines and, across forty miles of quiet desert, 712 huge Pratt and Whitney engines coughed, sputtered, and roared to life, shattering the morning calm. The roar was incredible, and the prop wash from that many engines created a major dust storm. But at 0400 flares were fired and throttles were pushed forward as the great ships, with a thunderous roar, began to inch their way to the takeoff point. In a day that would have no end of crises, the first one was at hand. Every crew faced the challenge of getting a giant airplane, horribly overloaded with 3,100 gallons of high octane gasoline and 4,300 pounds of bombs, off the ground. Slowly *The Duchess* began moving down the runway, straining against its overload, but gradually gaining speed, as Ramsey Potts pushed the throttle forward. Copilot Timmer's eyes darted from dial to dial as he called out the increasing speed. At 95 mph the wings began to help the wheels with the weight, and at 130 mph, amid a swirl of dust, *The Duchess,* grasping for height, lumbered into the air and was on its way to the rendezvous point over the Mediterranean.

It took over an hour to get all 178 heavily laden B-24s airborne. However, disaster struck almost immediately when *Kickapoo* lost an engine shortly after takeoff and attempted an emergency landing in the blinding dust. It struck a concrete pole, crashed and burned with only two of its crew escaping. Witnessed by many, it was a scary beginning to a scary day. But at 2,000 feet, the remaining planes formed up and began heading across the "Med" to Europe.

In front, with overall navigational responsibility, was the 376th Bomb Group called the Liberandos. The lead plane of that group was *Teggie Ann,* flown by Col. Keith K. Compton. With him was the only general on the mission, Uzal Ent, who sat on a stool slightly behind the pilot and copilot. Behind and slightly above the Liberandos in the formation was Ted's Travelling Circus. It was divided into two forces. The A group was led by their new commanding officer Col. Addison Baker and his copilot Major John Jerstad in *Hell's Wench.* Slightly behind them and to their right, was the B group, led by *The*

Duchess with Major Ramsey Potts and 2nd Lieutenant Robert Timmer in the cockpit. Behind the Circus were the planes of the 98th, the Pyramiders, led by Col. John (Killer) Kane in *Hail Columbia*. The Flying Eight Balls of the 44th Bomb Group were next in line but, like the Circus, they too were split. The A section was led by Col. Leon Johnson in *Suzy Q* and the B group by Col. James Posey in *Victory Ship*. Finally, bringing up the rear of the great armada, were the Sky Scorpions, the 389th led by Col. Jack Wood in *The Scorpion* who rode as an observer. Each of the seven task groups had specific targets at Ploesti.

Of the officers flying the seven planes who would lead the bomb groups into the Ploesti targets, there were, five colonels, three majors, three captains, one first lieutenant, and two second lieutenants. One of whom was twenty-year-old Robert Timmer. The lowest ranked, the least experienced and the youngest officer of those flying a command ship.

It was a multi-colored fleet of airships that left Libya that day. The planes of the Liberandos, carrying desert camouflage, had a pinkish tint, and they were followed by the drab green planes of the Circus. The Pyramiders, having also been in the desert, were also pink, and behind them were the English-green ships of the Flying Eight Balls. The fresh new planes of Sky Scorpions were without paint and were therefore factory-metallic. Over the target, color was not going to matter.

Tidal Wave brought together the most experienced, talented, and courageous group of men to fly in the largest air armada ever assembled, and now they were embarked on the longest mission ever flown by heavy bombers. Most of their route would take them over enemy held territory to what they knew would be a tough target, especially at low-level. There was no possibility, of course, that short range fighters could give them any protection. They were on their own.

They flew low, from 2,000 to 4,000 feet above the sea, with the various elements of the massive formation staying tight in their basic three-plane unit. The lead group was lowest, with each following group layered higher. It was essential that they maintain visual contact of the planes in front of them, but slowly, after a few hours of flying, a separation in the task forces was becoming evident. Colonel Kane's 98th Bomb Group was falling behind the three groups in front of him.

There is much speculation as to why this occurred, but some attribute it to the different flying styles of the leaders. Kane, for example, cut his teeth flying in support of the invasion of Africa where encountering heavy flak and the fighters of the Luftwaffe was not as frequent as when flying over Europe. His missions were to destroy ammunition depots, tanks, supply ships, etc., that supported the Afrika Korps; strict formation flying was not critical. It was a different kind of flying than Colonel Compton learned while bombing the Nazi infrastructure from high altitude over Europe. Here, attacks from German fighters were frequent, and strict formation flying was necessary if planes were to fend off their attackers and return home. Others speculate that the Libs of the 98th and 389th, which had been in the desert for a long time, were beat up by the harshness of the desert and just simply could not keep up. Whatever the reason, if the gap kept widening, it would have dire consequences for the mission.

According to orders, strict radio silence was observed. The only communication allowed was via the intercom in each plane so that the members of the crew could talk to each other, but there was no communication among the planes. For about two hours the weather was good and the flying was smooth. As fuel was being used, the planes became lighter and less cumbersome. All was going well. Then, suddenly, *Wongo Wongo*, a plane from the 376th, flying in front of *The Duchess* in a lead element, wobbled, and veered to the left narrowly missing another plane, stalled, plunged into the water and exploded, with a loss of all of its crew. The explosion sent a plume of black smoke 900 feet into the air. Bob Timmer and the crew of *The Duchess* watched this tragedy unfold, and when Charles Huffman, the radio operator, stood up and said, "Look at that fire!" an angry Ramsay Potts turned around and pushed him back into his seat.[163]

Allied forces along the way needed to be informed that they were not to jump to conclusions if they spotted the large formation. The armada did not want to encounter "friendly fire." That notification was sent using the 9th Air Force codes as the planes left Africa. Unknown to the American forces, the Germans had broken that code and were monitoring their transmissions. The enemy did not know, however, where the task force was headed but, as the massive Tidal Wave formations approached the coast of Albania, an Axis spotter on the Island of Corfu, which they had just recently passed over, called the German defense command, alerting them to the location of the enemy formations.

Now they had a good idea where the force was headed. When they projected a line along a possible flight route, it came slightly north of Bucharest. The Germans and their Romanian friends then knew, with a fair degree of certainty, that it was going to be Ploesti. Immediately, they put their forces on a third stage alert, and the defenders around Ploesti took their positions. Anti-aircraft batteries began taking on men, and planes were being readied. Pilots who were not on their bases were on their way. The Americans, now crossing into Albania, didn't know it then but, when they got to Ploesti, the Germans and Romanians were going to be ready for them. Those in the seven task forces fast approaching the target areas had no idea how ready and waiting they really were. So much for all the planning and practice that had gone into a surprise attack. Colonel Gustenberg, who was vacationing in the mountains, summoned his car for a fast dash back to Bucharest..

As they approached the mountains of Albania, Col. Keith Compton, in the lead plane *Teggie Ann*, waggled his wings to signal the force to start the climb to 9,000 feet. Cloud cover became an unwelcome challenge as they approached the mountain tops. Formation flying in cloud cover, with limited or zero visibility, was dangerous; air turbulence or a slight change in course could result in collisions where falling planes threatened taking lower planes with them. The signal was given to stay in formation but to "loosen up" (fly farther apart) to avoid hitting a neighbor. There were other flying strategies to get through the clouds, but those would require more time, so Compton eventually took his Liberandos up to 16,000 feet before leveling off. At that height they picked up a nice tailwind. The two groups of the Flying Circus, with Addison Baker and Ramsay Potts in the lead, followed, maintaining visibility. However, the four task forces behind the Circus, led by Colonel Kane's Pyramiders, chose a different tactic for clearing the mountains and clouds and leveled off at 12,000 feet where the tailwind was limited. The dangerous gap between Kane and Compton widened further. They now were being picked up by German radar operators who could not believe the enormous amount of blips showing on their screens.

Compton, realizing that the task force was split, slowly made his way down to the foot of the mountains by zigzagging his force, using up gas, but taking time in hopes that the rest of his force would catch up. Unfortunately, at this point, they were hopelessly too far behind to close the formation. They had long been out of sight of the tail gunners in the planes bringing up the rear of the Circus.

Once out of the mountains, the leading Liberandos, with only the Circus in sight behind them, began their headlong dash across the Danube River plain toward Ploesti. Flying low, the men looked upon beautiful golden and green farms and fields, and even with the tension of the approaching battle, the men welcomed the sight after the weeks of the stark desert landscape and its blowing sand. Comments were made about the Blue Danube not really being blue. In fact, to Robert Timmer, the color wasn't any different than the brownish-gray Grand River back home in Michigan. There wasn't a man aboard the fleet, however, who, at that moment, would not have traded the sight of the pretty green plain for the welcoming, wicked desert of their African home.

As they hurtled on toward their critical navigational landmarks, the men watched as people on the ground reacted to the thunder only a few hundred feet over their heads. Horses bolted and people dove for cover into haystacks, ditches, and under wagons. Others smiled and waved a welcome as the invaders flew past, leading the flyers to believe that this mission wasn't going to be so bad after all. A few of the crews broke into song with "Don't Sit Under the Apple Tree," while others sang the "Doxology." They did not know (or if they did, they didn't want to think about it) that, while they were admiring the plains of Romania, German and Romanian fighter planes were taxing toward their runways and would, momentarily, close the glass over their cockpits and launch their fighters at the approaching fleet.

As the two lead bomb groups passed the first navigational point at Pitesti, they were now aware that they would be going to the target without the others. Far behind them, Killer Kane realized that the group in his rear was not the Circus (he thought that he had gotten in front of them in the clouds) but the Eight Balls of the 44th and the Scorpions of the 389th. They were in the order they should have been, but, for the first time, Kane and the rest of the pilots recognized that they were hopelessly split from the leading groups, and most dangerously, neither knew the location of the other.

The planners had correctly assumed that the Germans would have their strongest defenses on the southern approaches to the oil fields. Therefore, they had devised a plan that would bring the attacking forces into the target from the northwest. (They would actually fly past Ploesti and then turn southeast.) To guide the task force to the target from that direction, the planners had established three navigational checkpoints that the navigators studied endlessly back in Africa, using maps and mock-ups of the key features. The difficulty was that the points looked very much alike, all having rivers, bridges, and railroads. And at low altitude and 200+ miles an hour, things on the ground were pretty much a blur.

The second checkpoint was at a town called Targoviste, only twenty miles from the Initial Point (I.P.) at Floresti, where the task force would turn to the southeast for their run at the oil fields. On the intercom, Captain Claude Culpepper, *The Duchess's* navigator, was in constant communication with Potts and Timmer in the cockpit and gave them a time of nine minutes to the Initial Point, where they would make their turn and begin their bomb run.[164] However, as Compton's lead ship, the *Teggie Ann,* approached Targoviste, Compton unbelievably turned to the east. The others turned neatly behind him, but some were shocked by the move and recognized immediately that a mistake had been made.

Norman Appold of the 376th, in *G.I. Ginnie,* immediately broke radio silence and yelled "Not here! Not here! This isn't it!" and Ramsay Potts, in *The Duchess,* simultaneously cried, "Mistake! Mistake!"[165] Dozens of others joined in on the open radio. As planned, they descended to treetop level, but most knew they had to turn back to get on course. Now, down to thirty-four planes because of aborts, they were headed south and east of Ploesti towards the capital of Bucharest, where Compton mistakenly kept leading his force. Unknowingly, he was headed for the heaviest concentration of flak guns in Europe.[166] The guns that a northwest approach was designed to avoid. Those in the 93rd, like Potts and Timmer who wanted to turn back, were trapped; guiding their planes into a turn would risk collision with those flying around them.

So, on they dashed, a few hundred feet off the ground at over 200 miles an hour. Quickly, anti-aircraft batteries opened up at the approaching fleet and shrapnel spread among the leaders. Fighter planes jumped them from behind and tail gunner Sgt. Lychester Havens in *Jersey Bounce,* flying on the wing of *The Duchess,* became the first American KIA (killed in action) on the raid. The battle of Ploesti had begun, and the forces were not even near their targets. It helped that the .50 calibers put in the Liberators to ward off enemy fighters now were turned on the men in the batteries below. Nose, tail and waist gunners, and even the top gunners, raked men and gun emplacements on the ground with withering fire and even silenced some of the big guns. Still, on they went toward

Bucharest, blindly following their leader away from their target.

Col. Addison Baker, who turned the Circus with the misguided leaders at Targoviste, stuck to the wrong course, even though many of his men were pleading with him to turn. Then, off to the left, the unmistakable smoke from the stacks of the oil refineries at Ploesti came into view and, even though Compton's Liberandos continued blindly on towards Bucharest, Baker suddenly made a decision. He deftly executed a left turn, courageously broke away from the lead group, and led his beloved Travelling Circus into hell.

Chapter X Ploesti

Circus leaders Baker and Jerstad, in *Hell's Wench*, drove low and hard toward the White targets. Their file of planes was on the left of the formation, with Col. George Brown and his group on their right. On the right of Brown came Potts. They were now fifty feet off the ground in tight formation, literally skimming the tops of trees and blowing furrows in the high corn. But things were different from what they had studied and rehearsed. Their targets, now, were on the other side of the city. "The pilots and bombardiers searched for aiming points — distillation towers, stacks boilers, power sub-stations and housings of electric control panels. None were now in proper perspective and it was life or death."[167] A few minutes after the turn, the men in the German emplacements saw them coming and began to swing their enormous guns into positions where they could draw a bead on the onrushing Circus who, because of a series of costly mistakes, were first over the target–all by themselves. The barrage balloons, including those rigged with explosives, loomed ahead, while Germans opened up with a "devastating salvo."[168] Black Sunday had begun.

In front of *The Duchess*, Baker's contingent approached the first circle of batteries around Ploesti. Enoch Porter's *Euroclydon*, flying on Baker's left wing, took a direct hit in the bomb bay and erupted in flames as the reserve tank (for the trip home) exploded. Trailing flames over 200 feet behind his B-24, Porter struggled for altitude to allow his crew some space to parachute. The plane stalled and began falling, then broke in two and fell to the ground. Four crew members got out, and three of them survived. Bombardier Jesse Franks fell to his death when his chute didn't open in time to cushion his fall. The rest of the crew died in the crash. Ploesti had claimed its first Liberator—it would not be the last.

In the flagship, Baker and Jerstad, trying to get to their target on an improvised heading, ran into another ring of batteries. There, *Hell's Wench* took a direct hit in the nose, and the front of the ship caught fire. Baker and Jerstad held her on course, but then were hit in the right wing and it, too, caught fire. After another shell slammed into her just below the flight deck, the plane shuddered, wavered, but continued leading the Circus onward, even when hit with a fourth burst. It quickly became a ball of fire, slowly slipping lower and lower until the decision was made to jettison its heavy bombs in order to stay in the air and keep leading to the target. A badly burned crew member tumbled out, far too low for a chute to open, and died as he hit the ground. Baker and Jerstad, no doubt badly wounded and with their cockpit shattered and burning, miraculously kept their plane in the air, while men in planes around them prayed that they would attempt a belly landing in a nearby wheat field and try to save themselves and their men. It was too late, and they were too determined. With several of the crew jumping from the plane, the commanding officer of the 93rd, Addison Baker, and co-pilot John Jerstad, having kept their promise made that morning to lead their men to the target, rode the flaming, falling, *Hell's Wench* into the ground. None of the crew survived.

By now several of the Circus planes were trailing fire, with wounded and dying men bleeding on the decks, their screams unheard over the din of the battle. Cables from barrage balloons were ripping at their wings and, while fighter planes were filling the thin-skinned Libs with holes from above, the big guns were blasting them from below. Still, they flew on.

In *Utah Man*, the sole surviving plane of the lead element, pilot Lt. Walt Stewart, who entered the fray on the right wing of *Hell's Wench*, pulled up to sixty feet to get on top of a refinery. As Bombardier Ralph Cummings dropped the first bombs of the day on Ploesti, hitting a target assigned to the Flying Eight Balls, the plane was rocked by a tremendous burst of flak, which threw shrapnel into the left side of the plane. On they flew, narrowly missing a tower by putting their left wing down a city street between buildings, the high right wing was shredded by ground fire. Full of holes, *Utah Man* was treating the citizens of Ploesti to valuable "get-home gasoline," which was spraying over the city through numerous holes in its wings. Adding to the melee were the exploding bombs that the Circus was delivering, sometimes on their assigned targets and sometimes not. With Ploesti exploding below them and with flames and smoke billowing hundreds of feet into the air, pilots and navigators were faced with enormous difficulty finding targets.

Lt. Russell Longnecker, piloting *Thundermug*, saw a flash from a clump of trees and took his plane under the barrage. He describes what he saw: "A shell removed the left aileron, left rudder and half the elevator on Capt. Hugh Roper's ship to my right. Hugh looked like a flying junk yard. In the cockpit, Roper's eyes were fixed straight ahead. He didn't waver a bit. Our gunners were firing steadily. We were going in at 245 mph, about 65 more than our usual speed, pulling emergency power for so long that it became a question of how much longer the engines could take it. All I wanted was to get beyond this superheated mess of tracer, shrapnel, exploding storage tanks and burning aircraft."[169] Again Longnecker recalls, "We saw a B-24 sliding down a street with both wings sheared. Another bomber hit a balloon and both disintegrated in a ball of fire. We saw bombs from other planes skipping along the ground, hitting buildings and passing through blast walls leaving big holes in brickwork. Suddenly, a huge oil storage tank exploded in front of my wingman Vic Olliffe's *Let 'er Rip*. A solid column of flame, debris and burbling smoke rose to 200 feet. Olliffe couldn't possibly avoid it, crossing under us and Hugh Roper. Olliffe then put *Let 'er Rip* over a pair of stacks like a hurdler before placing his bombs in a cracking tower. How he ever missed the explosions, us and the stacks is a mystery. Always will be."[170]

German gunners were having a field day. Many were hidden, some even camouflaged as hay stacks, and as the oncoming fleet approached they let loose on the low-flying bombers, often at point blank range—calculations were not needed. *The Duchess* began taking some hits. As John Sherman crawled out of the tail to do his job of starting the on-board camera in the belly, a blast shattered the camera and smoke filled the area. John turned and hustled back to the "safety" of the tail, where at least he could fight back with his .50. However, even though the .50 calibers on the planes were spraying every gun emplacement they could see, often with great effect, they were no match for the fire power of the defenders.

Pilot Nicholas Stampolis of Kalamazoo, Michigan, and his crew, on their first mission, were flying *Jose Carioca*. They took a direct hit in the bomb bay fuel tanks about five miles from the target. Fatally on fire and with their control cables burned through, the young crew fought courageously to keep the plane airborne and on course. Flying into the inferno, they plunged into a refinery and emerged out the other side, still airborne but without wings. The fuselage, with the ten men still inside, smashed through a brick wall of the Ploesti

Women's Prison, killing not only all the men in the plane, but many political prisoners of the Nazi's as well.[171]

Ramsey Potts and Bob Timmer, flying the lead of the B Force, were to the right and slightly behind the A Force and watched as their Circus brothers entered the oil complex. Seconds later they, too, plunged into the inferno of burning oil tanks, flying steel, huge fireballs, smoke and crashing planes. John Sherman, the tail gunner on *The Duchess*, referred to those who flew in the rear formations and entered the targets last, when the defenders were ready for them, as the "Purple Heart Squadrons." There would be many of the medals no one wanted won that day.

Due to several aborts, Potts' squadron was down to eight planes as they entered the target area. Because they were entering the complex from the wrong direction, the targets assigned to B Force were on the far side of Ploesti. As they headed toward their assigned target, Potts spotted a huge refinery complex. It was Astro Romana, the largest oil producer in Europe, which had been assigned to Killer Kane's Liberandos, who were nowhere in sight. *The Duchess* made a slight course correction and headed for it. As they passed over gun batteries firing armor-piercing shells, *Pudgy*, piloted by Milton Teltser and Wilmer Bassett and flying on *The Duchess*'s left, took a flak shell, which blew a huge hole in her wing. Exploding shells also hit the waist area, wounding the gunners, and then the number 2 engine took a hit and *Pudgy* began to lose speed. They fought for altitude and dropped their bombs on a target. With wounded aboard and one engine out, Teltser had no chance to get back to Africa, so he set out on a course toward Turkey.

On the right wing of *The Duchess*, *Jersey Bounce*, flying with the body of tail gunner Sgt. Havens and piloted by Worthy Long, had most of its nose shot off, wounding the gunner and navigator. Then, with two of its engines on fire and the plane engulfed in flames, with Long and copilot John Lockhart dodging telephone poles and trees, *Jersey Bounce* crash-landed in a field. Six of the crew died, but four escaped the burning plane and became POWs, including Long and Lockhart.

With both their wingmen in flames, and with battered, broken Liberators crashing and burning around them, Timmer and Potts, in *The Duchess*, put the plane on the deck, attempting to avoid the hail of bullets coming from the ground. Sgt. Louis Smith, the nose gunner, was firing at anything that seemed to be firing at them. He heard the radio operator screaming, "Balloons, balloons, balloons!" and Potts' reply was, "Damn the balloons!"[172] Major Potts recalls, "I had no trouble with the barrage balloons but one plane in my group hit one, partially shearing off his wing. We made our attack but I don't think more than three airplanes in the unit actually hit the refinery they were supposed to."[173]

Author Michael Hill, in his book *Black Sunday: Ploesti* recounts, "Ground fire hit *The Duchess*'s tail, then a blast peppered the waist area. Sgt. Edward Bagby tumbled from his gun as shrapnel sliced deeply into his left thigh. He scrambled back to his gun, cursing the pain and the control cables that were flapping in his face, spoiling his aim. Potts and copilot Lt. Robert Timmer pulled the aircraft up so that Julius Stormer could put his bombs into a boiler house. The pilots then pushed down over the stacks and jammed the throttles forward trying to clear the refinery complex.[174] A flak burst had torn away the vertical stabilizer, and another had shattered the elevator control cables. With critical cables useless, the pilots fought to control the plane, and as *The Duchess* turned at low altitude, attempting to exit the target, Major Potts remembers, "... we came abreast of what appeared to be a distillation unit, a cracking plant. My left waist, a young fellow about nineteen years old, let loose with a barrage from a .50 caliber machine gun at the unit which suddenly burst into flames. That was sort of a dividend."[175]

The second wave of the B Force, under Potts, faced the same fate as the first. Lt. Roy Harms, in *Hell's Angels,* which was badly shot up and on fire, with several wounded crew members, abandoned all hope of getting to the target and headed for a nearby wheat field, hoping for belly landing in an attempt to save his crew. As the plane desperately tried to gain altitude in a fight for its life, a man jumped from the burning ship and a lone parachute floated to the ground as *Hell's Angels* dove into a small hill and exploded, killing all who remained aboard. *Bertha*, with William Meehan at the controls, also badly hit by flak and burning, broke up as she skidded along a wheat field and blew up with only a single crew member escaping. *Thar She Blows*, piloted by Capt. Charles Merrill, hit a barrage balloon cable, which badly cut its left wing. Flak punctured the plane as they dropped their bombs. Badly damaged and with several wounded, they stayed airborne and left the melee to the northwest. Of Major Potts's B Force, the last over Ploesti was Capt. John "Packy" Roche and crew, in *Ready and Willing.* With his ship full of holes, he dropped his bomb load and, flying near the ground and under high tension wires, exited the inferno with four wounded and a bad engine.

Finally, the mauled Circus limped away from the complex, leaving in their wake death and destruction. Ploesti was in flames with black smoke from the burning oil refineries billowing hundreds of feet into the air. But also burning in and around the oil fields were the crumpled remains of many Circus Liberators, and inside the flaming hulks were the bodies of their fellow flyers–their buddies, forever left behind.

Several of the planes still in the air were flying on two or three engines, with all hope gone for getting back to Africa. Every survivor was shot full of holes, with most trailing broken cables, wires, gasoline and, often, smoke from burning engines. They carried in them the bloody bodies of the wounded and dead, and the airmen's struggle to get the battered planes home to their bases in Africa, where there was help, would result in the loss of even more planes and men. Author Michael Hill, summarizes, "Colonel Addison Baker brought the famed Traveling Circus to Ploesti for a one-time performance. They had given a magnificent ad lib show of courage and heroism after being trapped into the wrong turn short of the IP. Baker and his crew had died bringing the Circus into town."[176]

Tidal Wave was far from over. As the heroes of the Circus penetrated the defenses of Ploesti and began inflicting damage, the leaders of the attack, the Liberandos, under Col. K. K. Compton, with General Ent onboard, finally, when the cityscape of Bucharest became recognizable, realized their mistake and began their turn towards the oil fields. Incredibly, only after they spotted the smoke and fire left behind by the retreating Circus did the leaders in *Teggie Ann* realize that their task force was not intact. At that point, General Ent went on the radio and called the 376th Bomb Group off their bombing run. They were told to strike "targets of opportunity." Most, including the leaders, did a hard right to the north "away from the belching guns of Ploesti."[177] Maps showing the routes that the various bomb groups flew indicate that, for the most part, the 376th avoided Ploesti altogether.[178] The exception was Major Norman Appold in *G.E.Ginnie* and two other ships. They broke away from Compton and headed into the inferno. The main group, however, took a route around Ploesti to the north, firing at tracks, trains, occasionally a gun battery, and anything having to do with oil that was outside of the real oil targets. As they began heading back to base, several planes needed to dump their unused bombs for the long trip. So cows were scattered and cornfields pocked with craters from the blasts. Soon after, still hugging the deck as they headed away from the targets, the Liberandos spotted the pink colored planes of the Pyramiders, Col. Killer Kane's group, leading the "lost" squadrons of the Flying Eight Balls and the Sky Scorpions into the fray of burning Ploesti.[179]

Liberator over Ploesti

No wrong turn for Kane. As late as he and his forces were in getting into the action, his navigator nailed the Initial Point at

Floresti, and turned there on the correct course toward their targets. Their target was White Four, the huge Astro Romana plant, while Col. Leon Johnson on his right, leading the 44th Bomb Group, the Flying Eight Balls, headed for White Five. Together, they had over 50 Liberators. Farther to the right was Group B of the Eight Balls under Col. James Posey, who had Target Blue, about five miles south of Ploesti. Breaking off from Kane's group and heading to Target Red, about eighteen miles north of Ploesti, were the 389th Sky Scorpions led by Col. Jack Wood.

Even though the majority of the planes in the armada followed the routes that the planners had devised and that the crews had spent hours learning to recognize, the entire operation was, at this point, close to being a fiasco. Planes were everywhere they shouldn't have been, adding to the danger.

Just as the battered Circus was reeling out of the oily conflagration, Norman Appold and his breakaway group of four were making their "target of opportunity" bomb run. Potts and his group were not aware that they were on a collision course with Appold, but Appold, seeing them, continued his bomb run and hoped for the best. At the same time, the huge, pink-colored ships of Kane's forces were lowering to make a run at their target, White Four, which, they were shocked to see, was already burning from the Circus attack. Once Appold had dropped his bombs he fought to avoid colliding with Potts and Timmer. They were headed at each other at rooftop level at a combined speed of over 500 miles an hour, while Killer Kane's group, coming from a different direction, was almost upon both of them. Below, General Alfred Gerstenberg watched in reluctant admiration as the planes of Potts' B Force stayed low, while Appold pulled up slightly and Kane flew over both of them, avoiding a horrible collision. The

Germans thought it was planned skillful flying instead of the horrible mistake it really was.[180]

While the other task forces tried to complete the job that the 93rd had started, the ventilated planes of the crippled Circus groped to find each other and form some kind of protective formation for the trip back. At the same time, Kane and his groups, now bombing Ploesti, were being ripped by the same merciless fire that had so wounded the Circus. The 93rd, now under its replacement leader, Col. George Brown, flew toward Benghazi, licking its wounds, with as many planes as could keep up. Flying at treetop level, they hugged the ravines and river beds, hoping to avoid as much anti-aircraft fire as possible and giving the enemy gun emplacements something they never expected, withering .50 caliber fire from speeding 70 foot green giants bristling with guns. Those who could not keep up or were short on fuel headed for secondary, prearranged landing sites in Turkey, Cyprus, or Malta.

Utah Man, piloted by Lt. Walt Stewart and his co-pilot Loren Koon, severely shot up and trailing gas from its number 3 engine, was limping along, unable to stay with the main group. Even though as a lead plane in Baker's A Group, they had dropped the first bombs on Ploesti, two five- hundred - pounders were stuck in the bomb bay and had to be jettisoned before they could land (which they believed would be happening very soon!). Working above and around the open bomb bay doors with nothing more than screwdrivers, several hundred feet above the blur of the ground, engineer Connolly and bombardier Cummings were able, after about ten minutes, to pry them loose and the bombs tumbled into a field.

As Lt. Stewart and crew were working hard to keep their

battered plane in the air, Walt was delighted when he saw his best buddy, Hugh Roper in the *Exterminator,* flying in an element of three planes, pass under his beleaguered ship. Walt then knew that his friend was going to make it back, and as this was his last mission, Hugh would be going back to Utah and his lovely wife Abbie very soon. Stewart watched as *Exterminator, Thundermug,* and *Let 'er Rip* disappeared into a cloud bank.

On board *The Duchess,* engineer and top gunner T/Sgt. Herman Clay was successfully splicing together shot up cables so that the pilots would have more control in their attempt to bring it home. Nose gunner S/Sgt. Louis Smith was struck by the silence, "Even though our engines were buzzing away, it seemed to suddenly be quiet. No shooting, no bombs going off, no hollering in the intercom. Peace!"[181] As they began their climb over the mountains through the clouds Smith recounts that Major Potts may have been relieved by the smooth buzzing of his four engines, but he was not happy with the way things had gone at Ploesti.

In those clouds, slightly higher and in front of *The Duchess,* an incredible tragedy occurred. Hugh Roper's *Exterminator* and *Let 'er Rip,* piloted by Vic Olliffe, collided, tearing away the tail section of the *Exterminator.* Both planes fell from the sky with only four men from *Let 'er Rip* getting out. One parachute didn't open, however, so only three survived. All aboard the *Exterminator* died, including observer Jack Jones, who had just come along for the ride and who was going home after this one. Six crew members, besides Roper, were on their 25th and last mission. Just a few more miles and they were going back to the States. *The Duchess* was close enough to the accident to observe pieces of the planes falling through the clouds.[182] Lt. Timmer was stunned as he watched the planes come apart. Both Roper and Jones had trained him on the B-24 and flew combat with him. He felt close to them and deeply respected them as men and pilots.

Like antelope on the African plain, where vulnerable stragglers are set upon by beasts of prey, the struggling ships of the Great Air Armada anxiously limped along, often alone, hoping to avoid the fate of the weak. German pilots in their ME-109s lurked in the clouds just waiting for the opportunity to pounce on an easy mark.

One of the marks was the badly damaged *Pudgy*, shot up over the target as it flew next to *The Duchess*. Its crew was struggling to maintain altitude by throwing everything that was not tied down out the bomb bay doors. Lt. Telster, with wounded aboard, had the ship on course for Turkey in an attempt to save his men. While still over Romanian air space, however, the crippled ship was jumped by two ME-109s. Gunfire riddled the waist and bomb bay areas and killed the left waist gunner. Slugs hit the number 1 engine, and it began to belch fire and smoke. Now, with two engines out, a raging fire on board, and with the plane impossible to control, Telster and copilot William Bassett bellied her into a cornfield. The nose of the plane pancaked, killing the nose gunner and navigator, and fuel tanks exploded, killing the top gunner, who had been firing his gun to the end. Four badly burned crew members, including Telster and Bassett, managed to crawl out of the exploding wreckage.[183] They were immediately surrounded by peasants with pitchforks who, after some tense moments, eventually brought them to a spotless clinic run by a beautiful woman doctor who treated their wounds, while villagers came to gawk at the burned Americans.[184]

Although sick at what they saw happen to Roper and Olliffe, things were still going smoothly for the crew of *The Duchess*.

As they climbed from the Danube plain over the cloudy mountains, Potts signaled the few remaining planes in his group to "fly loose" to avoid collisions. S/Sgt. Louis Smith crawled out of his nose position to check on his buddies in the waist and rear. He then noticed that he had left his parachute in the waist area. It was punctured with shrapnel holes. He was very thankful that he had not had to use it.

In contrast to the smooth flight of *The Duchess*, *Utah Man* was barely staying airborne, shedding pieces of plane as it limped along. Critically low on fuel and flying at 150 mph to avoid falling apart, it was becoming increasingly doubtful that it was going to make it back to base. Lt. Walt Stewart was hoping to land in Yugoslavia where there was a chance of avoiding capture by the Germans. But the forlorn ship flew on, falling further and further behind the others. As they approached the Greek coast and had to make a decision on whether to try crossing the Mediterranean and make it back to Terria, Lt. Stewart asked for another fuel report. Engineer T/Sgt. John Connelly reported, "Well, number 3 shows zero. Numbers 1, 2 and 4 are very low." Stewart wanted a more exact report. Connelly answered, "Skipper, I have never been so out of gas, either in the air or on the ground!"[185]

Walt polled his crew, telling them the fuel situation and that they had 500 miles of sea to cross, and asked them what they wanted to do, put it down on the beach or try to make it. Gunner Richard Bartlett, from Montana, asked to make a speech before they voted. Bartlett said, "You call this an ocean, we got rivers in Montana wider than this. Let's go!"[186] With that morale booster propping up the crew, the decision was made by Stewart and copilot Larry Koon to carry on. And while the believers prayed, Stewart invoking his Mormon God and Koon his Presbyterian one, *Utah Man* lumbered on over what could likely be her watery grave. At about 4:00 in the afternoon, to break the tension, radioman Harold Steiner attempted to pick up the musical program Command Performance on the shortwave. Suddenly, the ear phones of the crew were filled with the sounds of Dinah Shore singing the new hit song, "Coming In On A Wing And A Prayer."[187]

At Benghazi, anxious men awaited the return of what was left of the great armada. Col. Ted Timberlake, and planners Colonels Jake Smart, Leander Schmidt and Gerald Geerlings, played horseshoes near the radio shack in hopes of relieving the tension they felt over the fate of their ships and men. The only official communication they had received was from General Ent who radioed that the mission was a success, but then they began picking up aircraft-in-distress signals being sent to Malta, Cyprus, and stations along the way, including friendly ships at sea. Suddenly, in the distance, they could hear and then see the vanguard of the returning planes.

First to land were the Liberandos of K. K. Compton and General Ent. It was readily obvious from the looks of their planes that, except for Appold and his group, they had not encountered any major combat damage, which led to a false sense of relief among the waiting. But then the Travelling Circus came straggling in with a totally different look from the first group that had landed. Most of their planes were rickety "buckets of bolts" festooned with hanging pieces of metal and with cables and wires flapping through holes in their shattered fuselages. Many were firing flares to alert medical personnel of the wounded they were carrying, even though, for many of them, help would be too late.

The battered *Thundermug*, its gas gages on empty, flown by Russ Longnecker, who a few hours earlier had watched both his wingmen fall from the sky, followed Potts and Timmer to a smooth landing on the desert floor. As the crew exited *The Duchess*, Colonel Timberlake hurried up in his jeep to extend a relieved welcome back to the crew. He was met by a furious Ramsay Potts who, shaking with anger, unloaded his frustrations with the mission on his old friend and former boss, while Bob Timmer and his crew boarded trucks for the interrogation tents where they would relive their flight to the intelligence staff. Pop Hastings and his ground crew would count over fifty fist-size holes in the wings and fuselage of *The Duchess*.[188]

But *Utah Man* was still out there somewhere, and after he had gotten Potts calmed down somewhat, Timberlake joined Pastor Chappy Burris, Diarist Brutus "Pop" Hamilton, and the ground crew who were gathered to anxiously await the return of their plane. Finally, after 13 hours and 15 minutes of flight, Walt Stewart and Loren Koon softly landed the battered plane to a relieved, but sullen, crowd.

There was no joy in the desert that night. Pop Hamilton wrote in his diary that evening: "This is written late at night with a heavy heart and a bewildered and laggard pen. It's been the saddest day in the history of the 93rd Bomb Group. Seventeen planes are missing. It is feared there are no survivors in some planes. The fact the raid was considered devastating to the Romanian refineries does not repay us for the loss of our friends: at least, we feel that way tonight. Yet we know that sacrifices must be made in war and some objectives must be knocked out regardless of cost. We know, too, that soon we shall set our teeth against this hurt, carry on our just cause to victory, and set up a world where bullies can't start wars. I shall write more later. At present, I'm too close to those who aren't with us tonight."[189]

Michael Hill, in *Black Sunday: Ploesti*, summarizes, "The men who climbed into their planes that morning...have been called heroes and they were. The men of Tidal Wave were a cross section of America. They were ordinary men who stepped forward to defend our country and democratic way of life. This is the heroic legacy of the men who flew Tidal Wave. Their valor will be remembered as the price for our country's Freedom." [190]

They began tallying the losses to the fleet on Monday, August 2, 1943. It would take weeks to get an accurate account because of many unknowns, especially among those who were or could have been prisoners of war. Historians now know that of those who went on Tidal Wave, over 300 were killed out of about 1600 on the raid, approximately 1 in 5. Hundreds more were wounded or captured. From the 178 Liberators assigned to the mission only 33 were listed as fit for duty the following day.[191] Only 88 returned to Benghazi and 55 of those had substantial damage. The Ploesti oil complex was heavily damaged. A few of the targets were totally destroyed and never did come back on line. But it wasn't too many months later that the oil complex began reaching pre-raid production.

There were five Medals of Honor awarded that day—the most awarded for a single mission in World War II. No other bombing mission of the war received more than one.[192] There were more citations for bravery for the Ploesti mission than for any other mission in air force history.[193] In fact, it was the most decorated military force ever.[194] The mission also gathered 430 Purple Hearts for the men who flew it.[195] It is probable that it was the only urban bombing mission of the war where more airmen died than civilians.[196]

President Franklin Roosevelt felt it necessary to inform Congress of the terrible casualties incurred by the air force in the Tidal Wave operation. He said, "I am certain that the German or Japanese High Commands would cheerfully sacrifice tens of thousands of men to do the same amount of damage to us if they could."[197] While that statement may have helped Congress grasp the enormity of the sacrifice, it was of little comfort to the families of the lost.

~~~~~~~

Years later in an interview, when asked why, with all the carnage, *The Duchess* came through relatively unscathed, Ramsay Potts replied, "Luck. Pure Luck." He went on to point out that a good crew can give a plane a slight edge but reminded the interviewer that Addison Baker had an excellent crew and didn't make it.[198] In that same interview, recorded in 1980, Potts, then a major general, was asked about his copilot on the Ploesti mission. "My copilot was a big, good looking kid. I had great qualms about having him fly with me, because he was very inexperienced. But when we went on the mission, I couldn't have asked for a better co-pilot. He never flinched. He did everything right. He never got flustered and during the periods when I would ask him to fly the plane and hold a certain heading or an altitude heading, he always did it right by the book and did a super job."[199]

In another interview recorded in 1989, General Potts said that even though he had some real reservations about having Bob as copilot it was "the best thing that could have happened" and speculated that Bob's inexperience may have contributed to his coolness under fire, stating that his rookie copilot may have viewed the mission as more routine than it was and "therefore was not as intense as the rest of us."[200] Accolades aside, Potts thought Bob was Swedish!

So how did Bob Timmer view this experience of a lifetime? Letters home could not contain many details because of wartime censorship, but in a letter to Eileen he mentioned that he flew so low that brush from treetops was caught in the bomb bay doors. Several weeks after the Ploesti action, he wrote to his mother and father. He knew they were worried about not hearing from him for a while and hoped they hadn't "worried too much," but said that he had been in the Middle East. He told them that he "had been seeing some action" and that he had won an air medal. Even taking into consideration the fact that he did not want to cause more concern among his family members than necessary, describing his combat situation which included the Ploesti raid as "seeing some action" could be the understatement of the war!

The air medal he mentioned was created by executive order of the president on May 11, 1942. Bob's was awarded in August, 1943, and the citation reads: *In recognition of meritorious achievement while participating in aerial flight in the Middle East Theater, he having participated in five operational sorties of two and one half hours or more duration.* The medal for valor was given to bomber crewmen for flying five combat missions. Those who conceived it recognized the courage necessary to climb into one of those potential flying coffins day after day.

A month later on September 15, 1943, Bob was awarded the Air Force's highest award for valor, the Distinguished Flying Cross.

The commendation reads:

> "Second Lieutenant Robert Timmer 0-204427, Air Corps, United States Army, is awarded the Distinguished Flying Cross for distinguished and meritorious achievement while participating in the operations against the Ploesti Oil Refineries of Romania on 1 August 1943. In carrying out a low-level, long range attack on an enemy target of extraordinarily great importance, this man under conditions of great difficulty and danger, contributed immensely to inflicting on the enemy one of the most damaging blows it has yet received. Flying through one of the world's heaviest barrages of flak, and amid swarms of enemy fighter planes, the objectives were bombed and strafed, causing very extensive destruction. The fearlessness, devotion to duty and indomitable fighting spirit he exhibited constitute a magnificent example of heroism for all the men of the United States Army Air Force."

Thus, twenty-year-old Robert Timmer of Wyoming Park, Michigan became a certified American hero.

Chapter XI Utah Man

Black Sunday was followed by Blue Monday, and as the first faint streaks of orange appeared in the eastern sky, there was an unaccustomed silence in the Libyan desert. Planes were everywhere they shouldn't have been, having landed on runways of convenience rather than their own. Many did not have enough fuel to taxi to their places, and others stopped quickly to extricate their wounded. Soon, as the skies began to brighten, ground crews boarded trucks and began to search for their planes. They were appalled at what they saw. Sitting silently in the dawn, scattered near the runways, were their Liberators, once majestic in their ferocity, now beaten and broken. Their bodies were ripped with gaping, jagged wounds. Shattered wires and cables dangled from their holes, and oil dripped from their silent engines. Insultingly, vestiges of tree limbs and corn stalks protruded from their bellies. Climbing aboard the once healthy machines that they had sent off just 24 hours before, the men were sickened by the combined smells of leaking fuel, burned rubber, charred wiring, and seared flesh. Many wept at what they found–and cried at what they didn't find. Man and machine needed a lot of healing.

The flyers of the Circus were also hurting. Even hardened combat veterans who had witnessed their share of battered men, and who had previously suffered through the loss of friends, were shocked by the carnage of Ploesti. So many who, just a few days before, had shared their tents, played on their baseball teams, ate with them at the mess halls, told stories of home, and laughed over card games, simply, suddenly, were not there. And even more catastrophic than the void was the fact that many of those who were there had witnessed the horrible, fiery deaths of those weren't. There were no professionally trained counselors rushing to Terria to treat traumatized young men. They had only overburdened chaplains, each other, and faith, to help them deal with the emotional scars of the raid.

It has been said that there were no atheists in foxholes. There were not very many of them climbing aboard B-24s either, and prayer groups began forming soon after breakfast. Many were still missing, and prayers were given for their safety. It was hoped that they had landed safely in Sicily or Cyprus or Turkey. Preparations were made to get the most seriously hurt, but able to fly, to hospitals in Cairo or Tunis. Some, who were unable to be moved, had to suffer in the desert until they could be transferred to one of several hospital ships now en route to Libya. Chaplains quietly went about their business of contacting families of the lost and making preparations for burial of those whose bodies came back in their plane or who died after their return.

Later that Monday, Ramsay Potts called the men together. Incredulously, he talked to them about how to save gasoline and showed them charts to emphasize his points. There were no compliments, no heroics, no rehashing of yesterday's mistakes, and no therapeutic suggestions for traumatized men. Just a matter-of-fact presentation which sent the intended message: business as usual. Potts's nose gunner on *The Duchess*, Sgt. Louis Smith, stated, "My first thoughts were of sorrow. I felt the loss of very close friends. Then I thought the good Lord is the one I should be thanking. I should also go to Ramsay Potts and tell him how great I feel about him being my pilot."[201] That is the way it was for that generation: suck it up and get on with it.

Business as usual was not going to happen very soon, however. The mauled men and machines of the Circus needed fixing, and they had a ten-day stand-down to get that done. Work on the 55 battle-damaged planes began immediately. The strain on the repair management systems was immense. While ground crews were experts at patching and replacing torn planes and engines, they were overwhelmed with the business confronting them, and it was difficult to know where to start. But by using parts from some to repair others, they quickly got most of the Liberators ready for the next round.

Fixing the flyers was another matter. Putting a patch on emotional damage was not an option. However, going on leave was, so on Tuesday, August 3, several Liberators loaded with airmen headed for Cairo. Ah, Cairo, with all its wonders, ancient and otherwise, went a long way in pumping up traumatized men. For those, like Robert Timmer, who wanted a somewhat quieter leave, there was Tunis with its great accommodations, fine food and hot baths. Flying, for men who loved airplanes, was another great tonic, and soon Liberators were taking off on practice runs over the desert. This time it was at high altitude, no more of the low-level stuff. Church services the Sunday after the Black one were well attended.

With Colonel Baker's death, the Travelling Circus was leaderless. Lt. Col. George S. Brown, who led the second wave of Baker's A group, was named interim commanding officer of the 93rd. (Later, Brown, as a four-star general, became Chairman of the Joint Chiefs of Staff.) Soon, their newly appointed leader, Col. Leland Fiegel, arrived at Terria. Replacing aircrews also began immediately and new men arrived within a few days of the battle, some of them coming in new planes. The Circus was well on its way to rejuvenation.

A mission was scheduled for August 10, and the men were out of bed by 0300 to prepare for their 0515 briefing. Prior to takeoff, however, the mission was scrubbed due to the beginnings of a massive sand storm descending on Northern Libya. The storm raged for two days, blowing sand into the most sensitive parts of the men, their belongings, and the freshly fixed planes and engines. However, the mail that day came in bushels, giving a great lift to their spirits. Sadly, mail that was undeliverable filled many bags. Bob wrote his parents a few days later and mentioned that he received mail from them dated last November, along with forty other letters he should have received when he was in the RAF. Going that long without news from home for men in combat seems inexcusable, but could have been due to the frequent wanderings of the Travelling Circus. It was just the way it was.

Captain Morton Macks, from San Francisco, California, was one of the original Circus pilots. He earned a degree in history from the University of California at Berkley shortly before Pearl Harbor, and in a burst of patriotism after the Japanese bombing, he volunteered for the Air Corps flying cadet school. His motivation was not so much a love of flying but an aversion to foxholes, tanks and rifles. He also was aware that a flyer, when surviving a mission, got to sleep in a clean bed. He came to England with the Circus in the fall of 1942 and went on their first tour of Africa. By the spring of `43, the Circus was so short of flyable aircraft that Captain Macks and his crew, in *El Lobo,* were the only members of the 330th Squadron to fly on a particular mission.[202] After flying more than his mandatory 25 combat missions, Morton Macks was awaiting rotation back to the States when the Circus left for its second tour of Africa. Timberlake, who called him "our court jester" for his ready wit and quick smiles, asked Mort to perform the important task of orienting new crews to the desert way of life.[203] Occasionally, he was pressed into flying combat, even though he could have refused.

On August 13, Morton Macks climbed into the cockpit of *The Duchess,* next to copilot Robert Timmer, and began the countdown to takeoff. Ramsay Potts had been promoted to chief of staff at Timberlake's new headquarters and, having more than fulfilled his mission quota, would no longer be a member of the crew of *The Duchess*. However, several of the Ploesti crew--Smith, Stormer, Clay, and Huffman--were on board that morning. The target, that first mission after Ploesti, was anticipated to be a rough one: a factory that built the German fighter plane, the Messerschmitt, located in Wiener Neustadt, outside of Vienna, Austria. All of the depleted Bomb Groups that flew the Ploesti raid participated. The flight was long; so long, in fact, that orders were to land in Tunis on the return to shorten the trip. The weather was good over the target, and, surprisingly, there were no fighters, and flak was minimal. Bombing results were excellent with planes and buildings destroyed or damaged so effectively that Me-109 production was cut by one-third. All B-24s were accounted for and returned to Terria the next day. The mission was a good morale booster for the still reeling flyers.

Three days later, Bob and the crew of *The Duchess* were off again, this time with substitute pilot Lt. George S. Black. Black, from Oklahoma, was the former pilot and copilot of *Shoot Luke.* As copilot he was almost killed during a spring mission when three Me-109 slugs came through the right cockpit window and narrowly missed his head. At Ploesti, *Shoot Luke* had to turn back with engine failure. The day's target was, for the second time, the Foggia Aerodrome in Sicily, where General Patton and British General Montgomery were racing to be the first to capture the capital of Messina. Multitudes of enemy planes had been photographed on the ground, and destroying at least some of them would relieve pressure on the troops. The new commanding officer of the 93rd, Leland Fiegel, led his first attack, flying copilot in *Hells-A-Droppin II*. Enemy fighters, German and Italian, rose to meet them. Bombing was inaccurate, and only a few planes on the ground were destroyed. However, 12 or 13 enemy fighters were shot down. One, a FW-190, was claimed by Royce Magee, a new gunner on *The Duchess*. Several Circus ships were damaged, but all returned to base. That evening's entertainment featured a live performance by Jack Benny. He played to mixed reviews.

Things seemed to be going quite well with the ground forces in Italy; therefore orders came for the Travelling Circus to travel back to Hardwick. They left Terria, with prayers in their hearts for the families of the comrades they were leaving behind—men who had come to Africa with them two months before, but who were now buried in Libya, Malta, Turkey, and wherever else Tidal Wave had deposited its dead. The Group was given a few days to get to England where they would again join the effort to carry the war to the German homeland.

Robert Timmer's 330th Squadron flew to Marrakech in Morocco, passing over Tunis, where they again looked down on some of their previous handiwork. The once beautiful harbor, where much of the turncoat French fleet had been based, was now decimated, due to hundreds of sorties flown by the 93rd and their friends. They proudly observed that the residential areas of the city were untouched, even though there was a swath of destruction several hundred yards wide along the waterfront. Allied planes of every description now were parked at the Aerodrome where, only a few months before, the same planes had hammered it into uselessness. After landing at Marrakech, Bob and his buddies had time to shop the bazaar and bargain with the Arab vendors for goodies to send home to wives and sweethearts. Bob bought himself a red Fez which made him look like a Dutch Shriner hosting their annual circus in Grand Rapids. That night, they slept in beds, had morning coffee and a good breakfast and, on a beautiful day, flew up the Atlantic coast of Europe to England. They did not encounter any enemy planes.

Hardwick, it was the next best thing to home and, for desert sojourners, the beautiful, lush green of it made up for the cloudy, rainy weather, which felt somewhat refreshing after the desert heat. Everyone on the base turned out to welcome back their valiant and famous flyers, whose exploits of heroism had been flashed around the world. They were also greeted by fresh smells, cool rain, decent food, and beds so clean and so unfamiliar that they caused many restless nights. They were given leave, lots of leave, in hopes that skinny and traumatized men would soon return to the healthy, cocky flyers that left just two months before. While ground crews worked to restore beat-up planes and engines, men began flying practice runs, only now, much to the relief of surrounding towns, it was done thousands of feet above civilization. It was obvious to all that they were again getting ready for more combat.

~~~~~~~

If Ted Timberlake was the engine that drove the early 93rd to effectiveness and prominence, then Walter T. Stewart was the sparkplug. His father was the twentieth child of a plural marriage, and Walt was born the tenth of twelve in a primitive cabin in rural Utah. (One of his grandfathers was 98 when

Walt was born.)[204] Walt moved to Salt Lake City, where he went to high school. He also learned to play the piano. He entered the University of Utah and studied speech and drama. He interrupted his studies and paid for his passage to England in 1940, to do missionary work for his Mormon church. He got caught in the bombing of London where, to stay out of harm's way, he was forced to hole up in air raid shelters. While huddled in a London church, dodging bombs during the Blitz, he decided to "fight fire with fire" and become a pilot.[205] Returning to the States, he married Ruth, enlisted in the Army Air Corp, and trained on B-17s. Later, whenever he encountered B-17 pilots, he could not resist telling them that he had started on 17s but had "graduated" to B-24s.[206] He was sent to Barksdale to join the 93rd, which had recently been formed. Fellow Utahan Hugh Roper was putting together a crew and asked Walt to be his copilot, and he flew copilot for Hugh until taking command as first pilot of *Joisey Bounce**. He renamed it *Utah Man*. (There was also a plane named *Jersey Bounce*. It too flew on the Ploesti raid.)

One of the famed Ploesti pilots, he dropped the first bombs on the oil complex and brought shot-up *Utah Man* back on a "Wing and a Prayer." Writers, in describing his exploits, gave Walt more descriptors during his short time with the Circus than most other mortal souls receive in a lifetime. He was adventure seeking, a man of courage, a man of deep faith, a musician, charming, a loyal friend, fun, funny, incredibly optimistic, talkative, humorous, energetic, sympathetic, and a great leader; and all this at the ripe old age of 25! He sparkled, he sparked and he cared; his personality getting him into (and out of) some unusual situations.

When not flying, he was a sought-after speaker on the English war bond circuit. Mr. Cowl, a gentleman in charge of one of the fund-raisers, wrote to Colonel Timberlake: "Lieutenant Walter T. Stewart came to our fund-raiser film show, spoke, and was far more popular than the flicks. We managed to raise the week's sale of British war bonds by 75 percent above our target."[207]

Cal Stewart, as Circus public relations non-com, attended one of Walt's speaking engagements. He describes what he heard. Walt, "like an auctioneer at a Western cattle sale went to work. He inserted lines tailored to the Brits' sense of humor, spilled a few parables, and sacrilegiously put-down the B-24." A self-described expert on bees (a relative had them), Walt went on, "The Liberator is sort of boxy," he said. "Its lines aren't neat and sleek. It's akin to the bumble-bee. Aerodynamicists tell us the bumble-bee can't fly. The bumble-bee doesn't know this and flies anyway.'" [208] (If B-17 pilots had ever gotten wind of Walt's B-24 critique, they would have gotten a real buzz out of it.) The sale that day helped raise $225,000 for the war effort.

In the audience were a 16-year-old girl and her younger sister, who Walt later described as "just like American high school girls. Pretty. Happy. Bashful as any when you first meet them."[209] They asked to meet him. So after the event, Crown Princess Elizabeth and Princess Margaret and their various ladies-in-waiting approached Walt and a conversation ensued. The topic got around to the current U.S. best-selling book, *The Robe*. Walt said he had a copy and if they would like to read it, they could borrow it. They said they would be delighted. Back at the base, he got plenty of advice on how to get the book to the princesses. The next day, after taking all the collective wisdom into consideration, Walt wrapped the book in newsprint and terry cloth, checked out *Fearless Fosdick*, the 93rd's Piper Cub, flew over the Royal Family's summer palace, Sandringham, in Norfolk County, and dropped the book on the palace. British security went nuts. Luckily, instead of shooting the small craft down, they noted the plane's numbers and turned the data over to the American command, which took care of the matter. It was the last time Walt violated royal airspace.[210] (They didn't realize how fortunate they were: he could have used *Utah Man* for the project!)

His mom was confused. She sent a letter. "Dear Walter, I'm glad you're flying one of those big Fortresses...be careful now...fly low and slow!" Walt replied, "Dear Mom, I DON'T FLY A FORTRESS!!!"[211]

In Africa, Walt was friendly with some of the Brits who manned the flak guns around Terria. They may have liked their beer warm but not their water. No problem, Walt gave their water a ride when flying high and returned with a rare, refreshing treat. He and his crew once flew six hours to Tunis to take a bath. While there, they learned of a new B-24 that needed to come to Libya. Again, no problem. Walt split his crew and had the new plane follow *Utah Man* home, somewhat justifying his expensive junket.[212]

Big Job, piloted by William McKelvey with a crew of ten, returning from a mission to Italy in July of 1943, lost its way back to Terria. Radio operators at the base were able to pick up a faint distress signal, indicating that the plane was out of gas over the desert, and that the crew was bailing out. Thinking that the plane was closer than it was, the British sent out special desert-worthy vehicles in an attempt to find the lost men. Several days went by, and hope was fading that they would be found alive. At desert church the first Sunday after the men went missing, Walt Stewart was sitting on an oil can in the sand, playing the final hymn of the service on his portable keyboard, when he suddenly bounced up from his seat and announced that he could not stand the thought of those lost men wandering in the desert without food and water. He asked for volunteers and, after organizing a Liberator search party, he began mapping out a strategy in the sand.[213] Walt gave each plane a huge search area, equivalent to the size of a state like Georgia. After reaching their assigned region, the volunteers flew back and forth through their designated grid. It seemed an impossible task. They were far from certain where the plane went down and didn't even know if there were any survivors; the search seemed fruitless. The land was barren and lifeless, and the searchers knew that survival was impossible after a few days without water. Guess who found them?

After four hours of boringly flying their grid with nothing in sight, Walt and his crew, in *Jersey Bounce—Utah Man* was in the shop—suddenly saw the white of a parachute. There were two men near it, the crew having split up to find help. Walt brought the plane around, came in low, and dropped several canteens of water, which did not survive the fall, smashing open when they hit black lava rocks. Walt and his crew sadly watched from above as the dying men ran, walked, fell and crawled to the broken canteens, where they licked the dripping water off the surface of the lava.[214] *Jersey Bounce* radioed its coordinates back to base and circled the area, waiting for other planes to arrive, until they ran low on fuel and had to leave.

Because the area was not suitable for landing, planes could not get within miles of the survivors, so, each day, Liberators carrying water and food (in large padded containers) flew over the site and dropped their life-saving cargo near the downed men, while the ground contingent slowly made its way to the site. Eventually, there were six men located and all were in bad shape. Tragically the other four, including the pilot, McKelvey, could not be found. Finally, after days of hot and difficult travel, the British vehicles, carrying a medical officer, arrived at the site of the men. The surviving six were given medical attention and taken about 60 miles to the nearest landing area, where a waiting plane flew them back to Terria. They were in the desert fourteen days. Walt's worrying had saved their lives. The four missing members of the crew were never found and died in the harsh desert.

Many of the legendary leaders of the early Circus were gone: Ad Baker, Hugh Roper, Jack Jones, and John Jerstad were dead, Ted Timberlake and Ramsay Potts were promoted, and others, like Walt Stewart, Mort Macks, and Lew Brown, having more than completed their mandatory missions, stood down from combat. The attack on Foggia on August 16 was Walt's 32nd combat mission, and he decided, at the urging of his family and friends, that he was pushing his luck with that many missions over the required 25. Instead of heading for home, however, he was made the operations officer for the 93rd, helping to plan missions and tactics. He also lectured new combat crews before they went into action. Bob Timmer got to know Walt in the desert, attending church services and prayer groups where Walt was one of the leaders. He also flew some practice missions with Walt in *Utah Man*, both in the desert and after they returned to Hardwick. Even though Walt was then twenty-six, six years older than Bob, they were friends.

A well-known photograph of B-24s from the United States Air Force collection. The first two are from the 330th Bomb Squadron. *Joisey Bounce* is the closest to the camera and was renamed *Utah Man* by Walt Stewart when he became its pilot. It went down in November, 1943 over Bremen, Germany, with Robert Timmer on board. Next to it is *The Duchess,* which is the plane that Bob flew on the Ploesti raid. It was shot down in February, 1944, on its 53rd mission. The other two planes are from the 328th Bomb Squad. The first is *Boomerang* and it is the plane that Walt Stewart flew on his war bond tour to the United States (see Epilogue). Next to it is *Thundermug* which was eventually so badly shot up that it was salvaged in October, 1943. All four dropped bombs on Ploesti. Some sources give the date of the photo as late June, 1943 at Hardwick. If that is the case, then Bob could have been flying *The Duchess* when this picture was taken.

Replacements, both men and planes, began arriving in Hardwick. Some of the planes that came were updated B-24s, H and J models, with new nose and ball turrets that gave them more fire power and a better field of protection. Most of the crew of *The Duchess* had completed their mandatory missions and were headed for home and Ramsay Potts was promoted, so a new team was assigned to *The Duchess*. With Walt's seat on *Utah Man* vacant, his copilot, Loren Koon, moved over to the left side of the cockpit. The battle-hardened and legendary *Joisey Bounce/Utah Man* and its experienced crew, was assigned a new copilot, Robert Timmer. For Bob, it was the second time in his fledgling combat career that he became the new kid on an established flying team.

In one of his rare surviving letters, sent in late August, Bob tells his family that he "hoped to have his own plane soon." He seemed impatient, telling them that he was getting bored being a copilot, but mentioned that he needed more hours before getting his own crew. He had flown six missions, and at twenty was still young, having left his teenage years only a short time before. Having come from Canada, Bob hadn't had the opportunity to be part of an original American crew, which typically would have been formed in the States and would have trained together; most having spent two months flying as a team before coming to England. The team was everything, and Bob had no sooner hooked up with Ramsay, than Potts and most of his crew left. This meant Bob had to "start over" as a member of a new team. Chances are that Walt had something to do with Bob being assigned to *Utah Man* even though it was no longer his plane. Walt was *Utah Man,* and he certainly had some influence with Loren Koon. Morton Macks speculated that, with a little more experience, and with Ramsay and Walt saying good things about him, Robert Timmer would have eventually gotten his own Liberator. "If he flew with Ramsay," Mort relates, "then Bob had to be good, or Potts wouldn't have flown with him."

The only photograph showing him with members of a crew was taken about the time of Bob's transfer to *Utah Man.* Eleven crew members are posed casually in front of the name and nose art of the plane. Why eleven instead of the usual ten? Because Walt Stewart got himself in the picture, even though he was a "retired" crew member. Standing on Walt's left, leaning towards him, is Robert Timmer, the new copilot, who essentially took Walt's place on the established crew. Bob has his arm behind Walt, whose left hand is on Bob's shoulder. There's affection there–signs of friendship. Carroll Stewart has published this photograph on page 181 in *Ted's Travelling Circus*.

~~~~~~~

Events of the first half of 1943 marked a turning point in the war. In the Soviet Union, the Nazi armies were going backwards, their advance having been stopped at Stalingrad, where an entire army had surrendered to the Soviets. In the Pacific, the Japanese had been kicked off the island of Guadalcanal in February, and the "island hopping" campaign had begun. This bloody strategy would ultimately lead to Japan's doorstep, where heavy bombers, including the B-29, could get at the dastardly perpetrators of both the sneak attack on Pearl Harbor and the Bataan Death March. North Africa was clear of fascist forces, and the island of Sicily had fallen to the Allies. In August, the United States was about a year and a half into the conflict, with two years yet to fight. Seven million American men and women were in the service, and the leviathan that was American industry was beginning to reach the incredible production numbers that began to make a difference. That same month, Churchill and Roosevelt met in Quebec, Canada, to discuss and plan the upcoming invasion of Normandy. Millions still had to die before the slaughter ceased, but the Allied forces were over the hump, and ultimate victory could now be realistically imagined.

As the 1943 calendar turned from August to September, the Ploesti Raid was still being discussed in the media and in military circles. Low-level attacks on a grand scale, using bombers designed for high flying, were never again attempted. The bombing of Germany, with B-24s and B-17s, however, continued unabated. Hitler's Germany was now routinely being bombed by several hundred plane flotillas, British and American, almost every night. The targets, for the most part, were means of production, ball-bearing factories, aircraft assembly plants, etc., and also included military targets, harbor facilities, railroad yards and aerodromes. Bombing of Germany entered a new phase. Heretofore, Allied planners tried to minimize civilian losses, e.g. Ploesti, but in July, Hamburg, a strategic port city, was pulverized with incendiaries. Even though the planners insisted that civilian targets were still off-limits, the bombs created a fire-storm that killed an estimated 40,000 people and virtually wiped Hamburg off the map.[215] Incendiary bombing of strategic German cities was becoming part of the Allied strategy.

The United States also began daylight raids into Germany and suffered catastrophic losses. The first daylight raid was carried out by 229 B-17s, when they hit ball-bearing production facilities at Schweinfurt. Fighters accompanied the bombers for some of the distance but ran out of range and had to turn back. The Heavies were then on their own into the target. Thirty-six planes and 352 airmen were lost.[216] Incredibly, daylight bombing by the Americans continued.

The island of Sicily fell to Allied forces in August, and on September 3, 1943, Germany's chief ally, Italy, surrendered, imprisoned Mussolini, and switched sides in the conflict. Germany would have none of that, however, and with German troops firmly entrenched on Italian soil, the bloody battle for Italy was far from over.

September, 1943, was an unusual month for the Circus flyers.

On September 6 the 93rd flew a diversion over the North Sea in hopes of drawing Luftwaffe fighters away from the main party of B-17s, who raided Stuggart. A diversion was an easy way for Lt. Timmer to begin adjusting to his new crew and plane. Combat credit was given for a diversion if it penetrated enemy airspace. This one, apparently, did not, because there was none given. On the 15th, the Circus' target was in France, the St. Andre de L'Eure Aerodrome. Twenty-two planes took off and bombed, but three, including *Utah Man,* had to turn back due to mechanical problems. The attackers did not bomb the primary target because thick cloud cover prevented them from seeing it, so they went after a secondary target near the cathedral city of Chartres. German fighters swarmed them and they lost a plane, with three killed, including the pilot, William Loveday. The rest of the crew survived as POWs. It was another sad night in the barracks at Hardwick.

Abruptly, the Circus was ordered back to Africa. They were given twelve hours to get ready and on the 17th they headed out for their third sojourn in Africa. No more desert living, however; this time they were based just south of Tunis, at a former French airbase, where they had clubs, a PX, a recreational facility, good food and plenty to drink. Earlier, the American Fifth Army had invaded the Italian mainland by landing at Salerno south of Rome. They were having trouble moving inland, and General Eisenhower called on Timberlake to send in the 93rd, in hopes of relieving German pressure on the bogged down troops by striking at supply and communication lines. (Timberlake was now in charge of the 20th Combat Wing of which the 93rd was a part.) The troops were told that the Liberators were coming and that may have sparked them enough to begin moving the Germans back. So, even with the hurry-up departure, the critical need for the Heavies was over by the time the Circus arrived in Tunis.

Pounding Germans, however, was their business, and missions were scheduled with that purpose in mind.

The weather in Italy that late September was awful, reminiscent of England's fog and rain, and it caused several planned missions to be scrubbed. However, Leghorn had an active harbor, filled with ships and boats, which was used to supply the German armies with men and equipment. Unfortunately for them, the weather cleared long enough for the Circus to pay them a visit. Led by their new commander, Colonel Fiegle, *Utah Man* and friends paid a visit to Leghorn on September 21. The harbor was plastered. The attackers met no fighters, and flak was light. All planes returned to Tunis without damage. It was the kind of mission everyone wanted, every time.

A few days later, the Leaning Tower of Pisa crookedly withstood Circus attacks on its city. The Tower and the priceless buildings surrounding it the marble cathedral, the baptistery, and the art museum – all housing treasures for the ages, were untouched by the precision bombing of the Liberator bombardiers. Not spared by those experienced bombers, however, were the railroad marshaling yards where hundreds of 250-pound bombs bounced around some freight cars and damaged the roundhouse, repair shop, and gas works. The aircrews were pleased with the results, but it wasn't the type of visit to the Leaning Tower that Robert Timmer envisioned as a kid when dreaming of faraway places. Again, there was little opposition to the raid, and all planes returned safely. The now deposed and despised dictator, Benito Mussolini, had been praised for his ability to get the chronically late Italian trains to run on time. But with attacks on yards in Foggia, Rome, Naples and Pisa, the Germans were faced with the challenge of getting trains to run, period.

The next day, September 25, eighteen of the Circus bombers, including *Utah Man,* roughed up the Lucca aerodrome north of Pisa. Lt. Timmer was not with them. His flight records indicate that he flew a secret mission of four hours duration. There is no indication of the plane he flew or of the purpose of the flight. Most likely, it was for photo reconnaissance.

The second trip to Wiener-Neustadt and its huge ME-109 factory took place on October 1 which also happened to be Bob and Eileen's first wedding anniversary. Seventy-three Liberators from four different bomb groups took part, with a third of them Circus planes, including *Utah Man.* Unlike the relatively easy attack of several weeks before, this one was rough. The long trip was made under heavily overcast skies until they approached the target. Then the clouds opened, improving visibility for the bomb-run, but also for the 65-70 Messerschmitt 109s that jumped the Libs from out of the clouds. At the same time, the bombers encountered heavy flak. An incredible air battle ensued, with at least forty-three Me-109s shot down, but the Tunis-based Liberators paid a high price, losing fourteen of their own. One of the fourteen was the Circus' own *Jerk's Natural,* the ship once flown by the late Ploesti hero, John "Jerk" Jerstad. Nine of its crew died. Of the seventy-three B-24s that took off that morning, in addition to those that went down, eight made forced landings and forty-one received battle damage, leaving only ten unscathed. The factory was hit, but far from destroyed.

It had been one year since LAC Robert Timmer joyously stood at attention and received his wings from Mayor Young in Brandon, Manitoba. He then knew, of course, that he would soon be leaving for England but never dreamt that he would be, in less than a year, in or over France, Gibraltar, Tunisia, Morocco, Libya, Italy, Yugoslavia, Romania, Albania, and

Austria. He would not have been able to comprehend, while standing on the tarmac at the Brandon aerodrome, the courage that it took each time young men crawled onboard a combat-bound bomber. He hadn't realized, then, that men he'd yet to meet, men who would become his friends, could make the sacrifices that he had recently watched them make. Now, he knew that he was one of them and that courage and sacrifice were what he, and the men flying with him, had and did. Like them, and those before him, he was ready to get on with it.

Chapter XII Bremen

Just as unexpectedly as they had been ordered to Africa, the Ninety-Third was ordered back to Hardwick. They left Tunis the evening of October 3, 1943, for an overnight flight. Walt Stewart hopped aboard *Utah Man,* joining his former crew for the flight home.[217] Lt. Timmer did most of the flying on the long trip back, while Walt blabbed with the crew. Again, for the second time in about two weeks, personnel at Hardwick, having been told at breakfast that the planes were on their way, gathered to watch them fly in from Africa, touching down one by one. Sadly, *Jerk's Natural* from the 328th Squadron was missing but nothing like the hacked-up formations they had observed coming in from the previous African venture.

The weather around Norwich was terrible that October. Hardwick was closer to the North Sea than many of the other bases in the area, and the fog was relentless. Along with the fog came rain, sleet and overall nastiness. Often, flying was impossible. The flyers were bored but realized that if they weren't flying, they weren't getting shot at, and that was some consolation at least, not getting shot at in the air. On October 7, the Germans paid another visit to Norwich, their bombs sending men on leave diving for cover at the Red Cross Club, and spilling beer and ruining dart games at the pubs.

The Circus did manage to make another run to Vegesack on the 8th, however, with sub pens, shipyards and power facilities the focus. Twenty-one Circus Heavies, including *Utah Man,* took a route into the target from the northwest, while over one hundred B-17s came in on a different heading. The

Germans, who knew they were coming, lit smoke pots and, with a favorable wind, much of the target area was obscured. The Circus then attacked a secondary industrial target and returned without a loss, but the main force of 17s were badly battered, losing thirty bombers to flak and enemy fighters. Thirty bombers lost equals potentially 300 men killed, although some may have parachuted into POW status. It's no wonder that the planners and senders were having second thoughts about daylight bombing. Unfortunately, their second thoughts never led to an alternate strategy.

New crews, fresh from the States, were arriving regularly but were barely keeping up with the losses. Once the rookies arrived in Europe, they were required to go through an orientation session of several weeks' duration to familiarize them with living conditions, English life, and combat realities. Despite the lecturer's wish to avoid the topic, someone always asked about the odds of surviving combat. They were told that the average attrition rate for the Eighth Air Force on each mission was four planes lost for each 100 flown, or 4 percent. The lecturer then asked, "Multiply the 4 percent by the required 25 missions and what do you get?" A hush fell over the room. The leader then pointed out that the formula under discussion really meant that a flyer would have a 100 percent chance of being shot down on his last mission. In reality, the speaker quickly added, many would complete their 25 missions because of the laws of probability.[218] Only then did it begin to dawn on the new guys that the carefree days experienced in stateside training were behind them. Navigator Lt. John W. McClane began to realize that "someone could get hurt" and that, up to now, they were just "big boys playing with expensive toys, not a care in the world nor a thought of danger."[219] McClane, who survived, had calculated that about a third would complete their missions. He kept track of the eighteen crews that trained and went overseas together. Six of those crews went home.[220]

> [Note: In a modern day perspective, it would mean that for every 100,000 deployed to Afghanistan (about the size of our present force there), 66,000 would be casualties!]

New arrivals assigned to the 492nd Heavy Bombardment Group noticed that there was a lot of tension, half-hearted greetings, and not much talk among the men who were there. The new guys soon realized that the cool reception was not due to something they had done, but that the stressful behavior was caused by incredible combat losses. The 492nd having been operational for only six weeks, had lost all but 11 of their 77 original crews. The morale problems were so great that they were deemed impossible to fix, and the Group was disbanded with the remaining crews assigned to other units.[221]

As winter approached, the dreadful weather only got worse. Planes rendezvousing above Hardwick for missions were having trouble finding each other and getting into formation, a dangerous situation. General Timberlake, now head of the 2nd Air Division, came up with an idea to address that concern which was so sensible that, eventually, it was used by many other bomb groups. The concept was to have a plane called a rendezvous or assembly ship hover in the skies over Hardwick so that the bomb formations could form around it. Ted ordered that *Ball of Fire*, a Circus original now on its last legs, be taken out of combat, painted white with brown and dark pink stripes, and hung with Christmas tree lights. Leaving ahead of the combat planes and circling above, the gaudy ship could easily be spotted by crews, who would rally to her and sort into formations, thus saving time, fuel, and mishaps.[222]

The Ninety-third's old *Ball of Fire* was the first rendezvous or assembly ship in the Air Force.[223]

The Circus put very few missions under its belt that stormy, foggy October, but it wasn't for a lack of trying. Several scheduled missions never got off the ground and others started out but turned back. Nevertheless, on October 9, while *Utah Man* stood down, Circus ships were part of a larger group that attacked German occupied Danzig, Poland. This was the longest trip to a target from England, thus far.[224] The bombing was effective, even though the target was obscured by smoke. The Ninety-third's old, beat-up *Boomerang* logged its 50th mission, the first B-24 to achieve that milestone.[225] It kept flying.

Despite the horrible losses suffered by B-17 groups on the August raid to Schweinfurt, they were sent back there on October 14. Again, they lacked adequate fighter protection. The results were even more deplorable than the first trip—sixty planes went down. That's 600 men killed or missing in just a few hours! And again, military planners decided that the losses, both to the USAAF and the RAF, were unacceptable.

Perhaps as a result of those losses, airmen began to notice changes that eventually helped the bombing campaign over Europe become more efficient. More effective electronic locating devices were being added to the bombers. Installed initially in lead planes, these radio and radar gadgets enabled navigators and bombardiers to hammer targets, even though masked by clouds, with some degree of accuracy. In addition, crews were noticing that more fighters were accompanying them for longer distances, often to the targets and back. American P-38 Lightnings and P-47 Thunderbolts, equipped with supplemental fuel tanks, were holding their own with the

German fighters. In fact, they were more than holding their own! Fortunately, as the need for deeper penetration into German airspace increased, so did the range of the fighters. The new P-51 Mustang fighter plane began arriving in force near the end of 1943, and its range (carrying auxiliary fuel tanks) was sufficient to provide protection for the bombers wherever they went in Germany. The vaunted Luftwaffe began taking huge losses from both American fighters and the expert gunners onboard the big ships. Simultaneously, factories that produced the German planes were taking regular hits from the Heavies. It would not be long before air superiority over Europe would tilt in favor of the Allies, resulting in less-costly raids.

Diversions are those missions flown in an attempt to draw enemy fighters away from the main attack force. Lt. Timmer and *Utah Man* flew two of them in October and received combat credit for both. On the 18th, on a diversion over the North Sea, the draw-off strategy worked tragically well when a Circus plane, attacked by Me-109s, was lost off the coast of the Netherlands. Nine of the crew were killed. Two days later they attempted to fly a diversion in such bad weather that, on the return, they could not land at Hardwick and had to put down at a less weather-bound field. For Bob and most others, flying diversions, especially in foul weather, or not flying at all was boring and took them away from their major focus: dropping bombs on enemy targets. The men were antsy and anxious sitting around the sparse barracks waiting for the weather to clear. Morale suffered.

Irritated men received a great lift, however, when a new officer's club was opened on the 19th. To celebrate, a festive dinner was served and General Timberlake was in attendance. Playing dice was the most popular event at the club, and the craps table was busy.[226] There is no indication that the general was inclined to wager on games of chance. He preferred taking his chances flying missions with his boys, which he did on a regular basis, especially if the target was a difficult one.

Finally, on October 30, it seemed that a viable mission was in the cards. *Utah Man* and friends visited the city of Gelsenkirchen, Germany, site of a huge iron and steel plant. The target was socked in, so the decision was made to turn back without release due to the likelihood of hitting civilian targets in the dense fog. The men were given credit for a combat mission.

The weather didn't change much as November came. There was still a lot of down time. On November 3, thirty Circus Liberators left Hardwick on a mission to Wilhelmshaven, a large German naval base on the North Sea. Although there was total cloud cover over the target, lead planes carrying improved radio and radar devices found the target area through the clouds. The planes released their bombs on signal from the leaders. With the lack of visibility, damage could not be determined. The planes returned safely, despite enemy flak.

Two days later, Munster, with its huge industrial complexes, came under attack by twenty-seven planes of the 93rd. This time the Liberators were accompanied by a host of Lightnings and Thunderbolts. They were needed. Swarms of German fighters of every variety rose to meet them, and a classic aerial dogfight ensued. While Koon, Timmer and navigator Ralph Cummings took *Utah Man* to the target, its gunners turned their .50s on the attacking Germans with some success. John Connolly, the left waist gunner, sent a Messerschmitt spiraling down in flames. The city was hit hard, and the Circus got away unscathed. Back at the base, a reporter for the *Stars and Stripes* interviewed Lt. Timmer as he was leaving the interrogation hut. In the article, Bob expressed his appreciation to the fighter pilots for the job they had done that day and observed that, "The numerous dogfights reminded him of the movies."[227]

Weather permitting, Allied bombing of the German homeland was relentless. With the British bombing at night and the Americans by day, not only was German production beginning to feel its effects, but the German people, especially those in the cities, were being subjected to horrible suffering. Fleets with bombers now numbering in the hundreds (and soon to exceed a thousand) were pulverizing what was once one of the world's most beautiful countries and the cradle of protestant Christianity. Now, centuries of cultural achievement in the arts, music, science, and architecture, so brutally hijacked by the Nazis, was being laid waste, not only by Allied bombs, but also by the systemic state murder of millions of its citizens. Still, Adolf Hitler and his henchmen kept the German nation and its people in their grip of terror. For the Allies, there would be no peace terms offered nor accepted. The devastation would continue until the Germans surrendered unconditionally. By then, there wouldn't be much left.

~~~~~~~

More often than not, flight crews would be roused from sleep in the wee hours of the morning to begin preparations for the day's mission - two to three o'clock was the norm. Typically, a corporal would have the honor of shining a flashlight into a sleepy face and telling the airman he was flying that day. The roused airman would then head to the necessary room to perform the day's toilette. A close shave was especially important to eliminate any possibility of a loose fitting oxygen mask. Fully dressed, the men would proceed to the mess hall for breakfast. Those flying that day would often be treated to real eggs, bacon and pancakes, along with lots of coffee. After breakfast they would make their way to the briefing room for instructions.

Two Nissan huts were used for the briefing: one for officers and one for enlisted men. At the front of the room was a lectern on a dais and against the wall behind it was a large curtain. Benches were arranged in rows on either side of an aisle in which a narrow, rectangular table stood. A slide projector was usually on the table. Windows in the hut were blacked out, making it difficult for new crew members to find the hut in the dark. Armed guards were positioned at the doors to ensure that only authorized personnel entered. Others would patrol the perimeter of the building.

Once the men had filed in and were seated, a chaplain would open the briefing with prayer. This was typically followed by a few remarks from the commanding officer. The curtain would then be pulled back by staff officers, exposing a large map of Europe pinned with red ribbons, revealing the route from Hardwick to the day's target and back. With the target identified, officers then discussed anticipated enemy resistance, weather reports, and aircraft assignments, including positions in the squadron. Sometimes, the slide projector was used to dispense information, with an occasional nude slipped in, just to get the attention of drowsy flyers. It worked - even at three or four a.m.![228] The announcement of the target was usually greeted by loud groaning. Sometimes, however, when the men realized the mission was going to be especially tough, the announcement was met by more silence than groans. With or without groans, emotions ran high among the men who were scheduled to fly. Given the horrible loss ratios occurring among flyers, that fall of 1943 many wondered if this foreign place was where they were going to die. Despite pre-mission stress, however, humor was always present among American airmen. At one particular briefing, when told by the presenting officer that, "The Krauts will be expecting you today" one of the flyers piped up, "If they're expecting us today, why don't we go tomorrow?"[229]

After the general briefing, the men gathered into groups, by position, to receive more specific information. Here, navigators, bombardiers, and radio men were given specialized codes and coordinates, while pilots met with the commanding officer for some final words of advice and encouragement. Flight crews then went to their lockers to don their amazing amount of flying gear. They yanked, stuffed, pulled, pushed, buckled and tied their; sheepskin jackets, pants, boots, gloves, flak vests, life preservers, helmets, goggles, oxygen masks and parachutes. Finally suited up, they waddled to the trucks, rode to their plane, and crawled aboard, exhausted, but for the pre-flight adrenaline.

Carroll Stewart called November 13, 1943, "a wretched day," and so it was.[230] At 0300 a determined corporal made his way among the cots lining each side of one of the officer's huts at Hardwick, using his flashlight when necessary to wake the men. Bob Timmer sleepily listened as he was told he'd been scheduled to fly that day. As he made his way to the mess hall for breakfast, he winced at the nasty weather. It was a cold, foggy, drizzly day, and winter was bearing down on Norfolk County, England. Although there was plenty of food for those flying, he never ate much for breakfast on mission days. A full stomach was often very uncomfortable when bouncing along in a Liberator at 22,000 feet. Bob had flown enough missions,

16 to date, to know that a light breakfast was preferable. In the officer's briefing hut, he found a spot on a bench next to *Utah Man* pilot, Larry Koon. Lt. Ralph Cummings, the bombardier, also sat with them.

When the black curtain opened, revealing the target, there were a few groans, but most were silent. It was going to be Bremen, Germany, a city with a huge commercial shipping fleet, U-boat pens, shipyards and factories. It would be heavily defended. The red ribbons indicated that the route would take them over The Netherlands; in fact, over the province of Groningen, Bob's ancestral homeland. They were told that the target was completely overcast but that B-17s of the 3rd Division, equipped with special radio and radar equipment, would be acting as Pathfinders, firing flares to alert the other formations when the target was located. Twenty-five aircraft of the Circus would join other B-24 groups and follow several formations of B-17s into the target area.

After putting on his flight gear and riding out to *Utah Man*, Bob greeted the rest of his crew, who were busy helping the ground crew top off the fuel tanks. *Utah Man* had a special feature that set it apart from other Circus B-24s. Because of the damage suffered at Ploesti, it had a pink right wing, a replacement "borrowed" from a pinkish colored ship of the Pyramiders. Koon and Timmer circled their plane, conducting their preflight inspection, noting that the venerable, battle-scared, old war bird looked in great shape, a credit to the maintenance men and a source of comfort to those who would fly her.

As he climbed into the cockpit, Bob felt some anxiety; not fear, but apprehension. He was experienced enough to know that flying a mission in such weather was going to test not only his ability but also the abilities of the individual members of the crew. He took satisfaction in knowing it was a very experienced crew flying *Utah Man* that morning, as well as the fact that they had been together since early September.

Second Lieutenant Loren J. Koon was the pilot and sat in the left seat of the cockpit. In the nose were tunnel gunner S/Sgt. Richard E. Bartlett, Lt. Ralph W. Cummings, who was the bombardier and the ranking officer on board, and Sgt. Benjamin Caplan, the navigator, in a position usually held by an officer. Behind the pilot was the radio operator T/Sgt. Paul E. Johnston; and the top gunner, Sgt. Robert L. Cox, was stationed behind and above the copilot's seat. Manning their .50s from the waist were gunners S/Sgt. William H. Major on the right and T/Sgt. John E. Connolly on the left. S/Sgt. Joseph R. Doyle was in the aft of the plane in the tail gunner's position. Only Connolly, Cox, and Caplan had not flown the Ploesti mission; the rest except for Bob, had come in on a "wing and a prayer" in *Utah* Man with Walt Stewart.

After taking off, they looked for the vibrant *Ball of Fire* to begin forming up. Even when they found her, the adverse weather conditions made it very difficult to get into formation, the whole business taking much longer than usual. On their way at last, trouble soon developed. The outside temperatures over Holland dropped to -50°F and planes began to experience various malfunctions. Ultimately, eight Circus planes had to abort, but *Utah Man* lumbered on. Other issues began to haunt the armada. In order to climb above the weather, the leading B-17 formations flew at altitudes up to 28,000 feet. Not designed to fly that high fully loaded, the Liberators struggled to keep up. In the cockpit of *Utah Man*, Bob and Larry fought the controls to keep the big ship in formation, while the rest of the crew watched the skies for enemy aircraft.

Then another disappointment. The B-17 Pathfinders, who had the critical task of leading the force over the target, aborted, leaving the remaining planes to find the target on their own.[231] As they approached the target area, Bob noticed that flak was lighter than expected and appreciated the expertise of his men, who keyed their bomb release to the area where they saw the most flak. He had a good feeling when Ralph Cummings yelled "bombs away" over the intercom as *Utah Man*'s bombs were salvoed, and the pilots began heading for home. There was joy in the plane as they saw P-58 fighters arrive just in time to provide a welcomed escort home.

Suddenly, hurtling out of a cloud in front and above them, a host of Me-109s jumped the formation. Spitting fire from its twin 20mm cannons, one headed straight at *Utah Man,* executing the dreaded forward pass, and, in a split second, rounds ripped into her cockpit, tearing apart the instrument panel and spattering the blood of the pilots. Others attacked her vulnerable sides, silencing the left waist and tail guns. Badly wounded, Bob slumped to the left struggling to maintain consciousness and control of the ship, while Koon, also wounded, checked with his crew on the intercom. Besides the silent gunners Connolly and Doyle, there were no reports from Caplan, Cummings, or Bartlett, all of whom were in the shattered nose. He gave the order to abandon ship.

Jumping down from his top turret, Robert Cox saw Paul Johnston, the radio operator, dazed and panic stricken, on the floor. He pushed and pulled Johnston to the open bomb bay, reminded him to pull his rip cord, and shoved him out. Cox dove out behind him. In the cockpit, Timmer and Koon soon lost their battle with the plane. *Utah Man* slipped quickly down and to the right, colliding with *Valiant Virgin* piloted by Richard Sedevic, knocking off her left wing and sending her spinning out of control. Three men, all in the nose of *Valient Virgin*, were able to bail out. Both planes careened into a death spiral, creating such centrifugal force that all who remained on board were trapped. The legendary *Utah Man*, veteran of so much heroic action, plunged from the sky, carrying the beloved son of Nick and Effie Timmer to his death. She hit the ground in a blinding explosion, sending up fire and smoke from the burning wreckage that could be seen for miles. Seconds later, *Valient Virgin,* with seven still on board, followed her into the ground.

Gone. The toddler who took his first steps holding his Opa's finger; the little boy who rode the sled behind his speeding dog; the precious son who snuck off to the airport because he loved planes so much; the brother that made his siblings proud with his academic, artistic and athletic achievements; the proud airman with the wings of two countries on his chest; and the husband and lover of a pretty girl who would soon begin her struggle to put her broken life back together - gone, just gone. Gone forever.

Chapter XIII Home

On a cold and snowy late November morning the nondescript Ford coupe pulled to a stop in the driveway of 1608 Porter Street in Beverly, Michigan. It was the 27th, the Saturday after Thanksgiving, 1943. The Western Union man, fully aware of what he was delivering, slowly got out of his car and, with his head down, walked toward the door of the Koopman house, fumbling to get the life-changing message out of the leather pouch hanging from his shoulder. Jennie saw him coming and knew. Doing her best to control the emotion in her voice, she called Eileen from the kitchen and they stood arm-in-arm as they watched the uniform make its way to their door. Eileen, numb with apprehension the second she saw him, lost color in her face, and felt her heartbeat quicken.

When the bell rang, Eileen with her mother by her side, opened the door and heard the heartfelt but wrenching words delivered daily by telegram men to all parts of the country, "Sorry Ma'am." She ripped open the envelope and with tears welling in her eyes, read,

"The Secretary of War desires to express his regret that your husband Second Lieutenant Robert Timmer has been reported missing in action since thirteen November over Germany. If further details or other information are received you will be promptly notified."

She turned to her Mother and softly said, "He's not dead, Mom. Missing is not dead." and as she hurried to her room she declared, "I know he's not dead!" She sobbed over the telegram in the privacy of her room.

Her growing brood of grandchildren called her "Granny" and with her small glasses, bunned gray hair, and a bosom so ample that little ones virtually disappeared when receiving her hugs, she was the quintessential grandmother. She was all about love. But now, the Reverend Jacob Blaaw, in the living room of the Timmer house on Avon Avenue, sat holding the hand of a crying mother. Effie Timmer, clutching a white hanky, dabbed at tears as her pastor prayed for the safe return of her son. Nick, "Pupup" to the grandchildren, silently listened, struggling to keep his worry under control. There is hope Pastor Blaaw told them. After all, men were seen bailing out of the plane. Surely, Bob was one of them and was now a prisoner of war somewhere in Germany. Have faith, pray, and find comfort in God and in your children and grandchildren.

Heaven was deluged with prayers from the Timmer and Koopman clans. But it seemed that God was taking His time answering them. "Nothing" was turning into reality. As the weeks went by, nothing became something. Communications smuggled out of POW camps often brought accurate information, but there was no mention of Bob. The anxiety of each member of the family increased.

Both Grand Rapids newspapers, *The Press* and *The Herald*, headlined the fact that local bomber pilot Lt. Robert Timmer, was missing over Germany, and Rev. Blaaw announced it from the pulpit. Once the word was out, letters of support and hope came pouring in to the family. A letter to Bob's parents, emphatically stated that crew members had a 50-50 chance of surviving if the plane went down and, even though he was probably a prisoner of war at least he was safe. Most letters simply offered sympathy and prayers and were a source of comfort for the families. The envelopes that really pulled at the emotions of the family however, were their own marked "Return to Sender" and stamped MISSING IN ACTION. They often imagined the worst, and it scared them. Those were distressing times, not knowing.

The army wouldn't, or couldn't tell her anything, so Eileen, desperate for news and determined as ever, began her quest to find out as much as she could on her own. She communicated with the families of *Utah Man's* crew, hoping they had information that she did not. Mr. and Mrs. Major, from South Bend Indiana, who were the parents of gunner William Major, responded to Eileen's entreaty, and told her that they had it on good authority that *Utah Man* was in a crash and went down, but that it "fluttered from side to side like a leaf," and therefore landed intact. Most of the crew survived and were taken prisoner Eileen was told. She quickly learned that Cox and Johnston were prisoners of war. Her emotions flipped between hope and fear. Hope that Bob like them could also be alive, and fear that if others' whereabouts were known, why not Bob's?

Eileen, not one to show emotion in the presence of others, did her best to go about her business. It was not business as usual however—her worry was contagious, and it bathed the Koopman house in anxiety. Bob's frequent visits seemed like they had been part of the family routine only yesterday, and though they always missed him, his unknown status intensified their awareness of his absence. Eileen's sister Jean recalled an occasion when two uniformed airmen, friends of Bob, paid a visit. As Eileen saw them get out of the car it was evident by the expression that momentarily flashed on her face that she thought one of them was Bob. How crushing it must have been. The family thought of him often and as they went about their normal routine, hope prevailed. If only they would hear something.

She did what she had to do for him as painful as it might be. On a warm Saturday in June, 1944, Eileen Timmer drove to Selfridge Air Force Base in Mt. Clemens, Michigan. There, airmen stood in rigid attention as the base commander, noting that 2d Lt. Robert Timmer was Missing in Action, handed nineteen-year-old Eileen Timmer her husband's Distinguished Flying Cross. Her apprehension was tempered by a tearful pride.

~~~~~~~

Dealing with death in the World War II American military was big business and large bureaucracies evolved to manage it. The various forms of apparatus engineered to kill young men produced thousands of them every month, and systems were developed for addressing the sheer volume of it all. Processing bodies, or body parts, took an incredible number of people. First, someone had to move the remains from the place of death, which was often a dangerous place, and transport them to a safe area where pathologists and morticians could do their work. Identification was critical and not always a matter of reading a "dog tag." A comprehensive intelligence network was necessary to make sure the correct name was placed with the right body. Military intelligence was also responsible for trying to determine the status of the missing, most of who were behind enemy lines, and they developed a vast network of informants to help with that task. Few of the dead were shipped home during the war; there simply was no way to do that, so most were interred near where they had fallen in temporary cemeteries. This meant that hundreds of thousands of burial boxes had to be made and graves dug. Internment services had to be planned and carried out which was generally the job of the chaplains.

Processing the effects of the men for shipment home took an inordinate amount of work, as well. Critical to the entire business was communication with the families of the lost and among the various military branches involved. In those days, communication up, down, and outside the military hierarchy was done with paper (enormous amounts of paper) to create or record: memos, directives, orders, letters, notes, lists, inventories, statements and reports. All of this took a multitude of clerks and a heavy toll on typewriters. It also required boxcars of typing ribbon and tons and tons of carbon paper, just to meet the mandate of having numerous copies of everything.

Whether KIA or MIA, it was clear after a few days that Lt. Timmer was never going to return to Hardwick. So under various rules and regulations, prefaced in memos by the "pursuant tos" and "directed bys," Robert Timmer's place in the officer's barracks was cleared of his effects. Replacements needed the space. Most of Bob's belongings were not unusual: photos, letters, a razor, a New Testament with Psalms, trench coat, his pipe, uniforms and other clothing, including eighteen shirts. He had left behind a number of RAF items, including: a kit bag, his Pilot Officer's cap, and two Canadian pilot wings. It would be interesting to know about the two pair of pink trousers (maybe he wore them with his red fez), the five wallets, all without cash (probably gifts), and the title of the book he was reading. All in all, it seemed to be an undue amount of "stuff" for one person, especially when most of the basics were provided by the military.

The entire process of packing, storing, and shipping, was

overseen by an Effects Quartermaster, whose office was located in a warehouse in Liverpool, England. A delay of six months was required before the effects of MIAs could be shipped home, and so all that was Bob lay boxed in an English warehouse, along with hundreds of other similar boxes, waiting to be returned to their families. Although the U.S. military did an amazing job with this difficult process, it was not perfect. Sadly, the address label on Bob's belongings began, "Return to: Eileen Timmer, mother."

Clearing his bank account did not go smoothly. In October, 1943, accountants in the Canadian Air Force notified the 330th squadron commander that Bob owed them $30.97 "due to a misunderstanding." In addition, £67.10 had been inadvertently deposited into his bank account by the RAF. They of course wanted reimbursement for the total converted amount of $332.70. Bob was informed of the issue on November 8, five days before his fatal flight. In late November, the fiscal office of the Canadian military was notified that Lt. Timmer was Missing in Action and that his bank assets would be frozen for six months from the date he was reported missing. After six months, the bureaucracies, Canadian and American, lumbered into bureaucratic inaction. For months, documents and forms were exchanged between them, finally resulting in a debt settlement in October, 1944, using money from his bank account. There was nothing left.

In May of 1944, Robert Timmer had been missing for six months and, with absolutely no word of his whereabouts, he was officially "presumed dead." Lt. Col. Edward Chayes, the Effects Quartermaster, thus began the task of removing Bob's box of personal property from the warehouse in Liverpool and getting it home to Eileen. It was sent first to the Quartermaster Depot in Kansas City, Missouri. In October,

Eileen completed and sent yet another form relative to her "next of kin" status, and on November 13, 1944, exactly one year to the day since the demise of *Utah Man*, two suitcases and a carton, arrived at 1608 Porter Street.

Alone in her room, Eileen, anxiously loosened the buckles on the straps of the first suitcase and slowly opened it. On top, folded neatly, with both sets of wings and insignias in place, was his Army Air Force jacket–the one he wore in her favorite photograph. She quickly raised it to her face and breathed deeply, searching for some trace of him. Her tears fell freely upon it as she clutched it to her chest, squeezing it, holding it up to her gaze, and then clutching it again, all the while sobbing "Bob, Bob, I miss you so."

The military has to do what it has to do and, in contrast to Eileen's heartbreaking episode which was taking place in the homes of wives, girlfriends and mothers across the country, the War Department coldly and efficiently removed Bob's MIA status. In one of those official documents, with its "pursuant to," etc., came the message:

> "The Adjutant General's Office, finds Second Lieutenant Robert Timmer, Army Serial Number 02044427, Air Corps, to be dead . . . For the purposes stated in the said Act, death is presumed to have occurred on the 14th day of November, 1944."

Military policy dictated a wait of a year before a missing person was declared deceased, and now that it was official, other events began to unfold. The little flag in the window of 2321 Avon, with its two blue stars denoting Gerald and Bob on active service, was removed and replaced with one displaying a blue and a gold star. By becoming a "Gold Star

Mother," Granny thus joined thousands of other American mothers. It was a tragic distinction, but one not without a touch of pride for having a son who gave the ultimate sacrifice. The little flag hung in the window long after the war was over.

Again, letters came to the Timmer and Koopman homes; now expressing sympathy rather than hope. John Hannah, President of Michigan State College, sent a certificate of honor, along with a personal note stating, "The death of your son, Robert J. Timmer in the service of our country has brought a feeling of loss to those of us at Michigan State College who knew him."

Eileen, emotionally spent, still had to correspond with the military. A package from Bob's effects was missing and she wrote to Kansas City asking where it was. She also wondered about the disposition of his papers, as both his folders and wallets were empty. She wrote, "If they have been removed for purposes of security, will they be returned to *him* or me after the war?" Him? Bob had not been heard from, or about, in over a year and had been officially listed as Killed in Action. What was she thinking? Eileen didn't seem the type given to denial. She wasn't. Even though she was just twenty, she was well grounded and definitely living in the real world. It was hope that was driving her life at this point. A strong belief that her present situation could still be rectified that Bob was over there, somewhere, alive and that he would return to her.

The package that was delayed contained a set of cuff links and Bob's first Air Medal. It was sent by separate post. The Quartermaster replied that all of Lt. Timmer's belongings had now been sent and that they had no information about any personal papers.

Eileen was not the only one who had not given up. The following notice appeared in a November, 1944, bulletin at First Church in Grandville. "Mr. and Mrs. Nick Timmer received word from the War Department this past week to the effect that their son, Lt. Robert Timmer, is officially reported "Lost in Action." They are still hopeful however, that he will be found alive, since no definite proof of his death has been discovered."

Eileen did not know, and could not know, about the classified attempts over the previous year to find information about Lt. Timmer and his crew. Every effort was made to ascertain their status, perhaps summarized best by a memo from the War Department to the Veterans Administration, dated November 14, 1944. After listing the names of *Utah Man's* crew, it reads, "An examination of all available, pertinent, War Department records, including status cards, burial records, prisoner of war reports, etc., indicates that none of the subject personnel have been seen or heard from by anyone during the twelve months which have elapsed since they became missing in action."[232] Finding nothing though was still a "probable" death. But a year and a half later, in April, 1946, a War Department document stated that information taken from captured German documents confirmed that Lt. Robert Timmer was, indeed, killed on November 13, 1943. That did it; the fading hope that was nurtured for so long was gone. It was over.

~~~~~~~

When the wreckage of the two burning planes cooled enough to allow nearby German villagers to approach them, there were only traces of human remains on the site. Despite the cold, inhumane reputation of Hitler's regime, the villagers frequently treated enemy dead with respect, giving them a proper burial, often in the village plot. They kept whatever identification they could glean from the wreckage, both of the men and the plane. In *Utah Man's* case, the fragments of the eight who were killed in her were mingled and buried together. It was possible the pieces found were from some of the men and not from others—without DNA it was impossible to know for sure.

After the war, the American Graves Registration Service began a continent-wide search for deceased American service men. When they came upon the *Utah Man* crash site, they only knew that the pieces in the native grave were from *Utah Man* and perhaps, from other planes that had crashed in that area. The remains were removed and sent to a temporary American Military Cemetery in Neuville-en-Condroz, Belgium, which was established in January, 1945 for just such a purpose. There the military would conduct more research in their attempts to identify the remains. Through their efforts they were able to identify several crew members of *Valient Virgin* whose remains were ultimately sent home to their families. Individual identification of the *Utah Man* crew was not possible. After the war, those buried in temporary cemeteries were either moved to one of fourteen permanent American cemeteries in Europe or sent home.[233] This was a monumental task and took time to accomplish. There is no indication that Eileen and other family members knew that any of this was taking place.

Finally, in October of 1950, Eileen and Bob's parents received information from the Graves Registration Services. The letter to Eileen told of the investigation into the identity of the remains and further stated, "… and it has been impossible to individually identify your husband's remains. It has been established, however, that the remains recovered are the only recoverable remains of your husband and the thirteen comrades with whom he lost his life. This group of remains is now casketed, and being held overseas, pending return to the United States for internment in Jefferson Barracks National Cemetery, located at Saint Louis 23, Missouri." Jefferson Barracks Cemetery, on the banks of the Mississippi River south of St. Louis, has been burying our military dead since 1826. World War II casualties introduced a new focus to the cemetery. It was given a special distinction, by becoming the central repository for group interment when individual remains could not be identified. More than 560 group burials have been held there—meaning that there are two or more veterans in a common grave.[234]

~~~~~~~

Slowly, quietly, the hearse carrying the boxed fragments of what was left of fourteen American heroes made its way on a lonely, cold, and snowy day, to Section 84 of the National Cemetery. Breaking the quiet were the tires of the black Cadillac as they crunched along the icy road, the footsteps of the honor guard, and the muffled sounds of a few crying people. It was Tuesday, February 6, 1951, the day that Robert Timmer and his comrades finally came back to American soil. It had been seven years and fifty-four days since *Utah Man* had fallen, and eight years and five months since Bob waved good-by to his teen-aged bride at the Grand Rapids train station.

While the few present stood silently by, airmen in full ceremonial dress carried the remains to a small chapel near the grave sites. No bells tolled, no bands played, and no joyous people lined the streets. No headlines blared the news, no mayors spoke, and no Air Force planes roared overhead. In a perfunctory service, a chaplain prayed and said a few words, then an honor guard of three active-duty airmen, symbolizing "Honor, Duty, Country," fired three rounds of salute. Taps was played on a mournful bugle and then it was over. The site guarded then, as now, by a fluttering half-staffed flag.

Epilogue

Robert Timmer fought in two planes, *The Duchess* and *Utah Man*. The pilots most identified with those planes, Ploesti legends Ramsay Potts and Walt Stewart, are mentioned frequently in this story. They were not only deservedly welcomed home as heroes, but also are examples of the successes that many flyers found after the war. One can only wonder what might have been for Bob and the thousands of others who did not return.

Ramsay Potts, a major when he flew with Robert Timmer, moved up rapidly in the military hierarchy as the war continued. Eventually, he made full colonel at the age of twenty-seven and became group leader of the 453rd Bomb Group. While serving in that position, the actor James Stewart became his operations officer. Even though Jimmy was eight years Ramsay's senior, they became and remained good friends for the rest of their lives. Potts became Director of Bombing Operations for the Eighth Air Force and, in that position after the war, was able to interview many top Nazis to gather data about the effectiveness of American bombing. Potts stayed in the Air Force Reserve after the war and achieved the rank of Major General.[235]

Besides the general's stars on his uniform, Potts wore ribbons denoting a Distinguished Service Cross (the nation's second highest honor for valor awarded for Ploesti when he flew with Bob), two Silver Stars, the Legion of Merit (worn around the neck), three Distinguished Flying Crosses, a bronze star, and five air medals.

While in Europe, Potts courted a young British woman who was in the Royal Air Force Women's Auxiliary. While stationed in Belgium, he flew a plane across the Channel to see her. The airfield where she was waiting for him was closed due to a heavy rainstorm. He buzzed the tower at twenty feet and was given a red light, preventing him from landing. He did it again - same result. He kept at it, each time getting closer to the tower, until he finally got a green. She was waiting.[236] He married Veronica in 1945, and the union ended with her death in 1993.

After the war, Ramsay graduated from Harvard Law School and became a special assistant to the Secretary of the Air Force. He was president of Military Air Transport Association, a trade group for charter and cargo carriers. In 1958, he and three other attorneys founded a Washington, D.C., law firm that came to be known as Shaw, Pittman, Potts and Trowbridge. It specialized in corporate law and securities regulation and became a very prestigious firm. Potts became the firm's managing partner and, when he stepped down from that role in 1986, they employed 300 attorneys with offices in D.C., New York, Los Angeles, and London. President Johnson asked him to serve as White House Counsel, but Potts turned him down.[237]

A top collegiate tennis player during his undergraduate years at the University of North Carolina, the sport remained his life-long passion. He played and organized tournaments well into his later years. He was instrumental in raising money for the fabulous Mighty Eighth Air Force Museum in Savannah, Georgia, where he served on the Board of Trustees. In the memorial garden at the museum, Ramsay has placed a plaque dedicated to his fellow flyers of the Ninety-Third Bombardment

Group. He passed away of a stroke, at age 89, at his home in Florida in 2006.

~~~~~~~

Old beat up *Boomerang,* veteran of Ploesti and more than 50 other bombing missions, was still battle ready but due to take a break from being shot at. It was decided to send her stateside for a triumphant coast-to-coast tour to sell war bonds. Thus, it was slated to follow in the footsteps of the ill-fated *Hot Stuff* and the much ballyhooed B-17, *Memphis Belle.* Heading a hand-picked, all-star crew was the pilot Captain Walter T. Stewart of Benjamin, Utah.

On April 4, 1944, all the big-wigs from the area came to Hardwick to see her off. General Timberlake put his signature on her nose and the Red Cross girls served cake. The BBC and NBC were there conducting interviews with the crew, who told British and American audiences of the old bird's exploits. After the ceremony, folks lined the runway to witness her takeoff and waved the plane into the clouds. It refueled at Prestwick before the North Atlantic flight (no Iceland stops this time).

In the States, some of the tour's highlights included buzzing the Michigan Penitentiary at Jackson, loudly honoring the inmates for their war production efforts. They visited war production cities, where thousands came to the various airfields to see the plane and, of course, to hear Walt's stories. All veterans should have such a welcome home! Cal Stewart tells the rest. "*Boomerang* flushed thousands of Milwaukee people into the streets with a thunderous roar down Beer Town's main drag, barely clearing the tallest buildings and broadcast antennae. Technically, the stunt was a gross safety violation. In the hands of the ex-missionary, the B-24D was capable of simulating a pursuit plane. *Boomerang* buzzed and visited twenty cities. Hundreds of newspaper cuttings and photos filtered to Hardwick."[238]

After the war, Walt went back to school, got his doctorate's degree in jurisprudence (J.D.) from the University of Utah, and tried law for a while, but farming and ranching were more to his liking. He and Ruth moved back to the family homestead to do just that. He also formed a construction company. He continued flying with the Air Force Reserve, rose to the rank of colonel, and served as a flying instructor for the Civil Air Patrol. After thirty-six years, Walt retired from the Air Force.

In 1965, Walt, Ruth, and their four children (they eventually had five), were called by the Mormon Church to build a chapel in Germany. They worked only a few miles from where *Utah Man* went down, but didn't realize it until they returned home. Walt was very disappointed that he did not have a chance to visit the site and pay his respects to his plane and its crew.

In 1994, Public Broadcasting Stations (PBS) began airing the documentary film, *Wing and a Prayer: The Saga of Utah Man*. Eventually, it was shown on more than 200 stations nationwide. In the film, Walt "holds forth," giving his account of the early days of the 93rd, his buddy Hugh Roper, Ploesti, and *Utah Man*'s fall. He talks about his crew and mentions Bob Timmer (who was not on his crew). Jacob Smart is featured, as well as several members of the Circus. Carroll Stewart served as an advisor. Narrator Walt is at his effervescent best, and the film won a Rocky Mountain Emmy Award as best documentary.

In the fall of 1995, Colonel Walter T. Stewart, dressed in his blue Air Force uniform, was presented with his long-delayed

Distinguished Service Cross for his Ploesti heroism at a ceremony at the University of Utah. It had been fifty-two years since *Utah Man* had dropped the first bombs on the refineries, so the award was a long time coming. After the award ceremony, Walt entered Utah's stadium prior to the Ute's football game with the Air Force Academy and was introduced to the fans. They were given a brief summary of his heroism over the loudspeaker, and as the Utah band lingered on the last note of our National Anthem, four Air Force fighters in tight formation screamed over the stadium in a low-level salute to an American hero.[239] Goose bumps and moist eyes prevailed as the coin was tossed. Taking his seat in the president's box to watch the game, Walt remarked, "It's a win for me either way." (Utah scored 15 points in the last forty seconds to win it, 22-21).[240]

> [Unfortunately, General Potts passed away before I could interview him about this story. However, I did have the pleasure of talking to Colonel Stewart on a couple of occasions, once on his 93rd birthday, November 8, 2010. I can't help wondering if the Queen's library at Sandringham Palace still has a beat up copy of *The Robe*!]

~~~~~~~

Parts of the old Hardwick aerodrome still exist thanks to the efforts of the local gentry who years ago fought a government attempt to turn the land into a garbage dump—called a "disposal tip" by the English. A committee was quickly formed to combat the county effort. They called themselves RATS—Residents Against Tip Site—and were successful in heading off the degrading scheme.[241] Leading the attempt were David and Jean Woodrow who own an area farm which includes several of the old structures. In conjunction with their American friends, the locals have created a museum to the 93rd and housed it in several modern Nissan huts. They are filled with memorabilia from the war days, including a great print of *Utah Man*. Near the farm's main buildings, there is a marker devoted to the 93rd Bombardment Group (Heavy). Dedicated in 1988, it is the centerpiece of regular pilgrimages to the site by Ninety-third airmen and their descendants. Old Glory always flies over it. Here, streams of visitors are graciously hosted by David and Jean.

English writer Graham Smith perhaps best describes the affinity that many of his countrymen have for the Ninety-third. He writes, "The 93rd Bomb Group that occupied Hardwick for most of its time as an airfield had so many claims to fame that it almost seems to be an embarrassment of riches. Not sufficient that it was the oldest B-24 group in the Eighth Air Force but it also mounted the highest number of missions of any group, and all for an amazingly low loss of aircraft and men. But its greatest hour and fiercest test came with its participation in the famous raid on the Ploesti oil refineries, without doubt the most brilliant and courageous operation carried out by the USAAF throughout the whole of WWII."[242]

Slicing through fields of lush crops lies part of Hardwick's old runway system. Walking along it, one can hear the ghostly thunder of those huge Pratt and Whitneys that so long ago carried young men aloft to do the thing that they were trained to do. The planes that lifted from that runway carried Hardwick boys – boys from the Circus. Boys who had laughed, lived and played there. And boys like Robert Timmer, and hundreds like him, who lifted off that runway never to return.

~~~~~~~

Eileen Timmer, even after Bob's KIA status was declared, still harbored a flicker of hope and waited for him until the war was over. But with an increasing acceptance of what was, she began getting on with her life. In the fall of 1944, she was hired as a clerk by Lynn Clark, Kent County Commissioner of Schools. Her responsibility was child accounting. The following school year, 1945-46, her title was "Attendance Officer and Secretary"—an important position for a young woman.[243] Eileen's office was in the county courthouse and she was making a decent salary for that time, $1,700 a year, and living at home. [The Kent County Schools later became Kent Intermediate School District.]

When he'd transferred from the RAF to the USAAF, Bob had taken out a life insurance policy naming his wife and mother co-beneficiaries. It was called National Service Life Insurance and it would terminate after five years, but could then be converted to renewable term insurance for those who survived the war. Bob took out $10,000 worth, and it cost him $6.50 a month. The payments were administered by the Veterans Administration and, when notified, both Eileen and Effie chose to be paid in monthly installments based on actuarial tables. Effie received $34.90 a month for life, while Eileen got $27.55 until 1963, when the payments ended. When Effie Timmer passed away, her balance went to Eileen, even though Eileen wrote the VA telling them that it should rightly go to her father-in-law. The letter had no effect; she received the payments as co-beneficiary.

In addition to the life insurance, Eileen and Bob's parents were eligible for a pension. The pension, also administered by the VA, went to widows whose husbands died in the line of duty. Mothers and fathers of a deceased serviceman could also file a claim for a pension if they could prove that they would have had to depend on their son for some of their living expenses. To demonstrate the need, forms were filled out, doctors' testimonies were given, and financial statements were copied and mailed. Their request was granted, and each of Bob's parents received a lifetime monthly income, which started at $25. When Effie died, Nick's increased.

During the time the government was investigating what happened to Lt. Timmer after *Utah Man* went down, he was still being paid. Once he was officially declared dead, the amount of his back pay totaled $3,255.25. That amount was sent to Eileen in care of her mother, Jennie Koopman, who was the "administratrix" of Bob's estate. Jennie deposited an even $3000 into Eileen's account and received the remaining $255.25 "as fees for performing duty of administratrix."[244]

People who knew her at that time recalled that Eileen was a woman who knew what she wanted and was willing to do what it took to get it. Several months after the war, she resigned her job at the county schools office and, with the money from Bob's pension and insurance, enrolled in Michigan State College, with the goal of becoming a teacher. She joined the freshman class in January of 1946, for the winter term. English was her major, with minors in history and French. Incredibly, she graduated with a Bachelor of Arts degree in December of 1948. Three years, in and out, and nothing but 'A's along the way! While at State, Eileen and a girlfriend bought a house together and rented out a bedroom and a loft over the garage; the income from the rent made their house payments.

In 1946, Eileen met Bruce Wortley, who was studying

engineering at MSC. He was from Iron River in Michigan's Upper Peninsula. On August 26, 1950, Eileen and Bruce were married in Beverly Reformed Church by Rev. Gordon Girod. They moved to Ypsilanti, Michigan, where Bruce worked as an engineer for the Kaiser/Frazier Automobile Company. Eileen worked as a secretary and a fund-raiser for an area hospital. They lived in Ypsilanti for eleven years before moving to Racine, Wisconsin. Eileen did some substitute teaching and earned her master's degree in counseling and became a middle school counselor. She and Bruce were frequent golfers. In April of 2000, Eileen passed away from hepatitis, contracted a number of years earlier while in the hospital for surgery. She was seventy-five. The Wortleys had three children and several grandchildren.

Author's Notes

When my Uncle Bob last visited our home before going overseas, I was three years old. I vaguely remember that visit, probably because I was impressed with that blue Canadian uniform. I have many memories of my Aunt Eileen. She frequently visited with my parents at our home, and I remember that, on at least one occasion, she was crying. Sometime during her college years, she brought me a Michigan State College pennant. I wanted it for the wall of my bedroom. I was about nine at the time, and I vividly remember her giving it to me. She was so cute that even her kid nephew had a crush on her.

Over the years the contacts between Eileen and the Timmer family became less frequent. When there was correspondence, it was often with Bob's sister Anne. Sadly, at least for the purpose of this project, Eileen shared with Anne that she "did not keep any of Bob's letters." The letters of Eileen's that I mention in the story are from the few that my Aunt Anne kept and from Bob's military files.

~~~~~~~

"Section 84" is in a hilly part of the cemetery at Jefferson Barracks, a few steps off a round-about with a tall flag pole in its center. Mature maple trees line the road. Over plots 316-320 is a large marker carved with the names and ranks of fourteen men—that's five plots for fourteen men. One of the names on the marker is ROBERT TIMMER 2D LT. During my conversation with the overseer, I was told that, most likely, there were only five body fragments and no one knows to whom they once belonged, so they put one in each box. "Sometimes," he stated, "we get orders to dig 'em up so they can do tests, because the family wants to know. I say, let 'em rest in peace."

Of the fourteen names on the stone at the grave sites, eight are the deceased crewmen of *Utah Man*, but only three are crew members of *Valiant Virgin*—out of the seven who died in her. The other four crewmen who perished in *Valiant Virgin* were probably identifiable and sent home to their families. Where did the other three names/remains come from if they weren't from the two colliding planes? That is another research project.

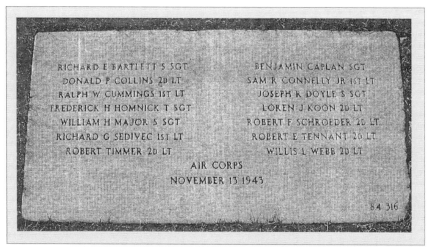

Section 84 Jefferson Barracks

In October of 1951, Bob's father received a letter from the War Department's Memorial Division. Enclosed was a photograph of the stone placed over the graves. Part of the letter reads, "It is regretted that because of the fact it was impossible to identify individually the remains of your son, you were deprived of the comfort and consolation which you might have been afforded by interring his remains at home." Be that as it may, Nick put an elaborately carved tombstone for his son on the family plot anyway. He went there frequently—often alone.

~~~~~~~

The story of the Ploesti raid has been told numerous times in books, articles and films. I did not attempt to retell it other than to give a general description of what the various bomb groups were doing, especially the Ninety-third. My focus in writing chapters nine and ten was to try to describe what was happening to Robert Timmer. What was going on around him? What did he see? What were the men on *The Duchess* experiencing? I treasure the stories told to me by Louis Smith about his shot up parachute, and John Sherman's account of the camera. Unfortunately, Robert Timmer did not live long enough to tell about his experiences at Ploesti, but the next best thing is the story in *The Mighty Eighth* where Ramsay Potts gives his account of the battle from the cockpit of *The Duchess*.[245] What Major Potts saw, for the most part, the guy next to him saw, and that, of course, was invaluable in putting together my chapters.

The venerated *Duchess* was shot down on a mission to Furth, Germany, on February 25, 1944, about six months after it safely carried Bob, Ramsay and the rest of the crew to Ploesti and back. Two of her crew died and the rest were taken prisoner. Among the survivors was the pilot, Lt. David Thompson who, a few months prior, was witness to *Utah Man's* last flight. *The Duchess* was on her 53rd mission—tied with *Boomerang* for the most missions flown by a B-24.[246]

A Liberator Crash Site

~~~~~~~

My story of the fall of *Utah Man* was pieced together from a series of eye witness accounts and Missing Air Crew Reports (MACR), many of them conflicting. MACR #2179 lists as witnesses three pilots of the 93rd who would have been in close proximity to *Utah Man*. Pilots Longnecker of the 328th and Weiss and Thompson of the 330th, all reported seeing a collision between *Utah Man* and an unidentified "other plane-not from this group." *Utah Man* was easily identified by the "L" on its rudders and its one pink wing. However, survivors, top gunner Robert Cox and radio operator Paul Johnston, said nothing about a collision when interviewed after they were freed from the POW camp where they spent the rest of the war. Cox, when filling out casualty questionnaires on each member of the crew, states, initially, that there was "nobody wounded" but then later speculates that gunners Connolly, Bartlett, and Doyle "may have been shot." Most telling is an interview with Robert Cox, conducted long after the war, when he stated, emphatically, that *Utah Man* did not collide with anyone, but was shot down.[247] From his perch in the top gun position, he had a 360° view of the action and reported that a head-on assault from an ME 109 did in *Utah Man*. He also stated that, when he climbed down from his position to the flight deck, he saw "blood in the cockpit" and that both Koon and Timmer were wounded. Walt Stewart, who lost most of his former crew in the tragedy, also stated, many times over the years, that *Utah Man* was shot down.

If there was a collision (which is the official military version of what happened) then another plane had to be involved. Given the fact that there were more than two planes from the 93rd lost that November 13, which was the plane "not from this group"? Researcher Paul Kooyer wrote to the Air Force History Support Office in an attempt to find out if there, in fact, was another plane that was reported downed by collision that fateful day. His request was handled by Colonel (Ret.) Thomas S. Berkey who, after conducting a thorough search of military documents, concluded, "It is likely that a B-24D from the 329th Bomb Squadron collided with 41-24226 (*Utah Man*). This is reported in MACR #2184. The serial number of the B-24D is 42-40765." That would make it *Valient Virgin,* piloted by Lt. Richard Sedevic. Berkey ended his response, "When I researched the unit histories of the 93rd Bomb Group, the 330th Bomb Squadron, and 329th Bomb Squadron, there is no mention in any of them of a mid-air collision."[248]

Missing Air Crew Report #2184 indicates that three crew

members survived the loss of *Valient Virgin*: the bombardier Alfred Van Dame, the navigator Howard Wodey, and the left waist gunner Edward Gillespie--all became prisoners of war. Van Dame and Gillespie were interrogated after the war and have left different accounts of what happened. Van Dame's account states in part, "Suddenly there was a terrific impact. Another B-24 had collided with us, and smashed our bomb bays...The tail section broke off immediately after."

Gillespie penned an interesting paragraph and I'll quote it exactly as he wrote it, because he likely had a clear view of what happened. He writes, "I was left waist gunner that day and we were about 25,000 ft, in formation with another sqd. The ship on the left of us was a little bit higher than us but it started to sideslip and hit us. think it took off part of left wing or something but (we) started to spin to right and almost got into tailspin I tried to lift Cozzone but was to heavy had a flack suit and parachute and was heavy anyway saw that I was going to be trapped inside of plane for centrifugal force was getting worse for was harder to move I sat on left waist window and the force just through me out and clear of ship." Both witnesses on *Valient Virgin* say collision, but one says bomb bays and the other left wing.

How can we rectify the above account onboard *Valient Virgin* with the reports from *Utah Man*, especially those of Cox? Most of the reports fit, if we assume that Larry and Bob, severely wounded, were losing control of their damaged ship and gave the order to bail out. Most of the crew is wounded or dead but Cox and Johnston get out, the plane flies on, and then, the final loss of control where it slips to its right, falls out of formation and collides with *Valient Virgin*. Gillespie sees it coming. Cox and Johnston, far behind and falling, do not see the collision. That is essentially the scenario that I wrote.

There are other alternatives, but the eye witness accounts do not mesh as well. Keep in mind, all this happened in the midst of a fierce air battle. People had far greater priorities than pausing to visually record the scene around them. Besides, many of the accounts were recalled years, if not decades, later.

Gerald Astor, in his book *The Mighty Eighth*, notes the difficulty in writing accurate scenes of air battles. He states, "The discrepancy in the eyewitness reports . . . on what happened to the aircraft . . . exemplifies the difficulty in sorting out who did what unto whom and the results. As vexing as it is to determine which version is correct, there is no guarantee of the truth in the final Air Force summaries of actions. The personal accounts of those involved frequently vary from the official statements and the later are almost equally suspect in their accuracy."[249]

Crew of *Utah Man*. Left to Right, Kneeling: Richard E. Bartlett, KIA, nose gunner, (The guy who told Walt Stewart that Montana had rivers bigger than the Mediterranean); Ralph W. Cummings, KIA, bombardier, (He dropped the first bombs on Ploesti and was a pitching prospect for the Brooklyn Dodgers.); Benjamin Caplan, KIA, navigator, (He did his training with the RCAF.); William H. Major, KIA, right waist gunner, (His mother wrote Eileen that they came down fluttering like a leaf.); John E. Connolly, KIA, left waist gunner/engineer, (The guy who told Walt Stewart at Ploesti that they were out of gas.); Standing: Paul E. Johnston, POW, radio operator, (He was helped out of the plane by Cox.); Joseph R. Doyle, KIA, tail gunner, (New member of the crew);. Walt Stewart, ("Horning in" on the picture of his former crew.); Robert Timmer, KIA, copilot; Loren J. Koon, KIA, pilot (Walt's former copilot.); Robert L. Cox, POW, top gunner, (Lived to tell his story of *Utah Man's* end.)

~~~~~~~

I have long been interested in World War II and believed that I was quite familiar with its history. I was amazed, however, by some of the statistics I encountered during my research. Here are a few examples:

- The Eighth Air Force (one of several) suffered more fatalities than the entire U.S. Marine Corps in the Pacific Campaign of WWII.[250]
- The Eighth Air Force, just one command of the Army Air Force, had a higher percentage of casualties during the war than all the other branches of service combined. This means that the percentage of casualties of those serving suffered by the Navy, Marines and Army during World War II, added together, do not equal the percentage of casualties incurred by the Eighth Air Force.[251]
- Some statistics are difficult to gather, even after all these years, but according to conventional wisdom, an airman had less than a one in four chance to survive his mandatory twenty-five missions. That's more than a 75 percent chance that the men who served aboard those

planes were going to die before completing their mandatory number of missions.[252]
- Based on the above, there is little doubt that climbing into a heavy bomber and going on a mission over Europe was the most dangerous undertaking of the war.

~~~~~~~

The most thrilling part of working on this story was interviewing those who did beat the odds. When I started this project, I thought I would need a bit of Dutch luck to be able to talk to anyone who fought in a Liberator. Because so many have passed and with the youngest of the survivors around eighty-five years old, I did not think there was a chance that I would find anyone who actually flew with Bob. After all, most of his last crew died with him, and that left only a handful of possibilities, most from *The Duchess*. Even if they were still alive, how I would ever go about finding them? One day I Googled the "93rd Bombardment Group" and a big part of Bob's Liberator world opened up to me. It was a window to the Ninety-Third Nation, and all of its people and resources. On the website was a name and email address. I sent a quick note to Joe Duran and, within a week, I was talking to Ploesti veterans Louis Smith and John Sherman of *The Duchess*. Amazing!

Many of these guys (90 years old or pushing it) have a hitch-in-their-get-along, but their memories are sharp and they are willing to share their stories. And what great stories they are - some sad, some funny - but all a testament to the incredible courage of young men like Robert Timmer, who so long ago, stepped into those now ancient airplanes, and carried the war to Hitler's places.

Acknowledgements

Initially, a simple story of a young American pilot whose short life seemed like it would take a few pages to tell turned into a multi-year project and a normal-sized book. It also led me to search for information about that short life, in three different countries on two continents. Michele went with me, took professional notes, edited and proofed, suggested and cajoled, encouraged and loved, and it would not have happened without her.

Paul Kooyer, a young man with exceptional persistence, was able to pry Robert's documents from the most remote corners of officialdom in two countries where they had lain dormant for decades. His work was critical to reconstructing a life that was shrouded in mystery and myth. He was also instrumental in reminding the Canadian government that they owed Pilot Officer Timmer some medals, which they were honored to posthumously bestow.

There is no one left in Bob's immediate family but my aunt, Grace (Timmer) Van Hoeven, whose 97-year-old memory never failed as she told stories of her brother and the family they grew up in. There would have been no Chapter 2, or 3, without her. She was my partner for the telling of the early years, and I relished spending time with her and listening to her stories.

Also helpful in reconstructing Bob's school days were his teammate and friend Jay Van Sweden and classmate Dorothy DeWitt. Thanks for some great stories.

My Aunt Connie (Timmer) Koster, Bob's oldest sister who has passed, left me a scrapbook of family documents and photos along with some of her brother's memorabilia and medals. I was able to weave much of it into the story. It is a small cache but it held some fond memories and gave me fond memories of her.

I never met a library or museum that I didn't like and this quest took me to some good ones. Not only were the archives helpful but so were the people. I frequently went digging at the Ryerson Library in downtown Grand Rapids, and many there happily helped me with my tasks. The Wyoming Historical Commission is located in the Wyoming branch of the Kent County Library where Dorothy Simon-Tibbe and Bill Branz, authors themselves, pulled Timmer family stuff out of their files for me. Libby Morgan the librarian at the incredible Second Air Division Memorial Library in Norwich, England, not only helped us find some good stuff on Bob Timmer, but also served us coffee while we were working. The people at the Michigan State University Archives and at the registrar's office helped me get a fix on Bob's time at MSC, and my little library near my home in Newaygo, Michigan, was instrumental in quickly procuring books for me from the MeLCat system.

Nothing beats the real thing and so it is much easier describing a Tiger Moth and a Cessna Crane when you are standing near one (or sitting in one) than from a photo. The Commonwealth Air Training Plan Museum in Brandon, Manitoba, has both of these planes, as well as wonderful displays featuring the system that taught Bob to fly. Executive Director Stephen Hayter was a great host and introduced us to flyer Archie Londry, who spent a couple of hours with us telling stories of the pleasures and pitfalls of training young men to go to war in their flying machines. Their newsletter, "Contact," contained a poem by J.K.Gierson called "In Memoriam" that inspired me to write the verse, "Forever Twenty."

I found a B-24 at the Pima Air & Space Museum in Tucson, Arizona and it was very interesting. Hard to imagine that ten men crawled into that thing and went off to do their dangerous thing. Although the Mighty Eighth Museum in Savannah, Georgia features a B-17, it still is an amazing museum with a great display on the Ninety-third. It also has a beautiful new stained glass window in its chapel dedicated to our Bomb Group.

The museum at Hardwick is really special. Hardwick was home away from home for the 93rd flyers during the war and the sense of their long-ago presence permeates the place. They have great displays, and, of course, buildings and runways that were there back then. It also has a P-51 Mustang, a World War II fighter plane that was so instrumental in giving our bombers the protection they needed. Unfortunately, Bob was gone before they were in full production. This one still flies. Does it ever! Our visit, hosted by English contingent of the Ninety-third, was headed by David and Jean Woodruff, along with Collin Mann, our guide and driver. We were in good hands. We prayed in David's church and played darts in Collin's pub. It doesn't get much better than that.

Because of this project I was able to connect with Eileen's sister, Jean Vandermolen and her brother, Dave Koopman. We had a great time sharing stories and exchanging photos. There was a bond between us, almost like we were relatives.

I sought out people from the Ninety-third Bombardment

Group for help with a lot of book-related issues. Joe Durand was always there for me, mostly at the California end of my calls and emails, but also in Savannah, where he and Phyllis showed me around and introduced me to people like Don Morrison, and Blaine Duxbury. These experts on the history of the Travelling Circus patiently shared their knowledge with me. Most of the non-family photographs in this book came from Bill Sargent's incredible collection which he willing shared with me, and Editor JoAnne Sargent's *Ball of Fire* newsletter was also helpful.

The flyers were a special part of this project. The insights that I received from them about life in and out of a B-24 bomber were invaluable to this story. Sharing their experiences were Wayne Baker, Lew Brown, Raymond Eck, Carl Grigg, Morton Macks, Leo Sharp, John Sherman, Fernley Smith, Louis Smith, Walt Stewart and Vernon Swaim.

A special thanks also to Steve Caplan who sent me photographs and a lot of good information about the demise of Utah Man. Sadly, we share a unique bond. Our uncles, Benjamin Caplan and Robert Timmer, entered eternity together.

What did I know about the structure and punctuation of an English sentence? Not nearly as much as I thought! Fortunately, I have three members of my family whose professional expertise in editing the language was critical to making some sense out of what I wrote. Michele had the first crack at the roughness and made it smoother. My son Nick IV, a busy teacher of English, was able to give me some valuable insight into several chapters. My niece, Susan Kooyer, painstakingly poured over the manuscript, red pen in hand, making little squiggles, symbols and suggestions which led to changes invaluable to the final product. I am proud of the fact that whatever pleasure the reader may have found in my pages was due in large part to a family effort.

BIBLIOGRAPHY

Books

Ambrose, Stephen E. *The Wild Blue: The Men And Boys Who Flew The B-24s Over Germany.* New York: Simon & Schuster, 2001.

Andrews, Paul M. and Adams, William H. *Heavy Bombers of the Mighty Eighth.* Pine Grove, PA: Eighth Air Force Memorial Museum Foundation, 1995.

Anderson, Garth L. *Captain Hugh Rawlin Roper.* Rexburg, Idaho: Self Published, 1993.

Astor, Gerald. *The Mighty Eighth.* New York: Dell Publishing, 1998.

Bowman, Martin W. *B-24 Combat Missions.* New York: Fall River Press, 2009.

Bowman, Martin. *B-24 Liberator.* Shrewsbury, England: Airlife Publishing Ltd., 2003.

Doolittle, Gen. James H. with Glines, Carroll V. *I Could Never Be So Lucky Again.* New York: Bantam Books, 1991.

Dugan, James, and Stewart, Carroll. *Ploesti.* New York: Random House, 1962.

Dunmore, Spencer. *Wings for Victory.* Toronto, Ontario: McClelland & Stewart Inc., 1994.

Gilbert, Martin. *Churchill: A Life*. New York: Henry Holt and Company, 1991.

Hatch, F.J. *Aerodrome of Democracy: Canada and the British Commonwealth Air Training Plan*. Ottawa, Canada: Directorate of History, Department of National Defense, 1983.

Hill, Michael. *Black Sunday: Ploesti*. Atglen, PA: Schiffer Publishing Ltd., 1993.

The Holy Bible. KJV. Nashville, TN: Thomas Nelson, Publishers, 1990.

The Holy Scriptures. Chicago: Jewish Publication Society of America, 1955.

Jackiewicz, Jacek, and Bock, Robert. *Assembly Ships of the Mighty Eighth*. Gdansk, Poland: Atelier Kecay, 2007.

James, Robert Rhodes, Editor. *Churchill Speaks*. New York: Barnes and Noble Books, Inc. 1998.

Lydens, Z.Z., ed. *The Story of Grand Rapids*. Grand Rapids, Michigan: Kregel Publications, 1966.

Merz, Robert, ed. *The Wolverine*. Michigan State College Yearbook. East Lansing, Michigan: The Michigan State College Publications, 1941.

Mulder, Arnold. *Americans From Holland*. Philadelphia: J.B. Lippincott Co., 1947.

Olson, Lynne. *Citizens of London.* New York: Random House, 2010.

The Orbit. Wyoming Park High School Yearbook, 1938, 1939, 1940, 1941.

Peden, Murray. *A Thousand Shall Fall.* Toronto, ON: Stoddart Publishing Co. Ltd., 2000.

Pitt, Barrie, ed. *The Military History of World War II.* New York: The Military Press 1988.

Simon-Tibbe, Dorothy, Branz, Bill, and White, Kelly. *Wilderness to Wyoming: A History of Wyoming Michigan.* Wyoming, Michigan: Franklin Press, Inc., 2009.

Smith, Graham. *Norfolk Airfields in the Second World War.* Newbury, Berkshire, UK: Countryside Books, 2007.

Smith, Starr. *Jimmy Stewart Bomber Pilot.* Minneapolis, MN: Zenith Press, 2005.

Stewart, Carroll (Cal). *Ted's Travelling Circus.* Lincoln, NE: Sun/World Communications, Inc., 1996.

Van Hinte, Jacob. *Netherlanders in America.* Grand Rapids, Michigan: Baker Book House, 1985.

Vaughn, Charles, and Simon, Dorothy. *The City of Wyoming: A History.* Franklin, Michigan: Four Corners Press, 1984.

White, Elmer, ed. *The Wolverine.* Michigan State College Yearbook. East Lansing, Michigan: Michigan State College Publications, 1940.

Documents and Letters

Declassified Loading Lists/Sortie Reports for July, August, and November of 1943. National Archives and Records Administration. Washington D.C.

Documents relating to the November 13, 1943 Bremen Raid. Department of the Air Force: Air Force History Support Office, Bolling Air Force Base, Washington, D.C.

Documents relating to Pilot Officer Robert Timmer's Canadian Medals. Veterans Affairs Canada. Ottawa, Canada.

Documents relating to Pilot Officer Robert Timmer's Canadian Military Service. National Defense Headquarters. Ottawa, Canada.

Documents relating to 2/Lt. Timmer's National Service Life Insurance. Veterans Administration. Washington D.C.

Federal Census Reports for 1880, 1900, 1910, 1920. State Census Report for 1894. Grand Rapids Public Library, Grand Rapids, Michigan.

Letter from Col. Thomas S. Berkey to Paul Kooyer. October 14, 2005. Family documents.

Letter from LAC Frank to Winnie. January 17, 1943. Commonwealth Air Training Plan Museum, Brandon, Manitoba.

Letter from Major Mathew Joost to Paul Kooyer. December 7, 2005. Family documents.

Missing Air Crew Report # 2179. Department of the Air Force: Air Force History Support Office. Bolling Air Force Base, Washington, DC.

Missing Air Crew Report #2184. Department of the Air Force: Air Force History Support Office. Bolling Air Force Base, Washington, DC.

Pilot Officer Robert Timmer's Royal Canadian Air Force Service Records. Library and Archives Canada: Access to Information and Privacy. Ottawa, Canada.

Robert Timmer's Individual Deceased Personnel File. Department of the Army, U.S. Army Human Resources Command. Fort Knox, KY.

2/Lt. Robert Timmer's Individual Flight Records. National Personnel Records Center: Military Personnel Records. St. Louis, MO.

Timmer family documents and photographs in the possession of the Wyoming Historical Commission. Wyoming Public Library, Wyoming Michigan.

Timmer/Zwyghuizen family records: births, marriages, deaths. Office of the Kent County Clerk. Grand Rapids, Michigan.

Unit History Card of the 330th Bombardment Squadron. U.S. Army Military History Institute, Patron Services Division. Carlisle, PA.

Newspapers

Articles with information about Robert Timmer. *The Grand Rapids Herald*. Various editions from 1937 to 1943.

Articles with information about Robert Timmer. *The Grand Rapids Press*. Various editions from 1937 to 1943.

"Ramsay Potts: Lawyer and World War II Pilot." Adam Bernstein, *The Washington Post*, May 31, 2006.

"Long-Range Fighter Escorts Lauded as Bomber Saviors." *The Stars and Stripes*, November 5, 1943.

Microfilm and DVDs

Ramsay D. Potts interview. *American Patriots Series*. VHS. 2nd Air Division Memorial Library. Norwich, UK. November, 1989.

Ninety-third Bombardment Group (Heavy) Histories 1942-1945. DVD. Office of the Group Historian, Mighty Eighth Air Force Museum, Savannah, GA.

93rd Bomb Group Unit History, March 1942-December 1943. Microfilm, Roll No. 183. Air Force Historical Research Agency, Maxwell Air Force Base, Alabama.

330th Bomb Squadron Unit History, March 1942-November 1949. Microfilm, Roll No. 582. Air Force Historical Research Agency. Maxwell Air Force Base, Alabama.

Wing & A Prayer: The Saga of Utah Man. DVD. Salt Lake City, Utah: Spike Productions, 1993.

Magazines, **Newsletters and Directories**

"The British Commonwealth Air Training Plan: 1939-1945." Bruce Aleman, *Lethbridge Under Graduate Research Journal*, Vol. 1, No. 1, 2006.

Contact. Newsletter of the Commonwealth Air Training Plan Museum, Brandon Manitoba, various issues beginning in October 1998 through May, 2011.

"Getting There: Churchill's Wartime Journeys." Christopher H. Sterling, *Finest Hour*, Autumn 2010.

"Getting There: With Fond Memories of Commando." William Vanderkloot, *Finest Hour*, Autumn 2010.

The Grandville Courier. First Reformed Church, Grandville, MI. October 1945.

Kent County School Directory, 1944-45 and 1945-46. Lynn H. Clark Papers. Archives Collection, No. 120. Grand Rapids Public Library.

"U.S. 93rd Bomb Group: The Traveling Circus." Sam McGowan, *World War II Magazine*, May 1997.

Oral History

DeWitt, Dorothy. Telephone interview. December 7, 2009

Caplin, Steve. Telephone interview. December 17, 2009.

Eck, Raymond. Personal interview. May 29 and 30, 2011. Norwich, England.

Koopman, David. Personal interview. February 6, 2011. Grant, Michigan.

Londry, Archie. Personal interview. September 15, 2010. Brandon, Manitoba.

Macks, Morton. Telephone interviews. December, 2010.

Puryear, Edgar F. Jr. Interview with Ramsay D. Potts. *U.S. Air Force Oral History Program.* Transcript of an audio recording. Historical Research Center, Air University. Maxwell Field, Alabama. April 15, 1980.

Searles, Elizabeth. Interview with Walter T. Stewart. *Utah WWII Stories.* KUSD Radio. Benjamin, Utah. April 29, 2005.

Sherman, John. Telephone interview. February 17, 2009.

Simon, Dorothy. Interview with Ty Timmer and Martin Willdeboer, transcript. Wyoming Historical Commission. Wyoming, Michigan. February 19, 1982.

Simon-Tibbe, Dorothy. Interview with Grace Van Hoeven. Wyoming Historical Commission. Wyoming, Michigan. June 29, 2010.

Smith, Louis. Telephone interview. February 11, 2009.

Stewart, Walter T. Telephone interviews. December, 2010.

Vandermolen, Jean. Personal interview. April 6, 2011. Grand Rapids, Michigan.

Van Hoeven, Grace. Personal and telephone interviews on numerous occasions, 2009, 2010, 2011. Grandville, Michigan.

Van Sweden, Jay. Personal interview. October 13, 2009. Wyoming, Michigan. Phone interview. July 6, 1010.

Wortley, Bruce. Telephone interview. October 20, 2009.

Internet Sources

"A Bomber an Hour: Charlie Sorensen's Story." www.strategosinc.com/willow_run.htm.

"Airfields in the County of Norfolk, England." Frank Shaw, http://norfolk-airfields.co.uk/

"The Airspeed Oxford." John D.R. Rawlings, *Aircraft Profile No. 227,* n.d. www.scribd.com/doc/48260780/Aircraft-Profile-No-227-the-Airspeed-Oxford.

"Airspeed Oxford I MP425/G-AITB." www.rafmuseum.org.uk/london/…69-A-909%20airspeed%20oxford.pdf.

"The BCATP Training Programme." www.junobeach.org/e/4/can-tac-air-bca-tra-e.htm.

"Bombing of Hamburg in WWII." http://en.wikipedia.org/wiki/Bombing_of_Hamburg_in_World_War_II.

"British Commonwealth Air Training Program." Canadian Warplane Heritage Museum www.warplane.com/pages/ourstories_bcapt2.html.

"Consolidated B-24 Liberator." www.acepilots.com/planes/b-24.html.

"Consolidated B-24 Liberator Medium/Heavy/Bomber." www.militaryfactory.com/aircraft/detail.asp?aircraft_id=80.

"Jefferson Barracks National Cemetery." Department of Veterans Affairs Web site, January 6, 2001.

"Life in the BCATP." Canadian Warplane Heritage Museum. www.warplane.com.

"The Link Trainer and the British Commonwealth Air Training Plan." Frank MacLoon, *Atlantic Canada Museum News*, March 2001. www.atlanticcanadaaviationmuseum.com.

"Neuville-en-Condroz US Military Cemetery-Belgium." www.pegww2.net/Pages/Neuville.htm.

"No. 6 Group RCAF." http://en.wikipedia.org/wiki/No._6_Group_RCAF.

"Norwich Under Attack." www.visitnorfold.co.uk/explore-norfolk/norwich-history.aspx#attack.

"Pier 21: The First 75 Years." Canadian Museum of Immigration at Pier 21, www.pier21.ca/research/research.../the-first-seventy-five-years.

"RCAF Bomber Squadrons Overseas." www.junobeach.org.

"Saga of Utah Man."
www.alumni.utah.edu/continuum/winter95/UTAHMan.html.
October 21, 2005.

"Short Bursts." Comments by Maurice Shnider and John Moyles, May, 2001. www.airmuseum.ca/mag/exag0105.html.

"Tatenhill airfield." Lez Watson, 2005.
www.watsonlv.addr.com/tatenhill.shtml.

"Willow Run." Michigan Historical Museum's Arsenal of Democracy Gallery, Web site.
    www.hal.state.mi.us/mhc/museum/explore/museums/hisus/1900-   75/willowrun.html.

"WW2 Casualties." Jim Harker, web posting, Mar. 5, 2007.
www.historykb.com/Uwe/Forum.aspx/world...II/.../WW2-Casualties.

Family Archives

Photographs and documents; personal interviews; clippings, letters, and telegrams; pamphlets and booklets; church brochures, directories, histories, and bulletins; citations and awards; and Robert Timmer's, letters, personal effects and medals.

Notes

[1] Hill, *Black Sunday*, 25.

[2] Ibid., 27.

[3] Potts interview, *American Patriot Series*, VHS, 1989.

[4] Stewart, *Ted's Travelling Circus*, 133.

[5] Ibid., 152.

[6] Sherman, Telephone interview.

[7] Astor, *The Mighty Eighth*, 160.

[8] Ibid., 16.

[9] Hill, *Black Sunday*, 37.

[10] Ibid., 35.

[11] Van Hinte, *Netherlanders in America*, 92.

[12] Ibid., 371.

[13] Ibid., 263.

[14] Mulder, *Americans From Holland*, 193.

[15] Van Hinte, *Netherlanders in America*, 368.

[16] Ibid., 365.

[17] Dorothy Simon interview with Ty Timmer, transcript.

[18] Lydens, ed., *The Story of Grand Rapids*, 135.

[19] *The Orbit*, 1938, 8.

[20] Van Sweden Personal interview.

21 Ibid.

22 *The Orbit*, 1940, 45.

23 "Holland Quint Whips Wyoming High Cage Five," *Grand Rapids Herald,* February 14, 1940.

24 *The Orbit*, 1940, 33.

25 Van Sweden Personal interview.

26 Ibid., 55.

27 Simon and Vaughn, *The City of Wyoming: A History,* 42.

28 White, ed., *The Wolverine*, 1940, 370.

29 Ibid., 200.

30 Hatch, *Aerodrome of Democracy*, 7.

31 Dunmore, *Wings for Victory*, 25-26.

32 *Life in the BCATP,* www.warplane.com.

33 Dunmore, *Wings for Victory*, 346.

34 Robert Timmer's Royal Canadian Air Force Service Records.

35 Aleman, *The British Commonwealth Air Training Plan: 1939-1945.*

36 Dunmore, *Wings for Victory,* 71.

37 Peden, *A Thousand Shall Fall*, 20.

38 Dunmore, *Wings for Victory,* 71.

39 Ibid., 9.

40 Peden, *A Thousand Shall Fall,* 4.

41 Letter from Frank to Winnie, Air Museum, Brandon, Manitoba.

42 Dunmore, *Wings for Victory,* 73.

43 Ibid., 74.

44 Ibid., 190.

45 Londry Interview, Brandon, Manitoba.

46 Peden, *A Thousand Shall Fall*, 15.

47 Dunmore, *Wings for Victory*, 78.

48 MacLoon, Frank, *The Link Trainer and the British Commonwealth Air Training Plan*, www.atlanticcanadaaviationmusuem.com.

49 *Life in the BCATP*, www.warplane.com, 3.

50 Ibid., 3.

51 Dunmore, *Wings for Victory*, 82.

52 *Contact*, May, 2009, 3.

53 Dunmore, *Wings for Victory*, 91.

54 Ibid., 90.

55 Peden, *A Thousand Shall Fall*, 41.

56 Hatch, *Aerodrome of Democracy*, 118.

57 Dunmore, *Wings for Victory*, 86.

58 Ibid., 346.

59 Ibid., 93.

60 Peden, *A Thousand Shall Fall*, 32.

61 Dunmore, *Wings for Victory*, 98.

62 Ibid.

63 Ibid., 102.

64 Peden, *A Thousand Shall Fall,* 35.

65 Ibid., 43.

66 Dunmore, *Wings for Victory,* 100.

67 Hatch, *Aerodrome of Democracy,* 142.

68 Ibid.

69 *Life in the BCATP,* www.warplane.com.

70 Ibid.

71 *The BCATP Training Programme,* www.junobeach.org/e/4/can-tac-air-bca-tra-e.htm.

72 Dunmore, *Wings for Victory,* 136.

73 Ibid., 131.

74 Hatch, *Aerodrome of Democracy,* 132.

75 Peden, *A Thousand Shall Fall,* 87.

76 Hatch, *Aerodrome of Democracy,* 91.

77 Ibid., 57.

78 Londry Interview, Brandon, Manitoba.

79 Hatch, *Aerodrome of Democracy,* 107.

80 Ibid., 108.

81 Letter from Mathew Joost to Paul Kooyer, December 7, 2005, Family documents.

82 "Too Young for U.S. Force, Wins Wings in Canada," *Grand Rapids Press,* October 1, 1942.

83 Londry Interview, Brandon, Manitoba.

84 Harker, Jim, *WW2 Casualties,* Historykb.com/Uwe/Forum.aspx/world…2/…/ww2-Casualties.

85 *Pier 21: The First 75 Years*, www.pier21.ca/research/research…/the-first-seventy-five-years.

86 Peden, *A Thousand Shall Fall*, 93.

87 Ibid., 105.

88 Stacy, "On the Path to London," *Contact*, May 2001, 4-5.

89 Olson, *Citizens of London*, 93.

90 Ibid., 237.

91 Ibid.

92 James, ed., *Churchill Speaks*, 720.

93 Shnider, Maurice, and Moyles, John, *Short Bursts*, www.airmuseum.ca/mag/exag0105.html.

94 Ibid.

95 Ibid.

96 *RCAF Bomber Squadron Overseas*, www.junobeach.org.

97 *No. 6 Group RCAF*, http://en.wikipedia.org/wiki/No._6_Group_RCAF.

98 Dunmore, *Wings for Victory*, 191.

99 Peden, *A Thousand Shall Fall*, 111.

100 Dunmore, *Wings for Victory*, 291.

101 Hatch, *Aerodrome of Democracy*, 149.

102 Watson, Lez, *Tatenhill Airfield*, www.watsonlv.addr.com/tatenhill.shtml.

103 "Airspeed Oxford I MP425/G-AITB.", http://www.rafmuseum.org.uk/london/collections/aircraft/aircraft-history/69-A-909%20Airspeed%20Oxford.pdf, 103.

104 Peden, *A Thousand Shall Fall*, 161.

105 Ibid., 148.

106 Ibid., 149.

107 Ibid., 157.

108 Ibid., 159.

109 Ibid., 161.

110 *93d Bombardment Group (Heavy) Histories 1942-1945*, DVD, June 1, 1942-September 30, 1942, 5-6.

111 Ibid., 10.

112 Ibid., 13.

113 Stewart, *Ted's Travelling Circus*, 8.

114 Ibid., 13.

115 Ibid., 75.

116 Ibid., 69.

117 McGowan, "U.S. 93rd Bomb Group: The Traveling Circus," *World War II Magazine*, May, 1997, 4.

118 Ibid.

119 Shaw, Frank, *Airfields in the County of Norfolk, England*, http://norfolk-airfields.co.uk/

120 *Norwich Under Attack*, www.visitnorfolk.co.uk/explore-norfolk/norwich-history.aspx

121 Bowman, *B-24 Combat Missions*, 103.

122 Ibid., 146.

123 Stewart, *Ted's Travelling Circus*, 96.

124 Bowman, *B-24 Liberator*, 6.

[125] *A Bomber an Hour: Charlie Sorensen's Story,* www.strategosinc.com/willow_run.htm.

[126] *Consolidated B-24 Liberator,* www.acepilots.com/planes/smallb-24.html.

[127] *Willow Run,* www.hal.state.mi.us/mhc/museum/explore/museums/hismus/1900-75/arsenal/willowrun.html.

[128] Ambrose, *The Wild Blue: The Men and Boys Who Flew the B-24s Over Germany,* 21.

[129] Ibid., 77.

[130] Bowman, *B-24 Combat Missions,* 30.

[131] Sterling, "Getting There: Churchill's Wartime Journeys," *Finest Hour,* Autumn 2010, 12.

[132] Vanderkloot, "Getting There: With Fond Memories of Commando," *Finest Hour,* Autumn 2010, 22.

[133] *Consolidated B-24 Liberator Medium/Heavy Bomber,* www.militaryfactory.com/aircraft/detail.asp?aircraft_id=80, 3.

[134] Stewart, Telephone Interview.

[135] Pitt, ed., *Military History of World War II,* 210-211.

[136] Anderson, *Captain Hugh Rawlin Roper,* 20.

[137] Stewart, *Ted's Travelling Circus,* 113.

[138] Ibid., 114.

[139] *93d Bombardment Group (Heavy) Histories 1942-1945,* DVD, June 1943, 8.

[140] Ibid., May 1943, 9.

[141] Stewart, *Ted's Travelling Circus,* 77.

[142] Bowman, *B-24 Combat Missions,* 52.

[143] Ibid., 53.

144 McGowan, "U.S. 93rd Bomb Group: The Traveling Circus," *World War II Magazine,* May 1997, 5.

145 Timberlake Memo of 25 November 1943, Robert Timmer's Individual Deceased Personnel File.

146 *The Holy Scriptures,* Job 40:7.

147 *93d Bombardment Group (Heavy) Histories 1942-1945,* DVD, June 1943, 10.

148 Ibid.

149 Stewart, *Ted's Travelling Circus,* 128.

150 Hill, *Black Sunday: Ploesti,* 21.

151 *93d Bombardment Group (Heavy) Histories 1942-1945,* DVD, June 1943, 20.

152 Dugan, and Stewart, *Ploesti,* 40.

153 Ibid., 36.

154 Ibid.

155 Hill, *Black Sunday: Ploesti,* 16.

156 Dugan, and Stewart, *Ploesti,* 42.

157 Hill, *Black Sunday: Ploesti,* 16.

158 Dugan, and Stewart, *Ploesti,* 26.

159 Ibid., 34.

160 Stewart, *Ted's Travelling Circus,* 41.

161 Ibid., 320.

162 Ibid., 159.

163 Astor, *The Mighty Eighth,* 161.
164 Ibid., 162.

[165] Ibid.

[166] Stewart, *Ted's Travelling Circus,* 171.

[167] Stewart, *Ted's Travelling Circus,* 173.

[168] Hill, *Black Sunday: Ploesti,* 58.

[169] Stewart, *Ted's Travelling Circus,* 174.

[170] Ibid., 177.

[171] Hill, *Black Sunday: Ploesti,* 63.

[172] Ibid., 67.

[173] Astor, *The Mighty Eighth,* 163.

[174] Hill, *Black Sunday: Ploesti,* 67.

[175] Astor, *The Mighty Eighth,* 164.

[176] Hill, *Black Sunday: Ploesti,* 69.
[177] Ibid., 79.

[178] Ibid., 76.

[179] Ibid., 78.

[180] Dugan, and Stewart, *Ploesti,* 142.

[181] Hill, *Black Sunday: Ploesti,* 149.

[182] Astor, *The Mighty Eighth,* 165.

[183] Hill, *Black Sunday: Ploesti,* 148-149.

[184] Dugan, and Stewart, *Ploesti,* 124.

[185] Hill, *Black Sunday: Ploesti,* 163.

[186] Ibid.

[187] Ibid.

188 Bernstein, "Ramsey Potts: Lawyer and World War II Pilot," *The Washington Post*, May 31, 2006.

189 *93d Bombardment Group (Heavy) Histories 1942-1945*, DVD, August 1943, 16.

190 Hill, *Black Sunday: Ploesti*, 193.

191 Astor, *The Mighty Eighth*, 165.

192 Ibid.

193 Hill, *Black Sunday: Ploesti*, 193.

194 Stewart, *Ted's Travelling Circus*, 205.

195 Hill, *Black Sunday: Ploesti*, 193.

196 Dugan, and Stewart, *Ploesti*, 244.

197 Astor, *The Mighty Eighth*, 166.

198 Puryear, Interview with Ramsay D. Potts, April 15, 1980.

199 Ibid.

200 Ramsay D. Potts Interview, *American Patriot Series*, VHS, 1989.

201 Hill, *Black Sunday: Ploesti*, 177.

202 Stewart, *Ted's Travelling Circus*, 96.

203 Ibid., 231.

204 Searles, Interview with Walter T. Stewart, April 29, 2005.

205 *93d Bombardment Group (Heavy) Histories 1942-1945*, DVD, January 3,1942-April 30, 1944, 142.

206 Ibid., 143.

207 Stewart, *Ted's Travelling Circus*, 119.

208 Ibid., 119-120.

[209] *93d Bombardment Group (Heavy) Histories 1942-1945*, DVD, January 3, 1942-April 30, 1944, 148.

[210] Stewart, *Ted's Travelling Circus*, 120-121.

[211] *93d Bombardment Group (Heavy) Histories 1942-1945*, DVD, January 3, 1942-April 30, 1944, 127.

[212] Ibid., 146.
[213] Stewart, *Ted's Travelling Circus*, 137-138.

[214] Ibid., 139.

[215] *Bombing of Hamburg in WWII*, http://en.wikipedia.org/wiki/Bombing_of_Hamburg_in_World_War_II

[216] Astor, *The Mighty Eighth*, 178.

[217] Robert Timmer's Individual Flight Records, October, 1943.

[218] Bowman, *B-24 Combat Missions*, 20-21.

[219] Ibid., 21.

[220] Ibid.

[221] Ibid.

[222] Stewart, *Ted's Travelling Circus*, 255.

[223] Jackiewicz, and Bock, *Assembly Ships of the Mighty Eighth*, 74.

[224] Stewart, *Ted's Travelling Circus*, 249.

[225] Ibid., 250.

[226] *93d Bombardment Group (Heavy) Histories 1942-1945*, DVD, October 1943, 9.

[227] "Long-Range Fighter Escorts Lauded as Bomber Saviors," *Grand Rapids Herald*, November 5, 1943.

[228] Bowman, *B-24 Combat Missions*, 25.

229 Ibid., 24.

230 Stewart, *Ted's Travelling Circus,* 256.

231 Timberlake Memo of 25 November 1943, Robert Timmer's Individual Deceased Personnel File.

232 Robert Timmer's Individual Deceased Personnel File.

233 *Neuville-en-Condroz US Military Cemetery - Belgium,* www.pegww2.net/Pages/Neuville.htm.

234 *Jefferson Barracks National Cemetery,* http://www.cem.va.gov/cems/nchp/jeffersonbarracks.asp

235 Bernstein, "Ramsey Potts: Lawyer and World War II Pilot," *The Washington Post,* May 31, 2006.

236 Ibid.

237 Stewart, *Ted's Travelling Circus,* 489.

238 Ibid., 207.

239 *Saga of Utah Man,* www.alumni.utah.edu/continuum/winter95/UTAHMan.html.

240 Stewart, *Ted's Travelling Circus,* 582.

241 Smith, *Norfolk Airfields in the Second World War,"* 128.

242 Ibid., 122.

243 *Schools Directory 1944-45 and 1945-46.* Lynn H. Clark papers, Grand Rapids Public Library.

244 Robert Timmer's Individual Deceased Personnel File.

245 Astor, *The Mighty Eighth,* 159-165.

246 Stewart, *Ted's Travelling Circus,* 285.

247 Steve Caplan Telephone Interview.

[248] Thomas Berkey to Paul Kooyer, October 14, 2005.

[249] Astor, *The Mighty Eighth*, 58.

[250] Olson, *Citizens of London*, 257.

[251] Stewart, *Ted's Travelling Circus*, 582.

[252] Olson, *Citizens of London*, 257.

ABOUT THE AUTHOR

Originally from Wyoming Park, Michigan, Nick Timmer graduated from Western Michigan University and began teaching in Marshall, Michigan. While there, he served as middle school principal and superintendent. He earned his Ph.D. at Michigan State University and his career path included time at Kentwood Public Schools and Kent Intermediate School District, both in Grand Rapids, Michigan. He and Michele have six children and eight grandchildren. He has traveled to all parts of the world, loves to golf collect books, garden and spend time with children and grandchildren.